OVERCOMING
ADDICTIONS

OVERCOMING ADDICTIONS

Skills Training for People with Schizophrenia

LISA J. ROBERTS, M.A.
ANDREW SHANER, M.D.
THAD A. ECKMAN, Ph.D.

W. W. NORTON & COMPANY   NEW YORK   LONDON

For information about permission to reproduce selections from this book, write to
Permissions, W. W. Norton & Company, Inc., 500 Fifth Avenue, New York, NY 10110

The text of this book is composed in Electra with the display set in Akzidenz Grotesk
Manufacturing by Hamilton Printing Company
Book design and desktop composition by Justine Burkat Trubey

Library of Congress Cataloging-in-Publication Data
Roberts, Lisa J.
Overcoming addictions : skills training for people with schizophrenia /
Lisa J. Roberts, Andrew Shaner, Thad A. Eckman.
p.   cm.
"A Norton professional book."
Includes bibliographical references.
ISBN 0-393-70299-5 (pbk.)
1. Schizophrenia—Patients—Training of—Handbooks, manuals, etc. 2. Substance abuse—
Prevention—Handbooks, manuals, etc. 3. Schizophrenics—Rehabilitation—Handbooks,
manuals, etc. 4. Training manuals. I. Shaner, Andrew. II. Eckman, Thad. III. Title.
RC514.R553   1999
616.89'8203—dc21   99-13341   CIP

W. W. Norton & Company, Inc., 500 Fifth Avenue, New York, N.Y. 10110
www.wwnorton.com

W. W. Norton & Company Ltd., 10 Coptic Street WC1A 1PU

1 2 3 4 5 6 7 8 9 0

FOREWORD

by Robert Paul Liberman, M.D.
Professor of Psychiatry, UCLA School of Medicine
Director, UCLA Center for Research on Treatment & Rehabilitation of Psychosis

Filling a void in the treatment of the dually diagnosed, substance-abusing persons with schizophrenia and other disabling mental disorders, *Overcoming Addictions* provides a much needed program for a wide range of mental health and substance abuse professionals and paraprofessionals. The authors have crafted their treatment manual, also known as the Substance Abuse Management Module (SAMM) through more than a decade of working directly with dually diagnosed individuals. This is a "tried and tested" program of procedures that recognizes the difficulties experienced by dually diagnosed individuals and those who provide service to them, as they ascend the "slippery slope" toward abstinence and control of serious mental disorders.

One of the great strengths of this skills training program is its anchorage in a phase-specific approach to dual diagnosis. Those who use the manual and *SAMM Skills Illustration Videotape* will first have to come to grips with the symptoms of the acute phase of schizophrenia or other serious mental disorder and bring those symptoms under control. Next, therapists use the "basic training" component of SAMM to enhance motivation and teach the basic principles of coping with substance abuse and mental disorder. Once patients are engaged in treatment and ready to change their drug-use behaviors, therapists use SAMM's "skills training" component to actively train the skills required to initiate and sustain abstinence and control schizophrenic symptoms. Finally, the principles and skills taught in SAMM are aimed at helping dually diagnosed individuals progress toward recovery and its associated goals of re-integration into family life, work, recreation and healthy pleasures, spiritual life, and the community.

The manual is user friendly and can be used with little preparation by those who have "natural teaching skills" and are experienced in working with this population. For those who lack experience with the dually diagnosed, consultation and training are recommended. In addition, the

5

skills-training procedures take into account the learning disabilities experienced by persons with schizophrenia and other serious mental disorders, with the liberal use of repetition, modeling, multimodal training, role-playing and behavioral rehearsal, and homework assignments. Those who employ *Overcoming Addictions* will be richly rewarded, as the prevalence of dual diagnosis is enormous, approximating 30 percent of all individuals who have mental disorders. The skills-training program will provide the practitioner with a tangible tool to work with this challenging population, made more difficult by the failure of social, substance abuse, and mental health agencies to coordinate and integrate their efforts on behalf of this population which so often "falls between organizational cracks." When imbedded in a comprehensive program of services for the dually diagnosed, *Overcoming Addictions* is an essential element in helping such individuals strive toward control over their disorders and eventual recovery.

FOREWORD

by G. Alan Marlatt, Ph.D.
Professor of Psychology and
Director, Addictive Behaviors Research Center, University of Washington

It gives me considerable pleasure to recommend this treatment manual. First and foremost, the material represents a cutting edge approach to the treatment of people with co-occurring mental health and addictive behavior problems, specifically patients who present with a dual diagnosis of schizophrenia and alcohol or substance abuse. Treatment professionals who seek an integrative approach to the treatment of these dual disorders will be particularly pleased with the program outlined here. The skills training model has been successfully implemented with a variety of mental health disorders and has also been documented as an effective treatment modality in the treatment of addictive behaviors. Now, patients who suffer from both disorders can benefit from a treatment model that provides a comprehensive set of clinical strategies that is both helpful and effective. Rather than treating schizophrenia and substance abuse as two separate disease entities, the skills-training model shows how the two disorders often interact and can be dealt with as an interlocking set of behaviors. For example, if patients use substances as an attempt to self-medicate symptoms arising from their psychotic disorder, this integrated treatment approach is designed to provide alternative coping skills that may serve as effective alternatives to drug or alcohol dependency.

The skills training approach described in this manual incorporates many key concepts of relapse prevention, a cognitive-behavioral therapy designed to prevent and manage relapse episodes for both mental health and addictive behavior problems. Therapists who adopt this treatment model will be able to help their patients to identify relapse triggers and to cope effectively with high-risk situations such as negative mood states and social pressures to use drugs. Many of the coping skills can be used to prevent backsliding or to recover from setbacks in recovery from both psychiatric and addictive disorders. In addition to teaching specific skills to prevent relapse, therapists who use this manual will increase their capacity to provide lifestyle-balancing skills in their treatment program. Relapse prevention promotes the use of alternative reinforcing behaviors that may substitute for addictive behaviors, such as relaxation training, exercise, and access to social support systems.

For patients who are unable to maintain abstinence from alcohol and drug use for long periods of time, *Overcoming Addictions* provides therapists with methods and techniques that are consistent with a harm-reduction approach. Although the harm-reduction model accepts abstinence as an ideal or long-term goal in the treatment of addictive disorders, any steps that can be taken to reduce the harmful consequences of active or ongoing drug use are also acceptable and promoted as short-term goals. This manual provides therapists with valuable tools and clinical techniques to help patients change their high-risk behaviors and to step-down the harm these behaviors cause for both the patient and his or her social environment. Relapse prevention and harm reduction share a common goal in the management of ongoing harmful alcohol or drug use: to help the patient get back on track and to live a safer and more balanced lifestyle.

Finally, I recommend this manual for therapists who are familiar with the application of the "stages of change" or "transtheoretical" model of habit change first described by Prochaska and DiClemente. This heuristic model provides a helpful guide for therapists who can match intervention techniques to the particular stage of motivation or action for each patient on an individual basis, from early "precontemplation" or "contemplation" stages to later "action" and "maintenance" stages. The psychoeducational aspects of the Basic Training section of this manual provides valuable information and concepts for individuals in the early stages of change (e.g., those in the precontemplaton stage), while the later Skills Training component contains methods that will be useful for those who are ready to take action and change their behavioral repertoire.

Lisa Roberts, Andrew Shaner, and Thad Eckman are to be congratulated for their hard work and efforts in developing this program and implementing it at the V.A. Medical Center in West Los Angeles. *Overcoming Addictions* represents the legacy of this work. It will prove to be of great benefit to individuals with co-occurring schizophrenia and addictive disorders.

ACKNOWLEDGMENTS

We are indebted to the many patients at the West Los Angeles VA Medical Center who shared their personal experiences and helped us learn what did and did not work. Special thanks to Stacy Suttmiller, Heather Barnett, Tom Fuller, and Karen Blair, who worked so hard to develop and test this manual. Other key contributors include David Gorelick, Doug Ziedonis, Jerry Vacarro, John Tsuang, Douglas Tucker, Jeffery Wilkins, Andrew Ho, and Jim Mintz. We also thank the entire staff of the Dual Diagnosis Treatment Program at the VA Medical Center in West Los Angeles (especially Maria Rosa, Gary Brown, and Shelley Reno). Finally we thank Robert P. Liberman and G. Alan Marlatt for providing inspiration and invaluable guidance.

Development was supported, in part, by the National Institute on Drug Abuse (NIDA RO1 DA09436-02) and by grant MH 30911 from the National Institute of Mental Health to the UCLA Intervention Research Center for Psychoses, Robert P. Liberman, Director.

CONTENTS

INTRODUCTION TO SAMM

Overcoming Addictions: Skills Training for People with Schizophrenia describes the Substance Abuse Management Module (SAMM), a course of behavioral skills training designed to help people with schizophrenia to stop abusing drugs and alcohol.

Schizophrenia and addiction. Many people who have schizophrenia are also addicted to drugs or alcohol. This combination creates special problems for patients, clinicians, health care systems, and social service agencies. These problems include uncertain diagnoses, learning difficulties, poorly integrated treatment, and frequent treatment drop-out. Direct payment of disability income can also facilitate drug use.

Comprehensive dual diagnosis treatment program. The best way to solve these problems is through a comprehensive dual diagnosis treatment program. In a comprehensive program, a team of clinicians treats both substance abuse and schizophrenia simultaneously. The team makes use of assertive case management, antipsychotic medication, and skills training. SAMM is designed as one of the skills-training components in a comprehensive dual diagnosis treatment program.

Behavioral skills training and schizophrenia. Behavioral skills training is a highly structured approach to teaching patients how to keep schizophrenia under control, recover from substance abuse, and enjoy life more fully. It relies heavily on having patients practice behaviors over and over again in the classroom and in real life. The UCLA Intervention Research Center for Psychoses has developed behavioral skills training modules like this one to help patients with problems associated with having schizophrenia. Various modules help patients understand and manage symptoms, use medications effectively, solve interpersonal problems, and enjoy life.

Substance Abuse Management Module (SAMM). This module, also developed by the UCLA Intervention Research Center for Psychoses, is designed to teach patients how to stop abusing drugs and alcohol. It is intended for patients in whom addiction to drugs and alcohol interferes with the treatment of schizophrenia, often leading to poor outpatient attendance, homelessness, and frequent hospitalization. Ten years ago, we set out to help such patients by collaborating in the development of the comprehensive dual diagnosis treatment program at the VA Medical Center in West Los Angeles. This program provides both acute inpatient treatment and long-term outpatient rehabilitation using the wide range of interventions described above. It soon became clear that merely *talking* with patients about overcoming addictions would not be enough. We would have to get them out of their chairs to practice the very behaviors required to quit using drugs and alcohol and replace them with healthy and rewarding activities. In the words of an old Chinese proverb, *talk doesn't cook rice*. Getting patients out of their chairs to practice skills can be difficult. Therapists must project a sense of acceptance, tolerance, and optimism. Liveliness and spontaneity are key.

Although we are enthusiastic about the module, as of this publication its effectiveness is still under investigation. We are making it available now because of the many requests we have received from clinicians treating similar patients.

Manual contents. This manual describes, in detail, how to conduct each skills training session. The sections below, *Module Overview, Key Concepts*, and *Test of Knowledge and Skills*, gives a quick summary of the treatment; *Materials Needed to Conduct Skills Training* describes what you need to have on hand to conduct skills training. The next three parts, *Basic Training, Skills Training*, and *Practice Sessions*, will tell you exactly how to conduct each session. There is also a *Glossary* and *Appendices* containing examples of the forms, flip charts, and other materials you will use as a guide for both yourself and your patients during each session. The *Appendices* include several tests you can use to gauge the progress of patients treated with SAMM.

MODULE OVERVIEW

SAMM treatment sessions. Patients learn how to avoid drugs and seek healthy pleasures by participating in group treatment sessions several times a week. Patients attend three kinds of groups:

- *Basic training* consists of eight 45-minute educational sessions designed to engage and motivate new patients while teaching basic relapse prevention concepts. These groups involve a lot of discussion but no role-play. Patients graduate to skills training.

- *Skills training* includes twenty-seven 45-minute sessions in which patients practice nine specific skills (for example, how to say no to a pushy dealer). The emphasis in these sessions is on learning skills through role-play.

- *Practice sessions* are twice weekly, 45-minute sessions for patients at all stages of treatment, including those who have just started basic training, those who have begun skills training, and even those who have completed skills training. This class focuses on applying the concepts learned in basic training and the skills learned in skills training to real-life situations that patients expect to face within a few days.

Figure 1 illustrates the timing of group treatment sessions.

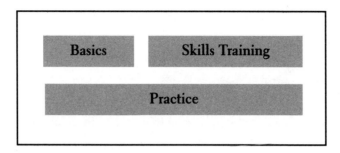

FIGURE 1. *Timing of Group Treatment Sessions*

Learning deficits and learning activities. People with schizophrenia often have trouble paying attention, remembering things, understanding concepts, planning future actions, and controlling immediate impulses. This can make it difficult for people with schizophrenia to learn new ideas and new skills. SAMM is designed to help people with schizophrenia learn new ideas and skills, despite these learning deficits. The teaching approach involves repeating information in different ways, having patients practice skills in various environments, and frequently rewarding or reinforcing new learning. For example, most sessions involve many of the following learning activities: viewing video-taped skills, rehearsing skills through role-play, solving problems, and homework assignments.

Overview of Module Concepts and Skills

How to avoid drugs (made simple). The concepts and skills taught in this module are designed to help patients follow these four recommendations:

- If you slip, quit early.
- When someone offers drugs, say no.
- Don't get into situations where you can't say no.
- Do things that are fun and healthy.

Key concepts and skills. Patients learn how to follow these four recommendations by learning key concepts and the skills. Here are the four recommendations restated in terms of the module's key concepts:

Plain English	*Module Concepts*
If you slip, quit early.	Practice damage control.
When someone offers drugs, say no.	Escape high-risk situations.
Don't get into situations where you can't say no.	Avoid high-risk situations.
Do things that are fun and healthy.	Seek healthy pleasures.

Patients learn the main point of each recommendation by understanding a few key concepts. They learn how to put the recommendation and the concepts into practice by rehearsing skills. Here are the four recommendations together with their main points, associated concepts, and skills:

- Practice damage control.

  Main point: If you slip and use drugs or alcohol again, stop early and get right back into treatment. This will reduce damage to your health, relationships, and finances.

  Concepts: Mt. Recovery, slip vs. full-blown relapse, harm reduction, abstinence violation effect, bouncing back into treatment

  Skills: Quitting after a slip, reporting a slip

- Escape high-risk situations.

  Main point: Some situations make it very hard to avoid using drugs. Be prepared to escape from these situations without using drugs. Realize that it would be much better to avoid these situations in the first place.

  Concepts: High-risk situations

  Skills: Refusing drugs offered by a pushy dealer, refusing drugs offered by a friend or relative

- Avoid high-risk situations.

  Main point: Avoid high-risk situations by learning to recognize the warning signs that you might be headed toward drug use.

  Concepts: Drug-habit chain (trigger, craving, planning, getting, using), warning signs, U-turns, removing triggers, riding the wave, money management, representative payee

  Skills: Getting an appointment with a busy person, getting a support person, reporting symptoms and side effects to a doctor

- Seek healthy pleasures.

  Main point: You can avoid drugs by focusing on the things that are most important and enjoyable to you. Do things that are fun and healthy.

  Concepts: Healthy pleasures, healthy habits, activity schedule

  Skills: Asking someone to join you in a healthy pleasure, negotiating with a representative payee

Additional recommendations and concepts. SAMM includes three additional recommendations. Here are the main points of these additional recommendations together with their associated concepts. These three additional recommendations do not have associated skills.

- Understand how you learned to use drugs.

  Main point: Drug abuse is learned and can be unlearned.

  Concepts: Habits, reinforcement, craving, conditioning, extinction, riding the wave
- Know why you decided to quit.

  Main point: Make sure you can always remember why you decided to quit using drugs.

  Concepts: Advantages and disadvantages of using drugs and of not using drugs
- Carry an emergency card.

  Main point: Make an emergency card that contains vital information and reminders about how and why to avoid drugs. Carry it with you at all times.

  Concepts: Support person, coping skills, why quit

KEY CONCEPTS

The most important concept in this module is called a U-turn. It refers to behaviors that decrease the likelihood, probability, or risk of drug use. The theory treats substance abuse as an unhealthy habit. This habit consists of a frequently repeated chain of behaviors or series of steps that lead to instances of drug use. Each step in the habit increases the probability of drug use. U-turns are alternatives to the steps in a drug-habit chain; they decrease the probability of use. Your job is to teach patients how and when to make various kinds of U-turns. You will use figure 2 often (flip chart 34) to help patients understand the concept of U-turns.

In this model of relapse, we imagine that patients are standing on a somewhat slippery slope that

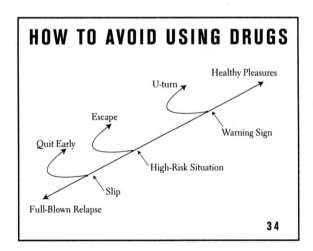

FIGURE 2. *How to Avoid Using Drugs*

can lead to a full-blown relapse of drug or alcohol dependence. However, patients don't simply slide down this slope. They take particular actions, such as accepting an offer to use drugs, and it is these actions that can lead to a full-blown relapse. U-turns are actions that do just the opposite. They reverse progress toward instances of drug use and instead lead to healthy pleasures.

For example, suppose a patient gets a call from a friend who invites the patient to his apartment to watch a football game. The patient knows that the friend will probably have a case of beer and that other friends will bring marijuana and possibly cocaine. So the phone call is actually a warning sign that a high-risk situation (a party involving alcohol and drugs) is ahead. Rather than accept the invitation and slide further down the slope toward the high-risk situation, the patient makes a U-turn. He declines the invitation to watch the game and instead calls another friend who does not use drugs and invites that friend to go to the movies (a healthy pleasure).

Note that quitting early and escaping high-risk situations without using (for example, by refusing drugs) are special types of U-turns. However, it is critically important to build skills that keep patients away from situations where drug refusal will be difficult (that is, a high-risk situation). Therefore, when teaching the module's concepts and skills, reserve the term *U-turn* to refer to things patients should do to avoid getting into high-risk situations in the first place.

SAMM assumes that drug-use behaviors are established and maintained by the reinforcing effects of addictive substances. The idea is to extinguish drug-use behaviors by promoting other behaviors that are incompatible with drug use and that will be reinforced in other ways. The simplest example is called "riding the wave." Patients are taught that when they get a craving for drugs or alcohol, they should take no action until the craving passes (just as a wave eventually passes). A more complex example involves talking with a psychiatrist about worsening symptoms instead of trying to reduce the symptoms with alcohol or addictive drugs.

Substance abuse and dependence are seen as unhealthy habits because they impair health, relationships, and functional ability. The behaviors that make up the habit are maintained by the reinforcing effects of the addicting substances. Often, the reinforcing effect is accompanied by pleasure. To use the terms of this module, the unhealthy habit of abusing drugs and alcohol is maintained by the immediate pleasure associated with use of addictive substances. This pleasure is considered unhealthy because it maintains a whole series of behaviors that are physically and psychologically damaging.

The opposite of drug-use habits (unhealthy habits) are healthy habits, like eating balanced meals, fulfilling family responsibilities, following medical advice, participating in regular physical exercise, and performing good grooming and hygiene. These habits tend to promote health, work, and social relationships. While drug-habit chains are maintained by the reinforcing qualities of addictive drugs, healthy habits are maintained by the reinforcing properties of food, exercise, and the approval of others. These reinforcers are termed "healthy pleasures."

The drug-use habit is maintained by the reinforcing properties of addictive drugs. The habit begins and grows because addictive drugs reinforce behaviors that occur prior to the drug's reaching the brain. These behaviors usually involve things like saying "yes" to a drug offer, buying drugs from a dealer, rolling a marijuana cigarette, loading a crack pipe, and opening a bottle of liquor. Shortly after a person does these things, the drug arrives in the brain and causes changes that make it more likely that the person will repeat these behaviors in the future. In fact, those behaviors that lead most efficiently and reliably to drug use will be more frequently reinforced and will therefore eventually dominate the addicted person's repertoire of behaviors. In this way, the drug essentially teaches the user to engage in a pattern of behaviors that will reliably lead to drug use. This effect probably extends beyond voluntary actions to include thinking as well. For example, the thought "I'll just use a little this time and then stop" will tend to be heavily reinforced and become part of the habit of drug use, even though the addicted person never uses "a little." As the drug-habit chain develops, it replaces healthy habits and the user stops working, ignores his family, and neglects his physical and emotional health.

The module is designed to teach patients how to reverse the drug-habit chain. The idea is to teach patients to think and act in ways that lead away from drugs and toward healthy pleasures that will reinforce the newly learned thoughts and behaviors. The drug-habit chain is seen as a series of behaviors, where each brings the patient a step closer to drug use. Once the drug reaches the brain, the entire sequence of behaviors is reinforced. The module teaches patients to recognize each step in the series. These steps toward drug use are called warning signs. For each step toward drug use (or at every warning sign), patients learn a variety of things to think and do that lead away from drug use and toward healthy pleasures. These alternative steps are called U-turns. They are the critical core of this module, the skills that the module seeks to train.

TEST OF KNOWLEDGE AND SKILLS

During development and pilot-testing of this module, investigators tested whether patients learned key concepts and skills. One way to appreciate what the module is intended to teach is to imagine a perfect score on this test. Below is an example of how a patient would have to answer the test questions and perform the test role-plays in order to score perfectly. The patient is real and did almost this well after completing the module. Topic areas are bold. The patient's responses are italic. (To illustrate the relationships among concepts, the sequence of questions differs somewhat from the actual test, which you can find in appendix B.)

Jeff is 40 years old and has had paranoid schizophrenia since he was 23. Later, he became addicted to heroin and amphetamines. When acutely psychotic, he's convinced that a "motorcycle Mafia" is hunting him. He once barricaded himself inside a building, which the police then surrounded to force his evacuation. The amphetamines worsen the psychotic symptoms, but those symptoms are present even when he has been abstinent for months.

Module Theme

"How are you going to avoid drugs?"

By saying no to drugs and yes to healthy pleasures.

"How are you going to say no to drugs?"

By avoiding high-risk situations.

High-Risk Situations

"What is a high-risk situation?"

A situation where it will be very hard for me to avoid using drugs.

"Describe one of your high-risk situations."

Hanging around the beach after I get my check. There are lots of dealers who know me. It's real hard.

Drug Refusal

"If a dealer offers you drugs, show me how you'd refuse. I'll be the dealer."

(Averts gaze, walks away quickly, waving his hand) Don't want any, don't want any.

"What if a friend offers? Show me how you'd refuse. I'll play your friend."

Jeff says no, suggests other activities; when pressed, levels with his friend (i.e., tells him why he must avoid drugs), then leaves.

Quitting after a Slip

"What if you end up using?"

I'll quit early before I spend all my money and make myself sick . . . and I'd stay in treatment.

"Show me how you'd leave a situation where you're sharing drugs with others."

(Puts drugs down, stands, walks quickly toward the door) Gotta go, gotta go.

Reporting a Slip

"How would you tell your case manager that you had used? I'll play your case manager."

Jeff gives a polite greeting, maintains good eye contact, and speaks in a pleasant voice. He reports the slip directly, and asks to discuss it. He describes the high-risk situation that led to use and explains that he quit early. He summarizes his current treatment efforts and asks for help in avoiding future similar situations. Finally, he thanks the case manager.

Avoiding High-Risk Situations

"Are you going to rely on being able to say no to drugs?"

No, that's too risky. I'm going to avoid high-risk situations.

"How are you going to avoid high-risk situations?"

By knowing my warning signs and by making U-turns.

Warning Signs

"What are warning signs?"

Things that tell me I might be headed toward using drugs.

"What are your warning signs?"

Getting my check; feeling like other people are watching and criticizing me; skipping my medication; calling friends I know use, or dealers; thinking that I'd feel better around people if I shot heroin; skipping treatment meetings.

U-turns

"What are U-turns?"

Anything I do that leads away from drugs.

"What U-turns will you make?"

Read my emergency card; talk to my doctor if I get paranoid; call my support person; work on my bike (motorcycle).

Reporting Symptoms and Side Effects

"Show me how you'd tell your psychiatrist about paranoia. I'll play your psychiatrist."

Jeff gives a polite greeting, maintains good eye contact, and speaks in a pleasant tone. He states the symptom character, duration, and effect on daily activities. He asks for help, then repeats the doctor's instructions. He asks when to expect relief and then thanks the doctor.

Support Person

"What makes a good support person?"

Somebody I know well, who I can trust; someone I can see often and get hold of in an emergency; someone who doesn't use drugs, who wants to help me.

Getting a Support Person

"Show me how you'd get me to be your support person."

Jeff explains the need for help, describes the role of a support person, is direct in asking the person to serve, answers questions about the role, shows his emergency card and asks to write name and number, thanks person.

Healthy Pleasures

"What's a healthy pleasure?"

Something that feels good and is good for you.

"What are your favorite healthy pleasures?"

I just want to feel comfortable around other people; not feel like I'm being watched and put down. I like talking to girls, like at Cocaine Anonymous dances. I also like working on motorcycles.

Healthy Habits

"What are healthy habits?"

Things that are good for me, that I have to do over and over. They're not always fun, but I need to do them so I can be comfortable around other people and so I can work on motorcycles.

"What healthy habits are important for you?"

Take my medication every day; go to my treatment program at least once a week; talk to my support person every week.

"What other healthy habits are important for you?"

I've got to get up on time every morning, shower, shave; I've already got my check going to my rep. payee; and I just started working out twice a week in the gym here.

Asking Someone to Join You in a Healthy Pleasure

"Suppose you wanted to ask a girl you know to go out with you. Show me how you'd do that."

Jeff offers a pleasant greeting, maintains good eye contact, and speaks in a happy tone. He says he enjoys the other's company, that she is fun to be with. He mentions at least two activities she would enjoy. He specifies when the activities would take place and is direct in asking her to join him. If there's a time conflict, he suggests another activity or other time. If she is clearly not interested, he says he understands and thanks her for considering his offer. If she accepts, he sets a time and place to meet.

Negotiating with a Representative Payee

"What if you wanted some extra money to buy motorcycle parts? Show me how you'd ask your payee. I'll be your payee."

Jeff offers a polite greeting, maintains good eye contact, and speaks in a pleasant tone. He explains that his request is part of avoiding drugs. He says how much money he needs and for what. He reminds the rep. payee of his therapeutic progress (for example, medica-

tion compliance) and he gives the rep. payee permission to contact clinicians to verify. He also says he'll provide receipts. Finally, he thanks the rep. payee and schedules a follow-up appointment to report progress and deliver receipts.

MATERIALS NEEDED TO CONDUCT SKILLS TRAINING

Here are the things you need to conduct skills training. You can find examples of some of these in the appendices. In addition, the *SAMM Skills Illustration Videotape* demonstrates the nine skills taught in the skills training sessions (see appendix A).

Supplies

- *SAMM flip chart.* This chart provides quick access to content from basic training and skills training. Therapists create the chart by copying the figures by hand from the appendices onto a blank flip chart pad attached to an easel. These are available from most office supply stores and catalogs. Attaching tabs to the pages helps the therapist find frequently used pages. The SAMM flip chart serves three purposes: (1) helps the therapist learn the material as he or she creates the flip chart, (2) increases patient understanding, and (3) keeps the therapist on track during sessions.
- *Blank flip chart or board.* Use this to list ideas that patients generate during brainstorming and problem-solving. Then compare the list to the relevant page on the prepared SAMM flip chart. (You can use a dry erase board but we prefer two flip charts, one prepared in advance and one blank).
- *Markers and eraser if using dry erase board.* Used to write on the blank flip chart or dry erase board.
- *Clipboards and writing utensils.* Used by the patients when completing the emergency card or activity schedule during class time.

Reinforcers

- *Candy for reinforcement.* Give candy to patients intermittently for desired behaviors, such as carrying their emergency card, arriving to class on time, or participating appropriately in group.
- *Graduation celebration treats (e.g., candy/baked goods).* Celebrate graduation from basic training or skills training with candy or baked goods. Some treatment programs have T-shirts or baseball caps with the program logo. Give these as symbols of graduation.
- *Poster of attendance.* Reinforce attendance by creating a poster with the names of all partic-

ipants and stickers representing each session attended. Those with the best attendance will have the most stickers following their names.

- *"Wall of Fame."* Post copies of each graduate's diploma on a wall of the classroom.

Forms

- *Clinical Urgency Form.* Use this form to tell a patient's psychiatrist about the patient's worsening symptoms.
- *Class Reminder Form.* Complete this form after each skills training or practice class to serve as a reminder to the therapist of what activities took place and what homework assignments were given. Begin every class with a brief review of the previous group and follow up on any homework assignments.
- *Basic Training Attendance Form.* Complete this form after each basic training class to keep a record of which classes the patient attended. This is important because the patient must complete all eight of the basic training sessions before beginning skills training.
- *Skills Training Attendance Form.* Complete this form after each skills training class to keep a record of the patient's participation in each role-play. This form helps determine when the patient is ready to graduate from skills training.
- *Graduation diplomas.* Give these certificates of training to the patients upon completion of the SAMM module.

Patient Materials

- *Emergency cards.* A personalized card completed by each patient (see appendix A). The card reminds patients of key phone numbers (e.g., clinic, support persons, crisis hotline), medical information (e.g., medication names and dosages), and key drug relapse prevention ideas (e.g., personal reasons not to use drugs). Patients fold the card twice and keep it in their wallets. They start filling it out in basic training session 2 and complete it during subsequent sessions.
- *Activity schedule.* A schedule completed by the patient listing all appointments, class times, healthy pleasures, and healthy habits. This is used to ensure that the patient is creating time to do things that are good for him rather than using drugs.
- *Skill prompt cards.* 4 x 6 index cards listing the steps of each role-play (see appendix A). The cards may be used by the patients outside the classroom to help them remember the skills.
- *List of healthy pleasures.* A list of healthy pleasures that can be used as a handout for the patients to assist them in creating a personalized list of healthy pleasures.

OVERCOMING
ADDICTIONS

BASIC TRAINING

WHAT IS BASIC TRAINING?

Basic training is eight 45-minute educational sessions designed to teach drug relapse prevention principles to small groups of individuals with schizophrenia. Each session can stand alone, so patients can drop into the series at any point. Patients attending basic training should also attend practice sessions. When patients successfully complete all eight basic training sessions they are ready to move on to skills training.

OVERVIEW OF EIGHT SESSIONS

Session 1: Damage Control

Main point: If you slip and use drugs or alcohol again, stop early and get right back into treatment. This will reduce damage to your health, relationships, and finances.

Related concepts: Mt. Recovery (Sobell & Sobell, 1993), slip vs. full-blown relapse, harm reduction, abstinence violation effect, bouncing back into treatment

Session 2: Emergency Card

Main point: Make an emergency card that contains vital information and reminders about how and why to avoid drugs. Carry it with you at all times.

Related concepts: Support person, coping skills, why quit

Session 3: Habits and Craving Control

Main point: Drug abuse is learned and can be unlearned.

Related concepts: Habits, reinforcement, craving, conditioning, withdrawal, extinction, riding the wave

Session 4: High-Risk Situations

Main point: Don't get into situations where drugs are hard to avoid. If you do, leave or escape the situation immediately.

Related concepts: Warning signs, U-turns, healthy pleasures

Session 5: Warning Signs

Main point: You can avoid high-risk situations by learning to recognize the signs that you might be headed toward drug use.

Related concepts: Drug-habit chain (trigger, craving, planning, getting, using), U-turns, healthy habits, removing triggers, riding the wave, emergency card

Session 6: Healthy Pleasures and Healthy Habits

Main point: You can avoid drugs by focusing on the things that are most important to you.

Related concepts: Extinction, U-turns, activities schedule

Session 7: Why Quit Drugs?

Main point: Make sure you can always remember why you decided to quit using drugs.

Related concepts: Advantages and disadvantages of using drugs and of not using drugs, support person

Session 8: Money Management

Main point: You may need someone to help make sure your money takes care of you, instead of going for drugs that hurt you.

Related concepts: Trigger, high-risk situation, warning sign, U-turns, representative payees, and fiduciaries

Session 1
DAMAGE CONTROL

OVERVIEW

In this session, help patients understand that if they do use drugs or alcohol again, it is important for them to stop use early so that they do less damage to their health, relationships, and finances. We call this concept **damage control**. It is similar to a concept in the substance abuse treatment literature known as harm reduction.

First, explain that learning to use drugs and alcohol took time—and it will also take time to unlearn those habits. Some people manage to stop right away and never use again. But most people who are trying to stop, even those who are working hard at it, will, nevertheless, use again. If this happens, it is very important not to let a minor slip turn into a full-blown relapse. Help patients understand the idea of damage control by asking them to recall their own previous slips and full-blown relapses. Have them discuss these experiences with respect to the quantity of drug used, money spent, and duration of use. Also focus on other negative consequences, including legal and family problems. This will help patients realize that the longer a relapse continues, the more damage is done and the more repairs will be needed.

It is important that patients focus on the negative consequences of their drug use. This is not an opportunity to recall the euphoria of using drugs. If patients begin to glamorize their drug use, return the discussion to the negative consequences.

SAMPLE THERAPIST SCRIPT

Introduce the goal (flip chart 5).

"It's good to see you all here today! Welcome to basic training. In today's class, you'll

SESSION SUMMARY

1. Introduce the goal (flip chart 5).
2. Make sure patients can repeat the goal.
3. Introduce the notion of successful techniques.
4. Define high-risk situation and damage control (flip charts 6, 7).
5. Contrast a minor slip with a full-blown relapse (flip chart 8).
6. Compare relapse prevention to fire prevention.
7. Use the Mt. Recovery metaphor to illustrate learning from a slip (flip charts 9, 10).
8. Discuss the abstinence violation effect (AVE) (flip chart 11).
9. Emphasize the importance of getting back into treatment despite slips and relapses (flip chart 12).

learn why it is so important to stop a drug relapse early. We call this idea **damage control**."

Make sure patients can repeat the goal.

"What is the goal of today's class?"

To learn why it is important to stop a relapse early.

"What is the main goal of the module?"

To say no to drugs and yes to healthy pleasures.

Introduce the notion of successful techniques.

"Quitting drugs or alcohol is one of the most difficult things you'll ever do. Lots of people try, and some succeed. Those who succeed use certain techniques. We will teach you those techniques. Just as an athlete would try to improve his skills by learning what the best athletes do, our goal is to teach you the techniques that others have used successfully to quit using drugs and alcohol."

Define high-risk situation and damage control (flip charts 6, 7).

"The goal of relapse prevention is, as the name suggests, to prevent a relapse from occurring. You'll learn to do this by anticipating and avoiding high-risk situations that led to drug use in the past. A high-risk situation is any situation in which it would be really hard to avoid using (flip chart 6). Abstinence is the ideal goal, but often it takes more than one try to reach an ideal goal. If you are able to quit using drugs and alcohol right away and never use again, that's great. However, if you do slip and use, you'll need to know how to stop a slip early on before it does lots of damage to your relationships, health, and finances. Remember, abstinence is the ideal goal, but if you do slip, it is important to reduce any damage by stopping a slip and getting back into treatment quickly. That is what we mean by damage control (flip chart 7)."

Contrast a minor slip with a full-blown relapse (flip chart 8).

"Let's talk about the difference between a minor slip and a full-blown relapse. Think back to a time when you had a full-blown relapse. How long did it last? How much money did you spend? What types of negative consequences did you experience? How did you feel about yourself and your behavior? Now think back to a time when you slipped and used drugs, but were able to regain control and get back on track without a full-blown relapse. How long did it last? How much money did you spend? What types of negative consequences did you experience? How did you feel about yourself and your behavior?"(Write group members' responses on the dry erase board or second flip chart.)

Compare relapse prevention to fire prevention.

"Because damage control accepts the fact that individuals who are trying to quit drugs may slip up and use, some people wonder if it is condoning controlled drug use, or 'chipping.' To see why this is *not* true, it is useful to compare yourself to a forest ranger. Your job is to prevent yourself from using drugs; his job is to prevent forest fires. Obviously, the ranger wants to prevent all forest fires from occurring. However, if a fire should occur he wants to get it under control and put it out right away. He knows putting out the fire is much better than letting the fire rage out of control for a long time. This applies to drug use as well. Like the forest ranger preventing fires, the recovering drug user wants to avoid all drug use. However, if a slip should occur, it is best to keep it contained and keep the damage to a minimum" (Brownell, 1990).

Use the Mt. Recovery metaphor to illustrate learning from a slip (flip charts 9, 10).

"Another useful analogy is to think of the recovery process as similar to climbing a mountain (flip chart 9). If you slip a little, you may lose a little ground, but you probably won't go back to the very bottom. In addition, you've already been over that ground before and so you are aware of the dangers that await you and have had a chance to think about and prepare for them. The goal of this class is to learn from setbacks and to help you keep climbing up your own personal Mt. Recovery (Sobell & Sobell, 1993).

"The forest ranger and the mountain climber have something in common in how they approach their situations: They anticipate dangers instead of waiting until the crisis happens. We call this 'thinking smart.' One aspect of thinking smart is realizing that a full-blown relapse causes much more damage than does a slip (flip chart 10)."

Discuss the abstinence violation effect (AVE) (flip chart 11).

"As we just heard, not all instances of drug use are the same. On the one hand, there

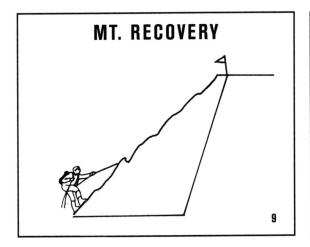

are times when using a little leads to using a great deal. If you have been trying to abstain, we call this a full-blown relapse. However, there are other times when you might use just a little bit and for whatever reason, don't have a full-blown relapse. We call this a slip. There are many differences between slips and full-blown relapses that are obvious. Such differences include amount used, how long you used, amount of money you lost, and negative consequences suffered. Despite these differences, many people feel the same after a slip as they do after a full-blown relapse. This is a problem because too strong a reaction to a slip can help turn a slip into a full-blown relapse. Here's what I mean. Suppose you slip and react too strongly. You are very deeply disappointed in yourself and feel like a hopeless failure who has messed up so badly that you are back where you started. You believe that you have blown the goal of abstinence and have failed completely. You tell yourself that you've already blown it, so you might as well keep using. Sometimes this is how a slip turns into a full-blown relapse (flip chart 11). It describes the reaction you might have when you violate or break a goal of abstinence. However, if you compare the negative consequences of a full-blown relapse to a slip, which has fewer negative consequences? We want you to understand how you react to having a slip, how these reactions can lead to continuing use, and how to stop the process before it gets completely out of control."

Emphasize the importance of getting back into treatment despite slips and relapses (flip chart 12).

"You can keep a slip from turning into a full-blown relapse by getting back into treatment as quickly as possible after a slip. This helps you break the cycle of drug use and avoid turning a minor setback into a major setback. We call this **bouncing back into treatment.** Can you think of other things that help you bounce back into treatment? *(Pause for responses.)* Right! Call your support person. Anything else? Okay. Let's see what's on the flip chart (flip chart 12)."

Session 2
EMERGENCY CARD

OVERVIEW

In this session you will teach patients the importance of an emergency card and get them started on creating their own. This card will contain personalized information about each patient's medications and health care providers. In addition, the card will remind patients how to avoid drugs and seek healthy pleasures. Patients should always carry this card with them. Like the ads for the American Express card said, "Don't leave home without it." Note that only the first three sections of the emergency card are filled in during this session. Patients will complete the remainder of the card during subsequent sessions of basic training.

SAMPLE THERAPIST SCRIPT

Introduce the goals (flip chart 13).

> "It's good to see you all here today! Welcome to basic training. In today's class, you'll learn about the importance of having an emergency card and will begin to develop your own personal emergency card."

Make sure patients can repeat the goals.

> "What are the goals of today's class?"

> *To learn about the importance of an emergency card and to create my own personal emergency card that will help me remember things so that I can avoid using drugs.*

> "What is the overall goal of the module?"

> *To say no to drugs and yes to healthy pleasures.*

SESSION SUMMARY

1. Introduce the goals (flip chart 13).
2. Make sure patients can repeat the goals.
3. Compare the emergency card to instructions for a fire drill.
4. Emphasize the need to carry the card at all times and review it before taking any steps toward drug use.

Compare the emergency card to instructions for a fire drill.

"Why do we have fire drills? So that in the event of a fire, everyone will calmly follow a predetermined plan. This plan is developed when everyone is in a calm state. In these classes you'll be learning and practicing what to do in a different kind of emer-

---

Name:

Social security no.:

Emergency phone no.'s:

Support person 1: (name & phone no.)

Support person 2:

Payee:

In case of emergency contact:

Treatment program: (name & phone no.)

Hospital ER: (name & phone no.)

Crisis Line: AA #

     NA #

     Other #

Prescribed medications (name, dose, freq.)

Healthy Habits

Things that I do over and over again that are good for me

-
-
-
-

Healthy Pleasures

Things that feel good and are good for me

-
-
-
-

EMERGENCY CARD *Front Side*

gency—the kind that leads you to use drugs or alcohol. Sometimes when faced with an emergency it is hard to think through a situation and make the best decisions. So today you will start working on a card that will help you remember what to do when faced with an emergency involving your use of drugs or alcohol. For example, it will remind you what to do when you start to crave drugs or alcohol. It will also list important information such as prescribed medications, allergies, and other health conditions. You should carry your emergency card with you at all times. Keep it in your wallet."

Emphasize the need to carry the card at all times and review it before taking any steps toward drug use.

"You'll notice that right now most of the card is blank. You'll fill it in as you learn new ways to avoid drugs. So it is very important to bring the card to each class because you will add new material. You'll choose what information and techniques will work best for you in an emergency, and then you will add that information to your emergency card.

High-Risk Situation I'm heading for a drug relapse if:	**Warning Signs** I'm headed for a high-risk situation if:
• People: • Places: • Things: • Thoughts: • Emotions:	• People: • Places: • Things: • Thoughts: • Emotions:
I've decided to QUIT because:	**U-turns and Coping Skills** Instead of using drugs I will: • Participate in a healthy pleasure • Call my support person • Ride the wave • Review why I decided to quit • •

EMERGENCY CARD *Back Side*

"You are probably wondering, 'Now that I have this card, what do I do with it?' This card is for two situations. The first is when you need to access medical information. With this card, much important medical information is readily accessible. When doctors ask you what medicine you take, you can tell them the exact medication and dosage. The second situation in which the card can be used is if you are experiencing cravings or urges to use drugs. Pulling out and reading your emergency card is the first of many coping skills you will learn in this class. Before thinking any further about using or taking any action, stop and look at the section of your emergency card that says "Instead of using drugs, I will" and pick a coping response and do it. If that does not work, try another. The goal is to cope effectively with urges to use, rather than using drugs automatically, as you did in the past."

Session 3
HABITS AND CRAVING CONTROL

OVERVIEW

Your goal is to help patients understand that they have learned the habit of using drugs through years of practice. This habit can be unlearned or, more correctly, it can be replaced by healthy habits. You'll help patients understand how brain physiology and learning theory can explain craving and how extinction can play a role in ending cravings.

You want patients to understand that each time they use an addicting drug, they are strengthening their drug habit. Every time they use the drug, they reinforce all the things they did to get the drug, and they strengthen the mental associations between the drug and all the people, places, things, thoughts, and emotions that accompanied getting and using the drug. These associations are often referred to as cues or triggers. By strengthening these associations and reinforcing drug-seeking, patients are teaching themselves to continue using drugs and to crave drugs when they try to stop.

You want them to understand that every time they avoid using drugs when it would have been their habit to use, they are weakening the habit and reducing the chance of cravings in the future. Use the "ride the wave" technique to emphasize the point that simply waiting for a craving to pass will weaken the habit and reduce future craving.

SAMPLE THERAPIST SCRIPT

Introduce the goals (flip chart 14).

"It's good to see you all here today! Welcome to basic training. Today's class is called habits and craving control. We'll show you that you can view your addiction as an unhealthy habit; a habit that you have *learned*. We'll also show you how you can *unlearn*

SESSION SUMMARY

1. Introduce the goals (flip chart 14).
2. Make sure patients can repeat the goals.
3. Point out that it took time to learn to use drugs and it will take time to unlearn the habit.
4. Define drug abuse as an unhealthy habit (flip charts 15, 16).
5. Define craving and discuss its relationship to breaking a habit (flip charts 17, 18).
6. Describe how withdrawal physiology leads to craving (flip charts 19, 20, 21).
7. Explain how conditioning can create craving.
8. Discuss triggers and get examples from patients (flip chart 22).
9. Explain Pavlovian conditioning (flip chart 23)
10. Explain extinction in Pavlovian terms.
11. Explain how to understand drug dreams in these terms (optional).
12. Explain the simple coping skill called "riding the wave."
13. Point out where to find coping skills on the emergency card.

the habit. We'll discuss what causes cravings and how to deal with them. We have a lot of material to cover so let's get started."

Make sure patients can repeat the goals.

"What are the goals of today's class?"

To see how drug abuse is learned and can be unlearned; to learn what causes cravings and how to deal with them.

"What is the overall goal of the module?"

To saying no to drugs and yes to healthy pleasures

Point out that it took time to learn to use drugs and it will take time to unlearn the habit.

"It is important to be realistic about drug use. Often people who abuse drugs have spent a large part of their lives learning how to get and use drugs. So trying to quit means learning a whole new way of life. Just as you had to learn to obtain and use drugs, now you will have to learn how not to use drugs. It will take time and practice."

Define drug abuse as an unhealthy habit (flip charts 15, 16).

　　"In some ways, you can think about drug abuse as a **habit**. Who can tell me what a habit is? Right, a habit is something you do over and over again (flip chart 15). Some habits are good for your health, like brushing your teeth. People tend to call these healthy habits. And there are habits that are bad for your health, like smoking cigarettes. People tend to call these unhealthy habits. Give me some more examples of habits, either healthy or unhealthy. *(Pause for responses.)* Right, drinking coffee and driving to work are examples of habits that have to be learned (flip chart 16). These habits have been learned the same way you learned to use drugs. You probably learned how to get and use drugs through years of practice. But, just as the habit of drinking coffee or using drugs has been learned, these habits may be unlearned too. The best way to unlearn an unhealthy habit is to replace it with a healthy habit. That's why the overall goal of the module is to avoid drugs *and* seek healthy pleasures."

Define craving and discuss its relationship to breaking a habit (flip charts 17, 18).

　　"When people try to break a habit, they often find that they get very strong urges to resume the habit. This happens even if they're absolutely sure they want to quit. When people try to break the habit of using drugs, they get very strong urges to use, called **cravings** (flip chart 17). Often these cravings are even stronger than the urges they had before they decided to quit. Why do you crave drugs even when you want to quit? Well, there are two reasons. One is called withdrawal and the other is called conditioning (flip chart 18)."

Describe how withdrawal physiology leads to craving (flip charts 19, 20, 21).

　　"First, let me tell you about intoxication, tolerance, and withdrawal. Addicting drugs tend to act like some of the brain's natural chemicals that are involved in feeling good (flip chart 19). Addicting drugs simulate the effect of the brain's natural feel-good chem-

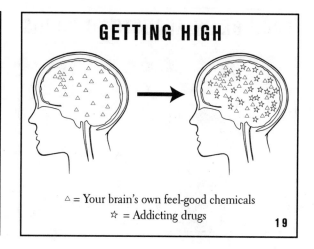

CRAVING

A strong urge or desire
to use drugs or alcohol.

17

GETTING HIGH

△ = Your brain's own feel-good chemicals
☆ = Addicting drugs

19

icals. Using an addicting drug causes a sudden increase in this feel-good effect and you are said to be *intoxicated*.

"When you use an addicting drug a lot and for along time, your brain adjusts to the presence of the drug. Your body senses that an artificial chemical, namely the drug, is present. It knows that the artificial chemical is doing the same thing usually done by one of its own natural chemicals. And it can tell that with both the artificial chemical and the natural chemical doing the same thing, some functions are overstimulated. To adjust for this, it cuts down on the production of its own natural chemical (flip chart 20). This means that you now need the drug just to feel normal and you need even more of it to get high. Addiction experts would say that you have developed *tolerance* to the drug.

"Then, when you stop using the drug, your brain senses the lack of the artificial chemical and has to start making its own natural chemicals again (flip chart 21).

"It can be a while before your body can make enough of the natural chemicals. Until then, there may not be enough of your natural chemicals to help your brain function properly. This condition is called *withdrawal*. It leads you to crave the artificial drug because it will quickly make things seem normal again."

Explain how conditioning can create craving.

"Now, let's talk about conditioning. Withdrawal is an important part of craving, but it doesn't tell the whole story. There is more to it. You have actually *trained* your body and mind to become dependent on drugs."

Discuss triggers and get examples from patients (flip chart 22).

"You might have noticed that even if you haven't used a drug for a long time you can still get cravings. This can't be because of withdrawal because your brain has had plenty

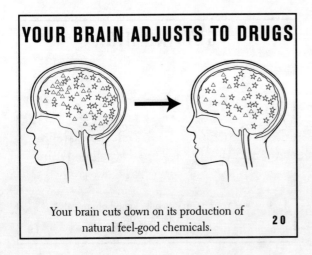

YOUR BRAIN ADJUSTS TO DRUGS

Your brain cuts down on its production of natural feel-good chemicals. **20**

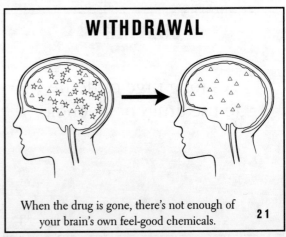

WITHDRAWAL

When the drug is gone, there's not enough of your brain's own feel-good chemicals. **21**

```
┌─────────────────────────────────┐  ┌─────────────────────────────────┐
│                                 │  │                                 │
│  LEARN TO PREDICT CRAVING       │  │  CONDITIONED CRAVING            │
│                                 │  │                                 │
│                                 │  │  • PAVLOV'S DOGS                │
│                                 │  │        Meat    ⟶ Drooling      │
│  • Do I crave in a particular   │  │   Meat + Bell  ⟶ Drooling      │
│    situation?                   │  │        Bell    ⟶ Drooling      │
│  • With certain people?         │  │                                 │
│  • At particular times?         │  │  • ADDICTION                    │
│  • When I am in a certain mood? │  │        Drug    ⟶ Craving       │
│                                 │  │  Drugs + Trigger ⟶ Craving     │
│                                 │  │        Drug    ⟶ Craving       │
│                           22    │  │                          23     │
└─────────────────────────────────┘  └─────────────────────────────────┘
```

of time to readjust and make the right amount of natural chemicals again. So what causes these cravings? The answer has to do with *when* you get cravings.

"Tell me more about your cravings (flip chart 22). *(Encourage discussion with the following questions.)* Do they happen in particular situations? With specific people? At particular times? In response to a particular emotion or mood? What are some of the obvious things that trigger your drug use? Some typical examples you might encounter include getting a large sum of money, such as SSI or general relief, being around another drug user, being with prostitutes, etc. These are the obvious triggers that cause craving and can lead to drug use. We will focus quite a bit of attention on the idea of triggers and by the end of this course you should have a good idea of your particular set of triggers.

"It is important to focus on triggers because if you know what prompts you to use drugs, you can think smart, anticipate the triggers, and either avoid them or cope with them when they happen. What makes the situation tricky, however, is that not all of the triggers are as obvious as the ones we've discussed so far. Have you ever had a craving and not been sure what caused it? *(Pause for responses.)* It may have felt like the urge came to you out of the blue. However, it is more likely that you were responding to something less obvious in the environment, which was causing you to think of using.

"A couple of examples might illustrate how these non-obvious or subtle triggers work. One man always bought his cocaine from a dealer who drove a black Mercedes. Eventually he decided he wanted treatment and entered a treatment program. He stopped using for several months. Then one day, walking down a familiar street, he suddenly had a strong desire to obtain cocaine. He felt angry and frustrated with himself, because he really felt committed to quitting, yet he felt this strong desire he could not explain. He shared this experience with his therapist. His therapist had him retrace his steps to try to discover what made him think of cocaine. He finally recalled seeing a black Mercedes similar to his dealer's car driving down the street and then feeling the urge to use cocaine. Even though he had not thought about the connection, the image of the black Mercedes stimulated his brain to crave cocaine.

"Another man shot heroin and used a necktie as a tourniquet. While in treatment, his doctor walked in to talk with him and the patient had a strong urge to use heroin. He later realized that it must have been the tie that reminded him of his heroin habit. Other examples include antennas, which can be used as pipes to smoke cocaine; steel wool pads, which can be used as screens; and even the local bus that you used to take you to places where you could buy drugs.

"To summarize, there are two reasons that you might get cravings even though you are trying to quit: First, if you have used within the last few days, your body may be used to the drug, and you may be in withdrawal; second, you may encounter triggers that remind you of drugs.

"One way to cope with cravings is not to act on them. If you can avoid using despite a craving, the craving will eventually go away."

Explain Pavlovian conditioning (flip chart 23).

"How many of you have heard of the Russian scientist named Pavlov? Pavlov was very interested in a kind of learning called conditioning. He studied how dogs respond to meat, but what he learned also applies to people and drugs.

"Pavlov noticed that if dogs smell meat, they drool. Pavlov wanted to see if he could train the dogs to drool to something that didn't naturally cause them to drool. So he let the dogs sniff the meat and rang a bell at the same time. He did this over and over and eventually found that he could get the dogs to drool just by ringing the bell. Pavlov concluded that the dogs had come to expect meat when they heard the bell, so they drooled even when there was no meat. He said that by always ringing the bell when the dogs sniffed meat, he had conditioned them to drool to the sound of the bell.

"How do you think that your experiences with drugs might be similar to Pavlov's experiment with the dogs? What's the equivalent of the meat? (*Pause for responses.*) Right! Drugs. The bell? (*Pause for responses.*) Sure! Money or the black Mercedes or the necktie."

Explain extinction in Pavlovian terms.

"Do you see any connection between Pavlov's theories and how the cravings may eventually be unlearned? Well, Pavlov found that he could teach his dogs to stop drooling to the sound of the bell. Do you think that Pavlov's approach might help you stop craving drugs? Here's what Pavlov did. He kept ringing the bell, but never brought the meat.

What do you think happened? At first, the dogs expected the meat and drooled anyway. But each time the bell rang and no meat came, they drooled less and less. They finally stopped drooling when the bell sounded because it no longer meant that meat was coming. Pavlov called this process extinction. How does it apply to drugs, triggers, and craving? *(Pause for responses.)* Right! If you keep encountering triggers, like black Mercedes or neckties, but you don't use drugs, your cravings will become less and less until they are extinct—like the dinosaurs.

"Let's look at a real life example. For one man, the first of the month was strongly associated with his drug use because he would receive his government checks and then spend all of his money on drugs. As the first of the month approached he would get stronger and stronger urges to use (like Pavlov's dogs' drooling when they heard the bell and thought food was on the way). So he arranged for the checks to go to a trusted friend who paid his rent and other bills so that he would not spend the money on drugs. At first, the man still got very strong cravings around the first of the month, but he no longer had a big chunk of cash to spend on drugs on the first of the month and his cravings gradually faded away."

Explain how to understand drug dreams in these terms (optional; teach if time allows).

"Patients often experience vivid and realistic dreams of drug use. Has this happened to any of you? *(Pause for responses.)* Based on information presented today, there are two reasons why people may experience drug dreams. One reason is that the brain may still be attempting to replace important chemicals, which at times can signal an urge to use. The second reason is that you may have been exposed to a trigger, possibly without even being aware of it, and it caused your brain to recall using drugs. The point is, when you have drug dreams, try to figure out if there was something that may have triggered the dream. Also, keep in mind that this may be a more vulnerable time for you and make plans to reduce the possibility of slipping into drug use."

Explain the simple coping skill called "riding the wave."

"If you can get through the cravings without using, eventually the cravings stop. There are many things you can do to help you get through the cravings. These are called coping skills. We will start with a coping skill that is easy to learn and that people have told us they find useful in dealing with cravings. It's called **riding the wave** (Marlatt & Gordon, 1985, p. 241). How many of you have been to the beach? When you think of the beach, what comes to mind? *(Pause for responses, such as people on the beach, suntan oil, sand, and eventually waves.)* When you look at a wave, what does it look like? *(Pause for responses.)* Right, the wave starts out small and develops momentum and becomes larger and larger until it eventually crashes onto the beach. Cravings are similar to waves. They start off small and become stronger and stronger, until you feel overcome by the craving or urge to use drugs. But just as the wave eventually crashes on the beach and disappears, cravings eventually disappear too. Instead of giving into the craving, one way of coping is to pretend to "ride the wave." Imagine you are a surfer, balancing on a surfboard as the wave is at its maximum intensity, only your wave is the craving. Remind yourself that, just like a wave, no matter how intense it is, your craving will subside over time. By riding the wave, you are buying yourself additional time, rather than impulsively using as you may have in the past. This provides an opportunity for you to think about whether or not to use drugs. Every time you ride out a wave of craving you are teaching your mind and body that the things that used to lead to drugs don't lead there anymore. You are teaching yourself *not* to crave. It's the same thing Pavlov would do to get his dogs to stop drooling when he rang the bell. He'd ring the bell, let them drool, and then not bring them any meat. Eventually, they stopped drooling when he rang the bell.

"In these sessions, you'll learn lots of things that will help you ride out the wave of craving."

Point out where to find coping skills on the emergency card.

"Look at your emergency card. You see a section called 'U-turns and coping skills.' In that list you'll see 'ride the wave.' When you experience cravings, look at this section of your card and it will remind you to 'ride the wave' instead of using. As you identify coping skills that are effective for you, it is important to write those down on your emergency card. Remember, it is easier to think of coping skills when you are calm and relaxed, but when you are in an emergency situation you are in a completely different state and you want to be prepared."

Session 4
HIGH-RISK SITUATIONS

OVERVIEW

Your goal is to get each patient to describe a high-risk situation that he or she must avoid if they are going to be successful in avoiding drugs. Have each patient write that situation on his or her emergency card. You'll help patients see how important it is to avoid getting into such situations in the first place. Finally, you'll briefly introduce the concepts of warning signs, U-turns, and healthy pleasures.

SAMPLE THERAPIST SCRIPT

Introduce the goals (flip chart 24).

> "It's good to see you all here today! Welcome to basic training. In today's class you'll learn about high-risk situations and why it is so important to avoid them."

Make sure the patients can repeat the goals.

> "What are the goals of today's class?"

> *To learn about high-risk situations and why it is so important to avoid them.*

> "What is the overall goal of the module?"

> *To say no to drugs and yes to healthy pleasures.*

Explain that it is harder to avoid drugs in some situations than in others.

> "In some situations it's easier to avoid drugs than in others. Don't you agree? For

SESSION SUMMARY

1. Introduce the goals (flip chart 24).
2. Make sure patients can repeat the goals.
3. Explain that it is harder to avoid drugs in some situations than in others.
4. Elicit examples of high-risk situations (flip chart 25).
5. Point out that situations are collections of people, places, things, thoughts, and emotions (flip chart 26).
6. Elicit more fully defined high-risk situations.
7. Introduce the idea of avoiding high-risk situations by making U-turns at warning signs and by seeking healthy pleasures (flip charts 27, 28).

example, how confident are you that you'll be able to get through the rest of this class period without using drugs or alcohol? (*Nearly all patients will say they are very confident.*) Why is that? (*Pause for responses.*) Right! You're not really interested in using drugs at this moment and you'd have to do a whole bunch of things you're just not in the habit of doing. In a sense, it would be a lot of effort. Can you think of other situations where you're very confident you wouldn't use?"

Elicit examples of high-risk situations (flip chart 25).

"At the other extreme, there are situations in which it is very hard *not* to use drugs. We call these **high-risk situations** (flip chart 25). These are likely to be the very situations in which you previously used drugs. Can you think of some of these? (*Pause for responses.*) Right! Hanging around old drug-using buddies or visiting in a neighborhood where you used drugs frequently would probably put you in a position where it would be hard to avoid using. Can you think of some things that would make those situations even more likely to lead you to use drugs? (*Pause for responses.*) Okay! If you had lots of money, that would make it even easier to use. Things that make it easy and tempting to use increase the risk that you will use. Give me some more situations. Some of you may have moved away from the old neighborhood, and you'll have to imagine what new situations you might encounter that will make it very hard to avoid using."

Point out that situations are collections of people, places, things, thoughts, and emotions (flip chart 26).

"Notice that these situations are made up of five kinds of things. Let's take a look at them and see if they remind you of any other situations that are very risky for you."

HIGH-RISK SITUATIONS

Situations that
make it hard
to avoid using drugs.

2 5

THE PARTS OF A HIGH-RISK SITUATION

PEOPLE: drug dealer, drinking buddy, strawberry

PLACES: liquor store, park, or neighborhood known for drugs

THINGS: paraphernalia (pipes, screens, lighters, brillo pads, syringes), cash

THOUGHTS: "I'm going to have just one beer."

EMOTIONS: angry, sad, nervous, lonely, worthless

2 6

Elicit more fully defined high-risk situations.

"With all this in mind, describe a situation that really could come up for you, and where you'd find it hard to avoid using drugs. I want you to provide lots of details, so that it would be as though I was watching the scene in a movie. Tell me about the people involved, the location, the things, what you are thinking, and what you are feeling—everything that contributes to making it hard to avoid using. *(Pause for responses.)* Wow! That's a good one. You just cashed your check, you feel lonely, you're walking through a drug-using neighborhood when a familiar prostitute comes on to you. Now if you actually get into that situation, what are you going to do? *(Pause for responses.)* Right! You'd have to say no and get out of there fast! You'd have to escape from the situation. Would that be easy to do? *(Pause for responses.)* No, it would be very hard and you're telling me that chances are you'd end up using. The risk that you will use in that situation is very high. That's what we mean by a high-risk situation. Write that one down on your emergency card. Who's got another high-risk situation?"

Note to therapist: Examples should be complete descriptions of real situations that patients are likely to encounter. For instance, if a patient says "the park" is a high-risk situation, ask for more information, including the name of the park. It is useful to remind them that you want to be able to see it as though you were watching it in a movie. Make sure that they describe the scene in enough detail (people, places, things, thoughts, and emotions) so that it is very clear why it would be hard for them to escape without using drugs. This is important so that you can later draw a distinction between high-risk situations (i.e., very hard to say "no") and warning signs (i.e., time to make a U-turn and avoid getting into a high-risk situation in the first place). Continue until everyone has described a high-risk situation they might run into and has written it on their emergency card.

Introduce the idea of avoiding high-risk situations by making U-turns at warning signs and by seeking healthy pleasures (flip charts 27, 28).

"If it is so very hard to say no in a high-risk situation, why is it good to know your high-risk situations? *(Pause for responses.)* Right! So you can avoid getting into them in the first place. How are you going to do that? For example, how could Joe avoid getting into that situation, where the strawberry makes the offer he can't refuse? *(Pause for responses.)* Of course! He can make sure he doesn't go to that neighborhood. But what if it happens in some other neighborhood? *(Pause for responses.)* Yes! He could make sure he doesn't carry that much cash around. So if Joe finds himself headed for that neighborhood with lots of cash in his wallet, what should he do? *(Pause for responses.)* Right! Turn around and head the other way. This brings us to two more terms I want to tell you about. The first is a **warning sign** (flip chart 27). A warning sign is something that tells you that you might be headed toward a high-risk situation. What warning signs should Joe watch out for? *(Pause for responses.)* Right! Getting on a bus for that neighborhood, cashing a big check, feeling depressed or lonely. What should you do when you see a warning sign that says you are headed toward a high-risk situation? *(Pause for responses.)* Sure! Turn around. Get off the bus. Put that money is a safer place. Do something you enjoy that doesn't involve drugs. We like to call all these things **U-turns** because when you see a warning sign that you are headed toward drugs, you need to make a U-turn and head the other way—toward **healthy pleasures**. What do I mean by healthy pleasures? These are things you really enjoy *and* that are good for your health and well-being (flip chart 28). Give me some examples. *(Pause for responses.)* Good! Now give me some examples of unhealthy pleasures, things that feel good but are bad for you. *(Pause for responses.)* Sure, drugs are the perfect example. Now, what's the overall goal of the module? *(Pause for responses.)* Right! Say no to drugs and yes to healthy pleasures. In this program, you will learn how to avoid the unhealthy pleasure of using drugs. You'll do this by learning the warning signs that you are headed for a high-risk situation and you will make U-turns that take you away from drugs and toward healthy pleasures."

Session 5
WARNING SIGNS

OVERVIEW

Your goal in this session is to get across the concept of warning signs. The idea is that patients usually take steps to use drugs. These steps take them toward high-risk situations. The closer they get to the high-risk situation, the harder it is to stop the process and avoid using drugs. However, during the early steps toward drug use it is much easier to quit the process and do something healthy instead. The trouble is that many patients take these steps without being fully aware that they are headed toward drug use. Your job is to help them figure out what steps they usually take before they end up in a high-risk situation.

Start out with a brief review of high-risk situations, then move on to a more detailed discussion of warning signs. Elicit examples of drug-habit chains and point out what steps can be seen as warning signs. Make sure that each patient records appropriate warning signs on his emergency card. Then go on to briefly explain U-turns and healthy pleasures.

SAMPLE THERAPIST SCRIPT

Introduce the goal (flip chart 29).

"It's good to see you all here today. Welcome to another session of basic training. Today you'll learn to avoid high-risk situations by recognizing the warning signs that you are headed toward drug use."

Make sure patients can repeat the goal.

"What is the goal of today's class?"

To learn how to avoid high-risk situations.

SESSION SUMMARY

1. Introduce the goal (flip chart 29).
2. Make sure patients can repeat the goal.
3. Briefly explain high-risk situations (flip chart 30).
4. Get patients to agree that it would be better to avoid high-risk situations.
5. Introduce the concept of warning signs (flip charts 31, 32).
6. Describe the usual steps in a drug-habit chain.
7. Note that these steps involve people, places, things, thoughts, and emotions (as do high-risk situations) (flip chart 33).
8. Ask patients to write a warning sign on their emergency cards.
9. Link the idea of U-turns to both warning signs and healthy pleasures (flip chart 34).

"What is the overall goal of the module?"

To say no to drugs and yes to healthy pleasures.

Briefly explain high-risk situations (flip chart 30).

"There are some situations that make it very hard to avoid using drugs and alcohol. For example, let's say you've gone to your friend's apartment to watch a football game, you quickly eat a bunch of BBQ potato chips, and then find out that the only cold beverage in the apartment is beer—and everyone else is drinking plenty of beer, and it happens to be one of your favorite drinks. We call this a high-risk situation (flip chart 30) because it will be hard to say no and the chance, or *risk*, that you will end up using is *high*. So it's a *high-risk* situation. Who can think of some other high-risk situations? *(Pause for responses.)* Okay, right. You've just cashed your check, you're feeling lonely, and a very persuasive dealer won't take no for an answer and puts a free rock in you hand. Would you all agree that this is a high-risk situation?"

Get patients to agree that it would be better to avoid high-risk situations.

"There are ways to get out of these situations without using, but wouldn't it be better not to get into them in the first place? *(Pause for responses.)* Sure it would. And that's what we'll focus on today: how to avoid high-risk situations; how to stay away from situations where it will be very hard to say no."

Introduce the concept of warning signs (flip charts 31, 32).

   "The way to do this is to watch out for signs that you are headed for a high-risk situation. We call these **warning signs** (flip chart 31) because they warn you that you are headed for a high-risk situation. Everybody has different warning signs, so you'll have to figure out what yours are. Here's a way to figure it out. Most people who are addicted to drugs or alcohol do the same things over and over again in order to get and use drugs. We call this a **drug-habit chain**. We call it a chain, because each step in the habit leads to the next step, just as each link in a chain is connected to the next link (flip chart 32). Think about your habit of using drugs. What did you tend to do over and over again in order to obtain and use drugs? What steps did you take each time you used? You might have called the same friends or dealers, used the same bus, or gotten some cash in the same way each time. Some patients have told us they worked so hard at it that it was almost like a job. Who can describe what they had to do in order to use drugs? I'll write a few examples on the board."

   Note to therapist: You may be wondering about the difference between the steps taken to use drugs during, say, a daily habit, and the steps that lead to a relapse following a period of abstinence. In our experience, relapses often closely resemble the drug-habit chain. Moreover, patients are much better at describing their drug-habit chain than they are at describing a recent relapse.

Describe the usual steps in a drug-habit chain.

   "As you can see from these examples, it's a little different for each of you. But there are some similarities too. Most of you encounter something that reminds you of drugs. Next, you start to crave drugs, then you make plans for money and transportation, then you carry out these plans. You go where the drugs are. You get some and you use."

WARNING SIGNS	DRUG-HABIT CHAIN
Things that warn me that I might be headed toward a high-risk situation.	Things I do over and over in order to use drugs and alcohol.
31	32

Note that these steps involve people, places, things, thoughts, and emotions (as do high-risk situations) (flip chart 33).

"Also, the things you've said that are part of your habit fall into five groups. You might have noticed that this list looks like the list of things that go into making a high-risk situation. That's because when enough of these things come together all at once, it becomes much harder to say no. It becomes a high-risk situation. What's a high-risk situation? *(Pause for responses.)* Right! It's a situation where it would be very hard to avoid using. But if you run into these things one or two at a time, you have a better chance of avoiding drugs than if you run into them all together in a high-risk situation. When you run into them one at a time, we call them "warning signs." That's because they warn that you might be headed toward a high-risk situation. Since you've been warned, you have a chance to do something to avoid using. Let's take Ed's habit as an example. Suppose he gets the thought 'A beer would really cut down on these voices.' We already know that's the thought he usually gets before having some beer. Then, after a few beers, he'd head for the park, and so on. So now if he gets the thought 'A beer would cut down on these voices,' that thought is a warning sign that he might be headed for drugs. If Ed's voices are getting worse, what should he do instead of having a beer? *(Pause for responses.)* Yes! He should make sure he's taking his medication, or he might arrange to discuss it with his psychiatrist."

Ask patients to write a warning sign on their emergency cards.

"On your emergency card there is a place to write down your warning signs. For example, one of the things Ed is going to write is 'A beer would really cut down on these voices.' I want each of you to write a warning sign in this spot. Enrique, what are you going to write? What about you, Leon?"

TYPES OF WARNING SIGNS

PEOPLE: calling your drug dealer or drug-using buddies, looking for strawberries

PLACES: taking a "walk" in the park or neighborhood known for drugs

THINGS: handling or buying paraphernalia (pipes, screens, lighters, brillo pads, syringes), cashing a check

THOUGHTS: "A beer would really cut down on these voices."

EMOTIONS: angry, sad, nervous, lonely, worthless

33

HOW TO AVOID USING DRUGS

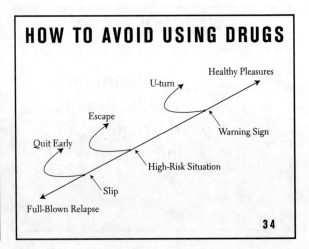

34

Note to therapist: Discuss warning signs with a few more patients before they write them in ink on their emergency cards. You are looking for warning signs that will be useful later, when patients learn how to make U-turns. So the warning signs need to be a few steps earlier in the drug-habit chain than the high-risk situation itself. The warning sign has to represent a point in the chain where it is possible to do something to avoid the high-risk situation. You won't have time to do this with every patient, but a few more examples will help all patients list the right warning signs.

Link the idea of U-turns to both warning signs and healthy pleasures (flip chart 34).

"So what should you do when you see a warning sign that says you are headed toward a high-risk situation? *(Pause for responses.)* Sure! Turn around. Get off the bus. Make sure you're on the right dose of medication. Put that money in a safer place. Do something you enjoy that doesn't involve drugs. We like to call all these things **U-turns** because when you see a warning sign that you are headed toward drugs, you need to make a U-turn. The U-turn takes you away from drugs and heads you the other way toward **healthy pleasures**. These are things you really enjoy and that are good for your health and well-being. Give me some examples of healthy pleasures. *(Pause for responses.)* Now give me some examples of unhealthy pleasures, things that feel good but are bad for you. *(Pause for responses.)* Sure. Drugs are the perfect example. Now, what's the overall goal of the module? *(Pause for responses.)* Right! Say no to drugs and yes to healthy pleasures.

"In this program, you will learn how to avoid the unhealthy pleasure of using drugs (flip chart 34). You'll do this by learning the warning signs that you are headed for a high-risk situation and you will make U-turns that take you away from drugs and toward healthy pleasures. Look at your emergency card. You can see a section called 'U-Turns and Coping Skills.' Some are listed and there is room to add more as you learn them. So, if you encounter warning signs, and you can't remember what to do, check your emergency card. It will remind you. That's why you must carry it with you at all times.

"The important point to remember is that the sooner you make a U-turn, the easier it is to avoid using drugs. So, be sure to pay attention to warning signs and make U-turns as soon as possible."

Session 6

HEALTHY PLEASURES
AND HEALTHY HABITS

OVERVIEW

Your goal in this session is to get each patient to identify several activities that would be reward-ing and healthy (healthy pleasures). You will also ask patients to identify the healthy habits they'll need in order to engage in healthy pleasures. For example, a patient who wants to take up photog-raphy (a healthy pleasure) will have to budget money (a healthy habit) for film.

SAMPLE THERAPIST SCRIPT

Introduce the goal (flip chart 35).

"It's good to see you all here today! Welcome to basic training. In today's class you'll learn about healthy pleasures and healthy habits. By the end of this session, you'll under-stand how healthy pleasures and healthy habits can keep you away from drugs. You'll also write your favorite healthy pleasures and most important healthy habits on your emer-gency card."

Make sure patients can repeat the goal.

"What is the goal of today's class?"

To learn about healthy habits and healthy pleasures.

SESSION SUMMARY

1. Introduce the goal (flip chart 35).

2. Make sure patients can repeat the goal.

3. Define healthy pleasures and give a few examples (flip chart 36).

4. Elicit more examples from the group and write them on the board.

5. Examine the flip chart for more examples (flip chart 37).

6. Ask patients to write on their emergency card a favorite healthy pleasure they'd like to do more often.

7. Define healthy habits and give a few examples (flip chart 38).

8. Elicit examples from the group and write them on the board.

9. Examine the flip chart for more examples (flip chart 39).

10. Elicit more personal healthy habits that are linked to individual healthy pleasures.

11. Have patients write one of these on their emergency card.

12. Have each group member complete an activities schedule (flip chart 40).

"What is the overall goal of the module?"

To say no to drugs and yes to healthy pleasures.

Define healthy pleasures and give a few examples (flip chart 36).

"You've probably noticed that saying yes to healthy pleasures is part of the overall goal of the module. That's because the best way to avoid using drugs is to seek healthy pleasures. So what are healthy pleasures? Let me give you a few examples: listening to a jazz concert, taking a walk on the beach, eating an ice cream cone, getting a compliment from someone you respect, and doing a job well. What do all these things have in common? They all feel good and they are good for you. A healthy pleasure is something that feels good *and* is good for you (flip chart 36)."

Elicit more examples from the group and write them on the board.

"Let's think of some more. *(Pause for responses.)* Yes, those are good examples. Now here's a hint to help you think of more. What do you really want to get out of life? *(Pause for responses.)* Okay. So you want to share your life with someone you care about. And you want to feel like you've helped others. Here's another hint. What would your life be like if there was never such a thing as drugs? What would you be doing now?"

HEALTHY PLEASURES

Things that feel good
and
are good for me.

36

HEALTHY PLEASURES

- Watching TV
- Reading
- Listening to music
- Fishing
- Taking a walk on the beach
- Eating an ice cream cone
- Teaching a child something new
- Getting a compliment from someone I respect
- Cooking
- Doing a job well
- Dating

37

Examine the flip chart for more examples (flip chart 37).

"Okay That's a good list. Let's see if there are any more on the flip chart. How about dating? Anyone enjoy that?"

Ask patients to write on their emergency card a favorite healthy pleasure they'd like to do more often.

"Now pick one or two healthy pleasures that you'd like to do more often than you do now. Write them on your emergency card."

Define healthy habits and give a few examples (flip chart 38).

"Now, you might have noticed that I listed some of your ideas under a category called **healthy habits**. Let me tell you more about that. Often, there are things you have to do if you want healthy pleasures. For example, suppose there's someone you'd really like to know better and ask out on a date. You're going to need to look presentable and you're probably going to need to look that way at least a few times. So, every day, you'll need to shower, shave, brush your teeth, comb your hair, and put on clean clothes. Those things are called healthy habits (flip chart 38); *healthy* because they are good for you and *habits* because you do them over and over. They aren't necessarily all that pleasurable all by themselves, but you need to do them in order to get something that would be fun. You can think of healthy habits as the steps you need to take to get healthy pleasures."

Elicit examples from the group and write them on the board.

"Give me some more examples of healthy habits. *(Pause for responses.)* Right! Taking your medication. You need to get into the habit of taking your medication every day. How about some more?"

HEALTHY HABITS

- Healthy = Good for me.
- Habits = I do them over and over.
- Not always fun but often lead to healthy pleasures.

3 8

HEALTHY HABITS

- Taking prescribed medication
- Buying food
- Buying clothing
- Waking up on time
- Going to bed on time
- Washing my clothes
- Combing my hair
- Taking a shower
- Brushing my teeth
- Shaving
- Saving money
- Attending meetings
- Exercising regularly

3 9

Examine the flip chart for more examples (flip chart 39).

"Let's look at the flip chart for some more healthy habits."

Elicit more personal healthy habits that are linked to individual healthy pleasures.

"Now, look at the healthy pleasures you've written on your emergency card. What healthy habits are you going to have to add in order to make sure you get to experience those healthy pleasures? Emilio, you said you wanted your uncle to hire you back at his motorcycle shop. What do you think it is going to take to get your uncle to hire you again? Show up every morning at 7 a.m. So how early are you going to have to get up in the morning? What about you, James?"

Have patients write one of them on their emergency card.

"On your emergency card there is a place to write healthy habits that you feel are important. For example, Emilio said he'd have to get out of bed at 6 a.m. every morning so that he could make it to his uncle's motorcycle shop by 7 a.m. Emilio, on your emergency card, under healthy habits, write 'get out of bed at 6 a.m. each morning.' James, what are you going to write?"

Have each group member complete an activity schedule (flip chart 40).

"Okay. You've decided what healthy pleasures are most important to you, and you've figured out what healthy habits you'll need to get those healthy pleasures. The next step is to set aside time to do those things. Actually make an appointment with yourself to do the things you think will make you happy and keep you healthy. Let's call this calendar of appointments your **activity schedule.**"

(Hand out activity schedule from appendix A) "This worksheet is called an activity schedule. You can schedule time for all the things that are important to your overall mental and physical health (flip chart 40). First, write in important set appointments, such as attending medication clinics, seeing your support person, going to school or work. Next, write in healthy habits, such as eating, managing your hygiene, taking your medications. Finally, schedule time for healthy pleasures, such as recreational activities and other things that are good for you and feel good. It is okay to schedule in time to watch television or take a nap, but you don't want to do that all day every day.

"The other important aspect of having an activity schedule is that if you notice you are *not* doing the things you know you should be, for example, if you stop taking your prescribed medications, then you can use that information as a warning sign that you may be headed back toward drugs.

"This schedule will also help reduce your desire to use drugs. It works like this: The more time you spend on healthy habits, the more often you'll get to enjoy healthy pleasures; the more time you spend on healthy habits and healthy pleasures, the less time you'll have for drugs, and the more you will have to lose if you are tempted. If you stop using drugs, your craving for them will gradually disappear."

Session 7
WHY QUIT DRUGS?

OVERVIEW

The point of this session is to get patients to compare the advantages and disadvantages of using drugs. There are four reasons to have them do this:

1. Discussing the advantages of using drugs will help patients understand why they continue to use a drug that ultimately has very negative consequences. Understanding that there are temporary advantages to using drugs provides a partial explanation for addiction.

2. A comparison of advantages and disadvantages sometimes convinces undecided patients that it is time to quit.

3. It will help those who have decided to quit to recall the down side of using drugs, even when they get a craving for drugs.

4. Obviously, the use of drugs is rewarding in some ways or people wouldn't use them. Acknowledging the positive aspects of drugs will enhance the therapist's credibility.

Some patients may be unable to identify any disadvantages of using. This may indicate that they are not ready to change their drug-taking behavior or they may have cognitive impairments that lead to poor recall. Gently encourage them to discuss the disadvantages by asking them to comment on the disadvantages that others describe.

SAMPLE THERAPIST SCRIPT

Introduce the goals (flip chart 41).

"It's good to see you all here today! Welcome to the basic training. The goal of today's

SESSION SUMMARY

1. Introduce the goals (flip chart 41).
2. Make sure patients can repeat the goals.
3. Explain the need to recall disadvantages whenever a craving is felt.
4. Elicit advantages of using drugs (flip chart 42).
5. Elicit disadvantages of using drugs (flip chart 43).
6. Weigh the advantages against the disadvantages (flip chart 44).
7. Elicit the advantages of not using (flip chart 45).
8. Have patients pick one to three main reasons for quitting.
9. Have patients record their main reasons for quitting on their emergency card.
10. Encourage patients to read this part of the card whenever they get an urge to use drugs.
11. Discuss the role of a support person (flip charts 46, 47).

class is for you to compare the advantages and disadvantages of using drugs. In other words, you'll compare your reasons for using drugs with your reasons for quitting. That's why the session is called 'Why Quit Drugs?' You'll write your reasons for quitting on your emergency card so you can remember them if you have an urge to use drugs. You'll also learn how a support person can help you avoid drugs and seek healthy pleasures.

Make sure patients can repeat the goals.

"What are the goals of today's class?"

To compare the advantages and disadvantages of using drugs; to add my reasons for quitting to my emergency card; to learn how a support person can help me quit using drugs.

"What are the overall goals of the module?"

To say no to drugs and yes to healthy pleasures.

Explain the need to recall disadvantages whenever a craving is felt.

"In today's class, we're going to discuss what you like about drugs and alcohol. That's right, what you like about them. What does that have to do with quitting? Plenty! There are reasons you use drugs. And there are reasons you want to quit. But you probably don't think about them at the same time. And that is one reason so many people continue to use drugs even though they know that the drugs are ruining their lives. When you get a craving to use drugs, are you usually thinking about how much trouble they have caused in your life? Or are you thinking about how good you'll feel and how much fun you'll have? The purpose of this session is to make sure that whenever you think about what you like about drugs, you'll also think about what you don't like. Whenever you have an urge to use drugs, you'll remember what you will lose if you use and what you will gain if you quit.

"The approach we are taking draws on the experience of people who have successfully quit using drugs. If there is one thing you will hear from these people over and over again, it is that they came to realize that the disadvantages of using drugs far outweigh any advantages of using drugs. You will know that you are making progress when you start thinking this way, too. Have you reached a point in your life where the disadvantages to using outweigh the advantages?"

Elicit advantages of using drugs (flip chart 42).

"It may seem odd to be coming up with reasons to use drugs in a class devoted to quitting drugs, but it is important to understand why you continue to use. What are some of the reasons you have used? For example, some group members have told us that they just liked the way the drugs made them feel. Others have said that when they are feeling bad, drugs make them feel better. Some have said that drugs made it easier to be around other people. Who can tell us what they like about drugs? I'll write them on the board. *(Pause for responses.)* Here's something that might help you think of some more reasons. Suppose you were trying to talk me into using drugs—what would you tell me?

"Now let's look at the flip chart and see if this reminds you of any more reasons you may have used (flip chart 42).

"That's quite a list we've got now. Sounds pretty good when we leave off the disadvantages."

ADVANTAGES OF USING DRUGS

- Euphoria: It feels good.
- Strawberries and sex.
- Feel like I fit in.
- Have fun with others.
- Worries go away, feel better fast.

42

DISADVANTAGES OF USING DRUGS

- Lose trust and respect of family and friends
- Lose job
- No money for rent, food, or clothing
- Become homeless
- Beg or steal from others
- Injured in accidents
- Get robbed or assaulted
- Get arrested; go to jail
- Voices and paranoia
- Depression
- Suicidal thoughts
- Physical illnesses, including HIV

43

Elicit disadvantages of using drugs (flip chart 43).

"Now let's talk about what you don't like about using drugs. What are the disadvantages or negative consequences of drug use? Are there any? Give me some examples. *(Pause for responses.)* Yes! Many people end up spending too much money on drugs and then they don't have enough money to pay bills, buy food, and pay rent. What else? *(Encourage discussion in the following manner.)* You say cocaine makes your voices louder. What about you, Alfonso? What are the disadvantages for you? You lost your job. Give me some more reasons. A few minutes ago, I asked you to imagine that you were trying to talk me into using drugs. Now imagine you are trying to talk me out of using drugs. What negative consequences can I expect?

"Okay. That's a pretty good list. Let's check the flip chart and see if we missed anything (flip chart 43)."

Weigh the advantages against the disadvantages (flip chart 44).

"If we were to put both lists on a scale, which one would be heavier? Which list would outweigh the other? *(Pause for responses.)* Right! There are definitely more disadvantages to using drugs."

Elicit advantages of not using drugs (flip chart 45).

Note to therapist: This is really just another way of examining the reasons to quit. For example, when asked about the disadvantages of using, a patient may have said, "After a full-blown relapse, I feel so stupid and worthless." Of course this can be restated as an advantage of not using: "If I quit, I will feel good about myself."

"We've been talking mostly about what you lose if you continue to use drugs. Now let's think about this just a little bit differently. Let's talk about the advantages of not using drugs. What will you gain if you stop using drugs? Enough money for an apartment. Okay. What else? Your family's respect. Good. Self-respect you say. Sure. What else? Okay. Let's check the flip chart (flip chart 45)."

Have patients pick one to three main reasons for quitting drugs.

Help them understand that they must have a reason to quit that is personally very important. The reason should be as concrete as possible.

"Okay. We've listed lots of disadvantages of using drugs and lots of advantages of not using drugs. These are all reasons to quit using drugs. But they might not all be *your* reasons. It is important that you have a reason or reasons to quit and that the reason be very important to you personally. Let's see if everyone has a main reason to quit. *(Encourage discussion in the following manner.)* Bob, what's the main reason or two that you want to quit? I see; you don't want your son growing up thinking of you as an addict and you want to help him grow up. What about you Barbara? You will lose custody of your children. Okay, that sounds like a big disadvantage, go ahead and add that to your emergency card."

Have patients record their main reasons for quitting on their emergency card.
Help them word the statement so that it will be a clear and potent reminder when a drug craving sets in.

"Now look at your emergency card. You'll see a space called 'I've decided to QUIT because.' Next time you get a craving to use drugs and you're thinking primarily about the advantages of using, I want you to pull out your card and read what you will lose if you do use again, and what you will gain if you don't. So you want to be sure you write something true and convincing. Let's try this out. Ed, what are you thinking about writing? *(Pause for response.)* That's good. Let me write that on the board: 'I won't be able to stop until all my money is gone.' Now why did you choose that? *(Pause.)* I see. You know that you always tell yourself you're just going to use a little. This will remind you that you won't be able to stop. What about something good that will happen if you don't use? *(Pause.)* Okay, you'll have enough money to buy a car.

"Some people remember better with pictures than words. So, if there are certain people that you will hurt by using drugs, put their pictures on that spot in your emergency card. You want to use whatever will quickly remind you of the real consequences of using."

Encourage patients to read this part of the card whenever they get an urge to use drugs.
"Be sure that you carry this card with you wherever you go. The next time you feel an urge to use drugs, don't do anything until you have read this part of your card. Ask anyone who has successfully quit drugs, and they'll be able to name their own set of disadvantages right away. And they can name the disadvantages even when they get an urge to use. Now you'll be able to do the same thing because you've written them on this card, you carry the card with you all the time, and you're always going to read it when you get an urge to use drugs."

Discuss the role of a support person (flip charts 46, 47).
"It is so important that you be very clear about why you want to quit using drugs. It is often a good idea to discuss it with your **support person**. What is a support person? Who can answer that? *(Pause for responses.)* Right! A support person is someone you can count on in a time of need. While quitting is your responsibility, it helps to have people who support you in this effort. A support person can help in a number of ways. I'm bringing it up now because a support person can help you clarify your reasons for quitting and, in an emergency, if the emergency card isn't working, help you remember the disadvantages of using and advantages of quitting.

```
┌─────────────────────────────────┐
│        SUPPORT PERSON           │
│                                 │
│  • Someone I can count on in    │
│    time of need.                │
│                                 │
│  • A support person can help me │
│    -deal with cravings.         │
│    -remember why I decided to quit. │
│    -develop healthy habits and healthy │
│       pleasures.                │
│                              46 │
└─────────────────────────────────┘
```

```
┌─────────────────────────────────┐
│   A GOOD SUPPORT PERSON         │
│         IS SOMEONE              │
│                                 │
│    • I know well.               │
│    • I trust.                   │
│    • I talk to frequently.      │
│    • Who does not abuse drugs or alcohol. │
│    • Who is available when needed. │
│    • Who will give me time when I ask. │
│    • Who wants to help me.       │
│                              47 │
└─────────────────────────────────┘
```

"Some of you may already have a support person, while others may be in the process of getting one. Does anyone have a support person? *(Encourage discussion in the following manner.)* Okay. Danny, who is your support person? How does he help you? I see, so you've been able to talk to your support person when you need advice and help. What are some other ways a support person can help? Right! You may be trying to deal with a craving and could talk to your support person about what caused the craving and how to cope with it. Just talking with a support person can be a coping skill. Other people may use their support person for advice on what type of healthy pleasures to add to their lifestyle. How else can a support person help? Okay. That's a good list. Let's check the flip chart and see if we missed anything (flip chart 46). As you can see, there are many ways a support person can help you with the challenge of quitting drugs.

"Now, what makes a good support person? What kind of traits would you like to see in a person that you would choose to be your support person? Great—that's a good list. Time to check the flip chart (flip chart 47).

"Now that we know what makes a good support person, can you think of someone who might be a good support person for you? What do you suppose are the steps involved in getting someone to be your support person? What would you have to do? Who already has one? How did you ask him to be your support person?"

Session 8
MONEY MANAGEMENT

OVERVIEW

Your objectives in this session are:

1. Focus patients' attention on money and the unique role it plays in their addiction.
2. Help patients develop concrete plans to ensure that their money buys necessities and healthy pleasures, not drugs. Many patients will conclude that, at least temporarily, they need help from someone else—either a support person, a representative payee, or both—to help them avoid drugs and manage their money. However, there are other options.

Initially, many patients don't appreciate the need for a strategy to avoid drugs. You may hear patients say, "I will just rely on my willpower to get me through." Such statements are an opportunity for you to encourage more specific planning. Help patients describe their money management habits—for example, how they anticipate receipt of a disability check, what they do when it arrives, how they feel when cashing it, and how they spend it. Given the resources, this is an opportunity to increase staff involvement to assist patients with handling their money, particularly if the individual does not have a representative payee or conservator. The topic of money is often a sensitive one. If patients resist discussing how they plan to manage future income, you can ask them what they did in the past that was both successful and unsuccessful. Patients may describe unique ways of ensuring that they do not have large quantities of cash, such as buying small money orders and mailing the funds to themselves throughout the month, or buying expensive jewelry or electronics that can be sold or pawned later in the month.

SAMPLE THERAPIST SCRIPT

Introduce the goal (flip chart 48).

"It's good to see you all here today! Welcome to basic training. In today's class, you'll

SESSION SUMMARY

1. Introduce the goal (flip chart 48).

2. Make sure patients can repeat the goal.

3. Get patients to talk about the connections between money and drugs.

4. Reframe patients' ideas in terms of triggers, warning signs, and high-risk situations (flip chart 49).

5. Encourage a discussion of solutions.

6. Encourage a discussion about representative payees.

7. Describe representative payees and explain how they can be helpful.

learn ways to make sure that your money takes care of you instead of going toward drugs that ultimately harm you."

Make sure patients can repeat the goal

"What is the goal of today's class?"

To make sure my money takes care of me instead of going to drugs that harm me.

"What are the overall goals of the module?"

To say no to drugs and yes to healthy pleasures.

Get patients to talk about the connections between money and drugs.

"Let's talk about money and drugs. Tell me, in your experience, how money and drugs go together. Right! You usually can't get drugs unless you have money. What else? Whenever you get your check, you get very strong cravings."

Write their ideas on the flip chart or board. Divide the paper or board in half. Use one side to write statements about money as a problem (e.g., "Sometimes I feel high if I just touch a $20 bill"). Use the other side if anybody brings up coping strategies at this time (e.g., "I figured out I just couldn't carry more than $20").

Reframe patients' ideas in terms of triggers, warning signs, and high-risk situations (flip chart 49).

"So money is connected to drugs in several ways. For most of you, it reminds you of drugs, sometimes so strongly that you feel a little high even before you use. In this sense, money is a **trigger**, sort of like what happens if you see some drug paraphernalia. Some of you said that if you leave the house with more than $20, it is a **warning sign** that you are headed for drugs, even if you are saying you need the money for something else. Most of you said that cashing a monthly check puts you in a **high-risk situation** where it is really hard to avoid using drugs. So money can be a trigger and a warning sign, and it can create a high-risk situation (flip chart 49). And, of course, money is what you exchange with the dealer in order to get drugs."

Encourage a discussion of solutions.

"So money is a big problem. It makes you crave drugs, it makes it hard to refuse drugs, and it is what you need to buy drugs. On the other hand, you need money to buy necessities, like a place to live, food, and clothing. So what do you do about a problem like this? If you get your hands on much money, you buy drugs; but if you avoid money, you're hungry and homeless. Any ideas? I'll write them on the board."

Encourage a discussion about representative payees.

"Several of you have heard of representative payees, or rep. payees. Tell me more about what you've heard. *(Pause for responses.)* So Bob, you're concerned that they'll be paid out of your money. And Liz, you knew a patient who did so well he didn't need one after a while."

Describe representative payees and explain how they can be helpful.

"A rep. payee is someone who receives your disability income and has the responsibility of spending it for your benefit. A rep. payee can be a good friend or family member, an accountant, an attorney, or an employee of an institution, such as a hospital or a community mental health center. You meet regularly with your rep. payee and discuss how best to spend your disability income. You and your rep. payee may decide that it would be best if the rep. payee wrote checks to your landlord and utility companies so that you didn't have to handle large amounts of cash. You might also decide on ways to limit the amount of spending money you have at any one time.

"How do you get a rep. payee? There are two ways. First, you can ask the Social Security Administration or the Veterans' Benefits Administration to send the disability income to someone who has agreed to serve as your rep. payee. The second way to get a rep. payee is if your doctor asks that your disability income be sent to a rep. payee."

SKILLS TRAINING

WHAT IS SKILLS TRAINING?

Skills training reinforces and extends the information learned during basic training. During skills training, patients learn specific skills for avoiding drugs and for developing healthy habits and healthy pleasures. Each skill helps patients with one of the module's four basic recommendations. Below you can see how these skills (in bold) relate to the four basic recommendations, main points, and related concepts.

OVERVIEW OF NINE SKILLS

- Practice damage control.

  Main point: If you slip and use drugs or alcohol again, stop early and get right back into treatment. This will reduce damage to your health, relationships, and finances.

  Concepts: Mt. Recovery, slip vs. full-blown relapse, harm reduction, abstinence violation effect, bouncing back into treatment

  Skills: **Quitting after a slip**

  Reporting a slip

- Escape high-risk situations.

  Main point: Some situations make it very hard to avoid using drugs. Be prepared to escape from these situations without using drugs. Realize that it would be much better to avoid these situations in the first place.

Concepts: High-risk situations

Skills: **Refusing drugs offered by a pushy dealer**

Refusing drugs offered by a friend or relative

- Avoid high-risk situations.

Main point: Avoid high-risk situations by learning to recognize the warning signs that you might be headed toward drug use.

Concepts: Drug-habit chain (trigger, craving, planning, getting, using), warning signs, U-turns, removing triggers, riding the wave, money management, representative payee

Skills: **Getting an appointment with a busy person**

Getting a support person

Reporting symptoms and side effects to a doctor

- Seek healthy pleasures.

Main point: You can avoid drugs by focusing on the things that are most important and enjoyable to you. Do things that are fun and healthy.

Concepts: Healthy pleasures, healthy habits, activity schedule

Skills: **Asking someone to join you in a healthy pleasure**

Negotiating with a representative payee

These skills are taught in twenty-seven 45-minute training sessions. Roughly, three sessions are devoted to each skill area. Some can be completed in two sessions; others require as many as four. In the first of each of these sessions, the therapist pinpoints a specific problem related to substance abuse (e.g., friends and relatives who offer drugs and alcohol). Group members then engage in a problem-solving process to generate plausible solutions to the problem. With some guidance from the therapist, the patients evaluate the proposed solutions to determine which is likely to be most effective in solving the problem. Next, the specific skills and steps required to implement the solution are enumerated. Resources that may be needed to use the requisite skills are also identified.

The remaining sessions related to each skill are dedicated to constructing and carrying out role-play scenarios designed to give each participant an opportunity to practice these skills as the therapist supervises. "How to Conduct Skills Training Sessions" and "How to Conduct Practice Sessions," which appear later in this manual, detail the procedures involved.

RATIONALE FOR SKILLS TRAINING

Quitting drugs and staying abstinent require taking action. Many of these actions involve social interactions. Interpersonal skills are essential in refusing drugs, reporting a slip, describing medication side effects to a psychiatrist, and asking for a date. Most people acquire social skills naturally as they grow up. However, when severe mental illness intervenes, skills acquired early in life may be lost and opportunities to learn new skills are often stymied. Mastery of interpersonal skills is a complex developmental process honed by the challenges encountered in the face of novel or difficult situations requiring intricate social and emotional responses. However, for those who have failed to learn essential social skills because they have never been exposed to appropriate models or because burdensome life events and stress evoke anxiety, depression, or other symptoms that interfere with interpersonal and emotional expressiveness, such challenges may be overwhelming. When these deficiencies and the ability to articulate one's needs and concerns persist, relationships deteriorate and symptoms may emerge in a person who is vulnerable to mental illness. People who have schizophrenia or other severe mental illnesses have deficits in attention, memory, abstract thinking, and executive function that impede learning. Substance abusers without mental illness may be able to translate recommendations into actions without being taught skills explicitly through modeling and behavior rehearsal. For people with schizophrenia, even relatively simple social encounters often pose insurmountable barriers. Consequently, social skills deficits play a substantial role in the development and maintenance of substance use disorders among the mentally ill. Nevertheless, even people who are grossly deficient in the skills needed to combat drug abuse can overcome the challenges involved if they learn the nine essential skills specified below.

These are the main points and related concepts for each skill:

1. Quitting after a slip

   Main point: It's never good to slip, but if you do slip, leave the situation before you go too far. This is a big part of practicing damage control.

   Related concepts: High-risk situations, U-turns, warning signs, cravings, damage control

2. Reporting a slip

   Main Point: If you slip, get back on track as soon as possible. Knowing how to discuss the slip with your support person and members of your clinical team can help you learn how to prevent slips in the future.

   Related concepts: Abstinence violation effect, reinforcement, high-risk situations, U-turns, warning signs, cravings

3. Refusing drugs offered by a dealer

   Main point: When you encounter a drug dealer, get away as fast as you can. Removing yourself from the situation reduces the risk that you will use drugs and it helps you feel like you're in control of your life.

   Related concepts: High-risk situations, U-turns, warning signs, cravings

4. Refusing drugs offered by a friend or relative

Main point: Don't worry that your friend or family member will be offended if you refuse drugs from them. People who really care about you don't try to force you to do things that are bad for you.

Related concepts: High-risk situations, U-turns, warning signs, cravings, healthy habits, healthy pleasures

5. Getting an appointment with a busy person

Main point: Knowing how to get a person's attention when you need assistance is an important skill to have in preventing drug use.

Related concepts: Support person, representative payee, reinforcement, U-turns, warning signs, cravings

6. Getting a support person

Main point: Quitting drugs can be easier with the help of someone you know and trust.

Related concepts: Advantages and disadvantages of using drugs, emergency card, healthy pleasures, high-risk situations, U-turns, warning signs, cravings

7. Reporting symptoms and side effects to a doctor

Main point: Symptoms and side effects may increase the temptation to use drugs or alcohol. Knowing how to report symptoms and side effects to your doctor can help you to stay on track.

Related concepts: High-risk situations, U-turns, warning signs, cravings, healthy habits, healthy pleasures

8. Asking someone to join you in a healthy pleasure

Main point: Healthy pleasures make it easier to avoid using drugs. You're less likely to think about drugs or experience cravings if you have lots of healthy pleasures in your life.

Related concepts: Healthy habits, healthy pleasures, high-risk situations, U-turns, warning signs, cravings

9. Negotiating with a representative payee

Main point: Negotiation skills come in handy when your payee resists giving you money because he or she is worried that you might slip and use the money to buy drugs. Knowing how to reassure your payee and gain that person's confidence is essential.

Related concepts: Healthy habits, healthy pleasures, U-turns, reinforcement, coping skills

Patients with dual diagnoses often attend treatment sporadically, so we have designed the skills so that they can be taught independently of each other. As with basic training sessions, the skills can be taught in any sequence. This means that patients can drop out of treatment at any point in the training sequence and re-enter the group at any point along the way.

HOW TO CONDUCT SKILLS TRAINING SESSIONS

Instructional Tasks

Skills training covers nine skills. Each skill is covered in two to four 45-minute sessions. A sequence of instructional activities or tasks is carried out to complete the training process for each skill. The tasks are as follows:

1. Introduce the goals of the skill topic.
2. Make sure that participants can repeat the goal.
3. Review terms and concepts introduced during basic training that relate to the skill to be learned.
4. Develop the steps required for successful completion of the goal.
5. View a video illustration of the skill.
6. Choose a person to role-play.
7. Describe the role-play and demonstrate the steps.
8. Conduct the role-play and provide corrective feedback.
9. Challenge participants.

This sequence of learning activities provides patients with a rationale for the training and promotes motivation for learning, demonstrates the skills to be learned, and helps participants to anticipate barriers to using the skills.

The objective of the introduction is to help participants actively identify the goals of the particular skill they are learning, the consequences that will accrue if these goals are achieved, and the steps necessary to achieve them. The overarching purpose of the introduction is to instill realistic and favorable expectations, introduce terms and concepts, and inspire enthusiasm. After introducing the skill area, the second step is to make sure that participants can repeat the goal. Next, the skill is related to specific terms and concepts learned in basic training. Once this is accomplished, participants are prompted to develop the specific skill steps required to accomplish the stated goal. These steps are elicited from participants with guidance from the therapist. For example, refusing drugs from a friend involves looking the person offering drugs straight in the eye, asserting the desire to refrain from using drugs, telling that person that drugs have caused problems in the past, suggesting an alternative, telling the other person that pressure tactics are offensive, and, finally, leaving the situation if the person won't take no for an answer.

Next, participants view a videotaped demonstration in which a model correctly performs the skill to be learned. Patients are then asked to practice the skill they have just observed in a role-play exercise. The therapist chooses a group member who is likely to be successful in the role-play. A scenario is devised in which the therapist, with input from participants, describes and demonstrates the skill steps and then conducts the role-play. The participant's performance is then reviewed by the therapist and other participants. Together they evaluate the performance for the presence and/or absence of the skill steps demonstrated in the videotape. Positive feedback is provided for the patient's performance and suggestions for improvement are given to highlight absent behaviors. The role-play is then reenacted and the process is repeated until the patient can perform all the requisite behaviors for that skill.

As patients perform newly acquired skills, they may encounter obstacles that make it difficult for them to achieve expected outcomes. Anticipating outcome problems helps patients learn appropriate responses to use when the environment or people they encounter fail to provide the expected response following the use of a particular skill. For example, if an individual arrives for an appointment with a representative payee who has agreed to help the patient manage his money, but finds that the person has been unexpectedly called away, the patient must decide what to do. Thus, the final step in the training process is to challenge participants by introducing obstacles requiring an extension of the responses learned during role-play. Practicing responses to "challenge scenarios" helps consolidate skills and prepare participants for real-life encounters.

Completion of these steps requires about three sessions per skill area. The first four steps can usually be carried out in one session. Two to three additional sessions are needed to complete the remaining steps and to ensure that all participants have had an opportunity to practice the skill. Typically, the first session ends with the development of the skill steps (task 4). The next session begins with a review of those skill steps and proceeds to the videotaped illustration (task 5). Next, the therapist conducts role-play with as many participants as time permits (tasks 6–9). If necessary, a third and even fourth session are added to ensure that all participants have an opportunity to master the skill.

Organize the Setting

Skills training generally takes place in a large room, larger than those used for most traditional group therapies delivered to the same number of patients. The room should be comfortable, with plenty of room for participants to move around freely. Arrange chairs in a circle with a large space in the middle for conducting role-play exercises. Use props to simulate the circumstances in which the skills to be learned will be used. A telephone, pencils and paper, items to simulate drug paraphernalia, and a few extra chairs that can be moved about easily are generally sufficient. An easel with large plain paper should be available for recording specific behaviors targeted for training, rating performances during role-plays, and documenting ideas generated during problem-solving segments of the training. Two such flip charts are used during the training process. On one of these, the therapist records the specific steps in the role-play exercises before the session begins. The other is used to document ideas generated by participants during each session. Later, these pages can be displayed on the walls of the training room as prompts and reminders to therapists and patients. Snacks and beverages encourage attendance and provide a more congenial atmosphere.

Conduct Role-Plays

Role-plays are brief scenes enacted by the therapist and a patient or by two patients. The purpose is to teach, in simulated situations, the skills needed in real-life situations. Role-play exercises are essential in that they give participants an opportunity to practice what they learn in the module by rehearsing, with the help of the therapist, what to say and how to say it. That the role-play situation is not "real" generally helps reduce anxiety, increasing the likelihood that the patient will use the skill in situations calling for that skill. Furthermore, while a correct performance of a skill in the clinic setting does not guarantee that the patient will use the skill in the natural environment, it is certain that if he cannot perform the skill during training, neither will he be able to perform it outside the clinic. Behavior rehearsal is the *key* component in the skills training process.

Tricks of the trade

When you conduct role-plays, provide instructions and guide the patient through the role-play by prompting specific behaviors, modeling responses, and providing corrective feedback. These actions by the therapist also help the more hesitant group members to engage in the rehearsal of specific skills.

During role-play exercises, patients execute scenes provided in the therapist's manual. When a patient practices a scene, the therapist is both a participant and an active observer. Most role-plays require that the therapist and the patient be out of their seats, moving about in the middle of the group, in plain view of other participants. If a co-therapist is assisting, both can be active during the role-play; while one participates in the scene, the other prompts or coaches the patient, reminds group members to pay attention, and points out aspects of the performance that will be discussed later. Alternatively, the therapist can perform the role-play with a group member or guide two participants through the exercise.

Assess Role-Play Performances

Evaluating a patient's role-play performance is a three-step process. Observe carefully, as the role-play unfolds. Identify the patient's behavioral *assets*, *deficits*, and *excesses*. Essentially, assets are the actions the patient does well. Deficits are desirable behaviors that are missing from the patient's performance. Examples include poverty of speech, expressionless face, restricted hand gestures, absence of eye contact, slouching posture, and social distancing. Excesses are behaviors that are overbearing, intrusive, flamboyant, or otherwise annoying.

Tricks of the trade

Focus your assessment on specific verbal and nonverbal *behaviors*. Pay particular attention to the patient's choice of words. Look for statements that may provoke responses that are inconsistent with the training goal or that could be inflammatory. For example, in teaching patients how to refuse drugs offered by a dealer, counter their tendency to respond politely to the dealer's greeting by stopping the role-play and offering alternative word choices. For example, the drug dealer might approach the role-player, make eye contact, smile, extend his hand, and say in a friendly voice, "Hey, what's happening?" A patient's typical response is to look into the dealer's eyes, smile back, shake his hand, and say, "Hey, how's it going?" By this time, the dealer will have slipped the drug into the patient's hand and begun haggling over the price. Identify words and phrases that are likely to facilitate goal attainment and reinforce them. If the patient fails to make any statements that will facilitate goal attainment, suggest one. For example, instruct the patient to dispense with the polite greeting and simply say, "No, I don't want any." Attend to paralinguistic aspects of the patient's remarks, such as voice tone, voice volume, verbal fluency, rate of speech, and unnecessary repetition (e.g., using a halting style of speech or ending every sentence with "you know"). Shape normal speech patterns as you have the patient integrate suggestions for improvement. Observe key aspects of nonverbal behavior, such as eye contact, facial expressions, hand gestures, body posture, body orientation, proximity to the person with whom the patient is interacting, and the degree to which the patient makes appropriate use of touch. In the example above, instruct the patient to avert his gaze, keep his hand by his side, walk briskly, and keep moving as the dealer approaches.

Give Positive and Specific Feedback

Always give patients positive feedback as soon as a scene ends. Even if the performance was grossly deficient, begin by praising the patient's efforts. State your remarks in specific behavioral terms. For example, the statement, "That was terrific, Henry! You looked your cousin right in the eye and firmed up your voice when you told him that you didn't want any drugs" is preferred to the more general statement, "That was great. You did a really good job that time." Avoid making value judgments. Focus on specific verbal and nonverbal *behaviors* when giving feedback. Rather than suggesting that aspects of the performance were "good" or "proper," indicate which elements of the patient's behavior were "effective" in attaining the stated goal. For example, instead of saying, "The way you handled the dealer was good," say "Keeping your eyes straight ahead, moving quickly, and using a firm voice were very effective in getting the dealer to back down."

Invite participants to comment on the role-play. Soliciting feedback from group members is an excellent way to keep everyone involved. Be sure to guide participants' remarks so that they, too, emphasize the effective qualities of the performance. Refrain from criticizing a patient's efforts. Similarly, do not allow other group members to make critical comments. Participants who feel judged are easily discouraged and become reluctant to participate.

Tricks of the trade

To be sure that everyone follows this method of giving feedback, demonstrate it yourself. Make suggestions for improvements, rather than pointing out deficiencies. For example, when soliciting feedback from group members, you might get them started in a positive way by saying, "Henry communicated very clearly about his intentions not to use drugs, didn't he? Did any of you notice how specific he was?" If a group member responds by saying something like, "Yeah, but he shouldn't stop and shake hands when the dealer sticks out his hand," say "So, you think this would be even more effective if he keeps his hand by his side and keeps moving." By consistently demonstrating positive feedback and by diverting criticisms quickly and politely, you teach patients to comment positively on one another's performances.

After praising the effective aspects of a performance, offer constructive suggestions that focus on what a person can do to improve a performance. You might say, "That was an excellent example of the way to report symptoms and side effects to the doctor. You smiled and introduced yourself. Now let's try it again and this time be sure to let the doctor know exactly which side effects you are experiencing and precisely in what ways they bother you." Also, rephrase criticisms from other group members to show alternative ways to provide positive feedback. For example, the criticism "He stared at the floor a lot" could be rephrased as "Mark thinks you can improve your approach by making more frequent eye contact."

Model Skills

Learning takes place more efficiently when you teach by example and imitation rather than by giving detailed instructions. *Showing* rather than *telling* is preferred when relatively complex behaviors are being taught. Also, patients tend to be less anxious about performing when they see you do it first.

Tricks of the trade

Before you model a sequence, tell patients what to watch for and what they will be expected to do when it is their turn. For example, when modeling how to report symptoms to a psychiatrist, say, "Notice how I greet the doctor politely by making eye contact, smiling, and shaking his hand. Pay particular attention to the way I describe the symptom and the way I tell him exactly how it interferes with my life." Ask them to imagine themselves performing the scene while you demonstrate. Then, let them try immediately after the demonstration is finished. A patient who already possesses the requisite skill can be encouraged to demonstrate. Asking one patient to model for another is an excellent way to keep patients' attention; it also provides additional practice and reinforcement for more advanced participants.

Modeling also can be integrated easily into a role-play. For example, as a patient completes the first rehearsal of a scene, you might say, "That was fine, Bill. You were able to describe your symptoms clearly to the doctor. You told him exactly how long it's been going on and how it interferes with your life. Now, let's work a little more on your style. That time you spoke in a clear voice. Let's see if we can help you to increase eye contact and improve your posture. Let me take your part for a minute. Watch how I look straight into your eyes as I explain the problems my symptoms cause me. Also, watch how I lean forward to show interest and keep your attention. Picture yourself in my place as I do this." Be sure to let the patient repeat the scene again as soon as you finish demonstrating.

Prompt and Cue Responses

Feel free to use verbal prompts or gestures to guide a patient throughout a scene, or to stop the role-play at strategic points to redirect the patient with further instructions. Again, keep your remarks brief and constructive; that is, focus on how the patient can improve his performance rather than on what he or she is doing incorrectly.

Tricks of the trade

Cueing a patient during the scene is a good way to elicit specific action or verbalization. A useful technique is to act as prompter while your co-trainer or another group member performs the role-play with the patient. For example, if the patient's eyes begin to wander or he fails to sustain eye contact, stop the role-play and say, "You're making your point well. I like your choice of words. You can make it even more effective if you look your friend right in the eye when you tell him that you don't use drugs anymore. Let's try it again. Only this time, I'm going to point to my eyes to remind you to focus on your friend's eyes as you let him know you aren't interested in using drugs anymore." Stay near the patient throughout the exercise, whispering in his ear or cueing him with gestures when necessary.

If the patient is on track and performing well, let him or her continue to the end. But if the exercise seems too difficult, stop the scene to provide constructive feedback, being sure to praise the patient for efforts made up to that point. As a patient progresses, you will gradually prompt less, give fewer instructions, and concentrate on encouraging him or her to rehearse an entire scene.

Shape Behavior

Shaping is the process of guiding a trainee through the behavioral sequence required to carry out a designated skill. Shaping a performance helps "polish" the skill by systematically reinforcing incremental improvements that successively approximate the desired result. Repeated rehearsal and feedback from the therapist help to increase self-confidence and efficacy expectations.

Tricks of the trade

Acknowledge and reinforce small increments in performing a skill, shaping the person's behavior so that each repetition comes closer to the desired result. Recognize and reinforce any behavior that moves the patient nearer to an ideal performance. Even the slightest improvement should be praised. For example, when helping a participant increase eye contact, say, "I noticed that you briefly glanced up when you told your friend that you don't want to use drugs. Making eye contact lets him know that you mean business. Increasing your eye contact will make it even more effective. Let's try it again and this time look him in the eye until you get the whole sentence out." When the patient accomplishes this step, say, "Excellent! You looked him right in the eye all the way through that sentence. Now, let's do it again and this time let's see if you can maintain eye contact for two sentences in a row."

Keep in mind that shaping can be effective only when the patient knows exactly what to do. This means that your instructions must be clear and concise, and you need to know when and how to prompt.

Overcome Resistance to Role-Playing

Patients sometimes experience performance anxiety when asked to do a role-play, but the anxiety diminishes with practice and as the number of successful experiences increases. Therefore, encourage patients to become involved in role-playing as soon as possible.

Tricks of the trade

A positive working relationship is the greatest asset in preventing resistance to role-playing. Projecting a sense of acceptance, tolerance, and optimism is key. Display warmth, enthusiasm, and empathy toward reluctant patients. Liveliness and spontaneity create a positive learning environment. Beginning a role-play exercise with the most enthusiastic patients establishes a participatory response for those who are more reluctant at first.

When someone displays reluctance, emphasize the constructive aspects of the role-play exercise and downplay that person's reluctance. Remind him or her that learning a skill is distinctly different from learning something on a verbal level. If a participant hesitates when called upon to role-play, say, "Have you ever heard the old saying 'practice makes perfect?' The skills we're learning here will help you to achieve your goal. Mastering a behavior requires practice. Think about how much practice it takes to learn skills like typing, driving a car, or bowling. Just a little bit of practice will make this seem like second nature to you." Then, begin the role-play immediately.

Another technique is to call on reluctant patients to give feedback to those who are role-playing. At the conclusion of a scenario, call the reluctant patient by name and solicit comments. For example, you might say, "Charles, tell James what you thought was the single most effective thing he did in that role-play." Sometimes it is possible to induce active participation by asking a reluctant person to describe a better way to do a scene; as he or she elaborates on the description you can subtly slip into role-playing with that person by saying, "I think I have the idea, but why don't you show me what you mean so I can be sure" or "Yes, that's it exactly. Show Bill how you would do it if you were in this situation."

Also, someone who is reluctant to take the major role in a scene may be willing to take a secondary role. A person who has performed a secondary role in front of the group finds it easier to take the major role next time. Of course, it is extremely important that he or she experience success and receive generous praise from you for efforts made. And be sure to elicit approval and reinforcement from other group members.

If a participant is strongly resistant to role-play, you can reduce performance anxiety by permitting the patient to remain in his seat rather than asking him to move to the middle of the group. Construct the role-play around him as he remains in place. It is usually easier for people to speak from their seat in a group situation than it is to stand and face the group. Then, after the person has successfully rehearsed the scene from a sitting position, make eye contact while giving praise and feedback, gently touch the back of the person's arm or shoulder and gesture toward the center of the group as you say, "Let's try it one more time. Only this time, stand a little closer to Bill as you begin."

If a group member claims that he or she already possesses a particular skill and declines to take part, point out that the role-play will provide a good opportunity to practice the skill. Remind him or her that the role-play exercises help you as trainer to assess progress in the module. You can also appeal to the person's altruism by asking him or her to help the other members of the group learn the skills by modeling effective techniques for them. Finally, you may want to call upon a more experienced role-player to describe how he or she felt the first time, and how different he or she feels after having participated in many role-play exercises.

While the suggestions above are effective in reducing resistance to participation, it is important that you never force patients into role-playing if they feel strongly that they do not want to participate.

Give Homework Assignments

Among the principle challenges to anyone learning new skills is the inherent difficulty in transferring the training from the classroom to the actual setting in which those skills are needed. For example, there is a big difference between refusing imaginary drugs from a therapist pretending to be a friend or family member and actually refusing real drugs from a person the patient knows well. Despite our best efforts at replicating the settings in which the skills we are teaching will actually be used, there is simply no substitute for practice in the patient's natural environment. Homework assignments help bridge the gap between the clinic setting and the patient's home turf. Instructing a patient to try a new skill in those places and with those people with whom the patient interacts in his or her daily encounters is one of the best ways to promote generalization. Additionally, homework assignments provide opportunities to monitor the patient's progress, occasion natural reinforcements, and, when successfully completed, give the patient a sense of accomplishment. The greatest reward a patient can receive for the effort invested in learning new skills resides in the eruption of spontaneous applause and the compliments offered by his or her peers when reporting the successful completion of an assignment.

Tricks of the trade

When giving assignments, start with simple tasks and then, as skill level and confidence increase, challenge the patient by gradually increasing the difficulty and complexity of the task.

Focus narrowly on *the next step* that will move the patient in the direction of fulfilling the overarching goals of the module. Don't hesitate to challenge the patient, but exercise caution. It's better to err on the side of too little than asking for too much, too soon. Avoid, at all costs, setting the patient up for failure.

When giving assignments, elicit the patient's participation and involvement by preparing him to accept the assignment. Start by asking, "Would you agree with me that practice makes perfect?" When the patient agrees, ask whether he feels that additional practice would be beneficial. Then say, "We need to figure out a way for you to get some more practice." Then involve group members by asking, "Does anybody have any ideas?" At this point, someone, often the patient himself, will suggest that an assignment might be a good idea. Then, use the technique of paradoxical intention by saying something like, "Gee, I don't know. Do you think that you would have the time?" Putting the emphasis on time availability rather than on whether the patient believes he has the ability to complete the assignment virtually ensures endorsement. Then, turn to the other participants and say, "What would be the best way to practice this skill?" Use a blackboard or flip chart to record the steps involved. Encourage participants to help formulate the assignment and make every effort to personalize the steps involved. Rehearse the assignment in class before sending the patient out to give it a try. After practicing the steps required to complete the assignment, ask the patient whether he can anticipate any problems that may arise. The process of checking to see whether there are any obstacles also provides a forum for problem-solving and encourages participation by other group members.

Once the assignment is made, prepare participants in advance for the possibility of failure. Remind them that practice helps to increase the likelihood of a favorable outcome but it doesn't guarantee success. Promote an attitude of experimentation by making statements such as, "I think this has a good chance to work, but if it doesn't, come back and we'll come up with a better way to get the job done." Emphasize that success will be gauged by the patient's efforts to complete the assignment, not by the outcome. Reinforce this notion by indicating that the best one can do is make the effort—there is no guarantee that others will respond in the expected fashion. Highlight this point by saying, "I think we've come up with a good plan, but if somebody throws you a curve, let us know next time and we'll come up with another option."

Teaching Tips

Consistency helps participants to organize their thinking and makes it easier for them to fit comfortably into the treatment program. The inherent structure of the groups and the regularity of scheduled activities fosters a sense of security and increases comfort by establishing clear guidelines and expectations. Here are a few pointers that help keep group meetings focused and on track:

- *Prepare the classroom in advance.* The group room should provide an appropriate atmosphere for learning. It should be organized and made comfortable before participants arrive. Arrange seating, set up the flip-charts, set up props, adjust windows, and erase the blackboard before beginning class. If using the optional videotaped skill illustrations, advance the tape to the appropriate vignette. Preparing in advance preserves precious class time and helps you to start on time.

- *Gather needed materials.* Make sure that materials needed are available and ready for use. Have handouts, pencils, and other items ready for distribution before the group begins.

- *Close the classroom door.* An open classroom door serves as an invitation for interruptions. It also signals participants that they can get up and leave the room while the group is in progress. Closing the door also screens out unwanted noise and commotion.

- *Take attendance.* Recording participants' attendance in scheduled activities ensures that they are following their prescribed treatment regimens. Progress in the program is generally measured by treatment adherence. Opportunities for participation in recreational outings and involvement in other desirable activities can be made contingent on attendance.

- *Start on time.* Beginning the group on time reinforces the expectation that everyone should be present and ready when it is time to start. It shows respect for participants and helps to maintain a good working relationship. It also reinforces the emphasis on punctuality and organization, which are integral to other aspects of participants' success.

- *End on time.* Concluding groups at the scheduled time is necessary to the efficient operation of any treatment program. Participants often must be available for other scheduled groups and activities, clinic appointments, or meetings with other staff members. Allowing groups to run over creates unnecessary disruptions for others who have scheduled their time around participants' group participation.

- *Use incentives.* Incentives such as credits, points, or tokens can be awarded for exhibiting appropriate behavior, participating in scheduled groups and activities, promptness, and fulfilling designated responsibilities in the treatment program. With respect to participation in skills training groups, credits can be earned for promptness and involvement. *Promptness* simply means that the participant has arrived on time for the group. The group leader should emphasize the desirability of timeliness while recording the attendance of those who were seated and ready to start at the beginning of the group. Participants who arrive late can be reminded that they will receive credits next time if they arrive on time. *Involvement* is loosely defined as relevant participation in the group. Basically, this involves asking questions or making comments related to the topic being presented or discussed in the group. Involve everyone in the process. This will require special effort on your part. The usual teaching techniques of prompting, asking questions, reinforcing comments and suggestions, or asking a participant to further elaborate on a statement made by another person can help foster an atmosphere in which everyone feels free to take part. Making a consistent effort to provide ample opportunities for group members to participate and to earn credits for their involvement ensures regular attendance and promotes active participation.

- *Demonstrate courtesy.* Polite and assertive interpersonal exchanges invite patients to do likewise. Every interaction with participants should be seen as an occasion to promote prosocial behavior. Smiling, complimenting specific aspects of participants' behavior, or acknowledging efforts consistent with the general aims of the treatment program will reinforce desirable actions. Many patients with dual diagnoses have been "hardened" by life on the streets. As a consequence, they frequently display antisocial behavior or actions that are offensive to the staff and to each other. Finding ways to promote prosocial behavior is among the most important goals of any skills training program.

- *Project a positive attitude.* A calm, pleasant demeanor sets the tone for an enjoyable learning experience. It relaxes and comforts anxious participants. A serious manner, while conveying a sense of importance, distances the instructor from group members and reduces motivation for learning. Sternness or haughtiness detract from the subject matter and leave participants feeling that the instructor "talks down" to them.

- *Model interpersonal skills.* The group leader should capitalize on the opportunity to model appropriate interpersonal skills by using social reinforcement techniques, such as making eye contact with the patient, smiling, and making statements that specifically reflect some positive aspect of the patient's behavior.

- *Deal with disruptions.* Disruptions in the classroom are disturbing to participants and group leader alike. However, if the class is well organized, clearly structured, and the leader presents him- or herself as clearly in charge without appearing to be overbearing or dictatorial, disruptions can be kept to a minimum. Disruptions come in a variety of guises, ranging from irrelevant or inappropriate questions or comments to patients suddenly getting up and leaving the room to expressions of inappropriate affect or behavior provoked by psychotic processes. Participants should remain in the group until it ends but may be excused if you determine that leaving is not a manipulation but, instead, represents a genuine concern expressed by the patient or a legitimate reason to leave the group. When a participant asks to be excused to use the bathroom, remind the patient of the time the group will end. Often participants will wait until then to use the bathroom. For example, if a patient suddenly gets up and starts to leave the room, you might say, "Where are you going?" "I gotta go to the bathroom." "Class will be over in five minutes. Can it wait until then?" "Yeah." "Great." Smile and gesture with a head nod toward the patient's chair. In rare instances, a participant may become agitated, argumentative, or difficult to interrupt. When this happens, politely end any interaction with that participant and focus your attention on group members who are appropriately involved in the group process. While speaking to one of these individuals, turn your back to the disruptive participant and shield him or her from view of the other group members. Exercise good clinical judgment when using this technique. Never turn your back on a potentially dangerous patient. If a participant is persistently disruptive or all else fails, ask him to leave the group until he feels that he can be courteous.

Skill 1
QUITTING AFTER A SLIP

OVERVIEW

This skill is a crucial part of damage control. Many patients will slip and use drugs or alcohol again. They need to know how to leave a drug-using situation early and thereby prevent the slip from becoming a full-blown relapse that greatly damages their health, relationships, and finances. People with schizophrenia may have special trouble in such situations because many addictive drugs and alcohol worsen the symptoms of schizophrenia. For example, even small doses of some drugs can worsen persecutory delusions and leave a patient paralyzed with fear. Your goal is to teach patients how to leave a drug-using situation despite intense cravings, worsened psychiatric symptoms, and pressure from acquaintances to stay and continue using. In a subsequent training session you will teach patients how to report a slip to a treatment provider and thereby return to treatment.

Patients may tell you that once they have used some drug, they can't stop using until they are out of drugs and money. They may tell you that it is impossible to leave after using some drug and therefore this exercise is pointless. Your job is to get them to practice the skill even if they think it is pointless. But first, get as many patients as you can to understand the point of the skill. You can do this by listening to their reservations about the skill and by explaining that while the ultimate goal is abstinence, slips may occur before they reach this goal. By practicing the skill, they can minimize the damage caused by each slip. Some patients won't be convinced. Have them practice the skill anyway.

Some patients may be concerned that you are encouraging *chipping* (using small amounts of addictive drugs). Remind these patients that the overall goal is abstinence but that it is important to take any reasonable steps toward abstinence.

83

SESSION SUMMARY*

1. Introduce the goal (flip chart 51).

2. Make sure patients can repeat the goal.

3. Review "damage control" and "Mt. Recovery" (flip charts 52, 53, 54).

4. Develop the skill steps (flip chart 55).

5. View the video illustration.

6. Choose a person to role-play.

7. Describe the role-play and demonstrate the steps (flip chart 55).

8. Conduct the role-play (set up, conduct, review, positive feedback, corrective feedback, repeat).

9. Challenge participants.

Usually requires 2–4 sessions (see p. 73).

SAMPLE THERAPIST SCRIPT

Introduce the goal (flip chart 51).

"It's good to see you all here today! Welcome to skills training. In the next few classes, you'll learn how to stop using before a slip becomes a full-blown relapse. In other words, quitting after a slip. Let's get started!"

Make sure patients can repeat the goal.

"What is the goal of today's class?"

To learn how to stop using before a slip becomes a full-blown relapse.

"What is the main goal of the module?"

To say no to drugs and yes to healthy pleasures.

Review "damage control" and "Mt. Recovery" (flip charts 52, 53, 54).

"Let's think about situations in which people are likely to slip up and use drugs. What is a **slip** anyway? (*Pause for responses.*) That's right! A slip is when you find yourself in a high-risk situation and you take a drink or a hit but catch yourself and get out of the situation before you have a full-blown relapse. Would you agree with me that it would be a good idea to be prepared for situations like this? (*Pause for responses.*) Of course, it's never good to slip, but if you can get our early, you can go a long way toward controlling the damage. This is what we call **damage control** (flip chart 52). Remember Mt. Recovery?"

It's important to remember that a slip will do less damage than a full-blown relapse (flip chart 53). So how can we reduce the damage? *(Pause for responses.)* That's right! By stopping drug use early and bouncing back into treatment (flip chart 54)."

Develop the skill steps (flip chart 55).

"Let's think about techniques that can help you quit after a slip and get out of the situation. What might be some of the steps?" *(Ask co-trainer to list steps on the board as you elicit them from group members. Shape responses into the following list. Show flip chart 55 only after the group has developed its own list.)*

Quitting After a Slip

1. Don't make eye contact with the person offering drugs.
2. Stand up and turn away from the person.
3. Start walking out of the room.
4. Say in a firm voice tone, "I gotta go."
5. Use the broken record technique by continuing to say, "I gotta go now."
6. Keep moving quickly, don't stop for anything.

"Okay, let's see if these techniques work. Imagine a situation in which you might have a slip. Where might such an encounter take place? *(Pause for responses.)* All right! Now let's see how this might actually go."

View the video illustration.

Introduce the video. Be sure that the videotape is wound to the beginning of the scene before starting the session. Briefly describe the video scene, emphasizing the steps involved in quitting after a slip.

"Let's see how a person might actually go about quitting after a slip. In the scene you're about to see, three men get together to watch a football game on television. As they sit on the couch and begin to watch the game, one of them lights a joint and passes it to the others. The man on the left has been participating in a substance abuse treatment program. He has been completely abstinent for 10 months. He slips and takes a drag on the joint. Watch how he handles the situation. See if he uses the techniques that you suggested for quitting after a slip."

Critique the model's performance. "Well what did you think? How did he do? *(Encourage discussion of the model's performance.)* Did he follow all of the steps? *(Focus comments on specific behaviors enumerated in the steps related to quitting after a slip.)* Did he leave anything out?"

Elicit suggestions for improvement.

"Can you think of anything that he might do to make his way of handling this situation more effective? What could he do differently?" (*Guide participants' remarks to contrast behaviors exhibited by the model with the requisite steps for quitting after a slip. Politely interrupt digressions from the criterion behaviors.*)

Choose a person to role-play.

Select a group member who you believe will be successful in the role-play. Encourage cooperation by modeling the role-play scenario with the co-trainer. If a co-trainer is not available, select a person who will effectively demonstrate the skills.

Describe the role-play and demonstrate the steps (flip chart 55).

"Okay, I want (*co-trainer or group member*) to play the role of a person who has drugs. (*Name group member*), you'll use the techniques listed on the board to get out of the situation as quickly as you can. Practicing these techniques will help you to stay in control and prevent a full-blown relapse.

"Let's review the techniques so that you don't leave any of them out." (*Point to items listed on flip chart 55. Provide the rationale for each item.*)

1. Don't make eye contact with the other person. Looking him in the eye makes it too easy for him to get your attention.
2. Stand up and turn away from the person. Turning away will help you to avoid eye contact.
3. Start walking toward the door. Moving quickly away from the person makes it harder for him to follow you. It shows him that you're not interested.
4. Say in a firm voice tone, "I gotta go." A firm voice will make it harder for him to interrupt.
5. Use the broken record technique by continuing to say, "I gotta go now." Don't let him get a word in edgewise. Use a loud voice. This way he can't give you an argument.
6. Keep moving, don't stop for anything. Moving away quickly show that you're determined.

Conduct the role-play.

The following is a sample role-play. The group member's responses are in italic. Use it as a guideline to conduct a role-play with each group member. Instruct group members to read the steps listed on the board as they engage in the role-play if they have difficulty remembering what to say.

Set up the role-play. "Imagine a situation in which you might have a slip. It's best to think of a situation that is quite likely to happen in the future or one that has happened in the past. Okay, now tell me, where would such an encounter most likely take place in your case? *(Elicit a specific site.)* Who would be involved? Who are you likely to be with? *(Remember, group members are often reluctant to mention specific names for fear of causing problems for others. Suggest that the group member make up a name to use in place of the person's actual name if need be.)* What emotions might you be feeling in this situation? *(Pause for responses.)* Is there anything else I should know about the situation to make it as realistic as possible?"

"What is *(trainer/co-trainer's)* role in this situation?"

To play the role of someone who wants me to use drugs.

"What is your role in this situation?"

To play myself.

"What is your task in this situation?"

To quit using immediately after slipping and to get away as quickly as I can so I don't use any more.

"Okay, let's give it a try."

Sample Role-Play Dialogue

"Hey *(group member's name)*, I'm really glad you came over. I've got some really good stuff. Let's get loaded. What do you say?"

(Reluctantly accepts) Uh, okay (takes one hit and passes to the other person).

"Here, take another hit."

(Immediately puts drug down) No thanks, I gotta go (stands up, turns away, and starts to walk out).

"Hey, where are you going?"

No, I gotta go.

"What do you mean, you gotta go? We're just getting started."

I gotta go (keeps walking toward the door).

"We've got enough here to last all night."

I gotta go.

"I don't believe you. Come back if you change your mind."

(Continues walking out the door)

Review the role-play: Elicit positive feedback from group members. Provide positive feedback with respect to specific behaviors that were effective. Elicit positive comments from group members by asking them to comment on specific verbal and nonverbal behaviors that increased the effectiveness of the performance. Politely interrupt or reframe negative comments. Follow these steps when reviewing the role-play:

1. First, ask the role-player what he or she thought was most effective about the performance. Embellish the group member's responses, emphasizing the criterion behaviors listed on the board

2. Elicit positive feedback from group members. Guide the process by eliciting remarks about specific verbal and nonverbal behaviors that enhanced the performance.

3. Ask the other player to give specific feedback to the role-player.

4. Summarize effective behaviors and reinforce the role-player with group applause.

Provide corrective feedback and repeat the role-play. Make constructive suggestions that will enhance the role-player's performance. Model skills (specific behaviors), annotating each suggestion as it is demonstrated. Repeat the role-play, giving constructive feedback as described above. Practice the role-play as many times as necessary to achieve an effective response. Practice with each group member until all have mastered this damage control technique.

Challenge participants.

After participants have demonstrated an acceptable level of mastery, challenge them further by repeating the role-play scenario, but this time introduce an obstacle that requires extending the responses described above. Having participants respond to a range of situations that involve quitting after a slip will help promote generalization of the skills learned and increase self-efficacy.

Challenge can be made more realistic by asking participants for suggestions about circumstances that are likely to require more skill to quit before a full-blown relapse occurs. Remember, learning is optimized by creating realistic, meaningful scenarios and finding ways to personalize them for each group member.

Suggest challenge scenarios if participants are unable to pinpoint useful examples.

For instance, you might repeat the above role-play, only this time have the person playing the role of the individual offering drugs question the role-player's friendship or loyalty. For example, as the role-player starts to leave the situation the person who is offering drugs might say, "Hey, I thought we were friends" or "What's the matter—my dope not good enough for you?"

Elicit challenge scenarios. "You seem to be catching on to how to quit and quickly get out after a slip. Now I want to challenge you a bit. What do you think would make it hard for you to stick to the techniques that you've learned for quitting after a slip?"

1. List suggestions on the board.
2. Ask what it is about each situation mentioned that makes it difficult for participants.
3. Identify a situation that the majority agree is likely to occur.
4. Determine whether the skill steps outlined above apply as they are or whether some modification is required.
5. Choose a person to role-play. Select a group member who you believe will be successful.
6. Conduct the role-play.
7. Review the role-play and elicit feedback from group members.
8. Provide corrective feedback.

Skill 2
REPORTING A SLIP

OVERVIEW

Most patients will slip and use drugs or alcohol at some point during treatment. Reporting the slip is critical to successful treatment because it provides clinicians with a detailed description of the chain of behaviors leading to drug use. This allows patients and clinicians to more readily identify warning signs and design more effective U-turns. Yet many patients find it so difficult to report a slip that they avoid returning to treatment. One reason is their fear of facing the clinicians who were helping them avoid using drugs and alcohol. Even when patients do report a slip, many clinicians respond in a punishing way that discourages patients from remaining in treatment and learning from the slip. You will teach patients to report the slip despite their shame, and to do so in a way that promotes helpful, rather than punitive, responses from clinicians. This will increase the chances that your patients will return to treatment and learn how to prevent future slips.

SAMPLE THERAPIST SCRIPT

Introduce the goal (flip chart 56).

"It's good to see you all here today! Welcome to skills training. In the next few classes, you'll learn how to tell a support person that you slipped and used drugs or alcohol. This is a very important skill to learn. Let's get started!"

Make sure patients can repeat the goal.

"What is the goal of today's class?"

To learn how to tell my support person that I slipped and used drugs or alcohol.

SESSION SUMMARY*

1. Introduce the goal (flip chart 56).
2. Make sure patients can repeat the goal.
3. Introduce the skill.
4. Develop the skill steps.
5. View the video illustration.
6. Choose a person to role-play.
7. Describe the role-play and demonstrate the steps (flip chart 57).
8. Conduct the role-play (set up, conduct, review, positive feedback, corrective feedback, repeat).
9. Challenge participants.

*Usually requires 2–4 sessions (see p. 73).

"What is the main goal of the module?"

To say no to drugs and yes to healthy pleasures.

Introduce the skill.

"We've discussed the fact that slips may occur from time to time, even when you are trying your hardest. It would be better to avoid slips altogether, but they can occur. The important thing is to get back on track as soon as possible. One way to get back on track is to let the people supporting you know about the slip. That way, you can get their help to prevent future occurrences. Now, who are the people who provide the support you need? (Pause for responses.) That's right, your support person, family members, friends, and the people on your clinical team. Discussing a slip openly takes courage, but, more than that, it also takes skills. Let's get an idea of what it might be like to report a slip."

Develop the skill steps.

"Help me to list some of the steps in the process. (Ask co-trainer to list steps on the board as you elicit them from group members.) Let's think about what's involved in reporting a slip and asking for help to prevent future occurrences." (Shape responses into the following list.)

Reporting a Slip

1. Greet the person politely. Maintain eye contact. Use a pleasant voice tone.
2. Be direct. Don't beat around the bush. Tell the person that you have slipped.

3. Tell the person that you would like to discuss the circumstances surrounding your slip.

4. Describe the high-risk situation and how you escaped from it. Emphasize the fact that you escaped before you went on a full-blown relapse.

5. Remark about the things that you have been doing recently to keep your sobriety program intact (attending groups, carrying your emergency card, meeting with your support person).

6. Ask the person to help you figure out how to prevent entering into similar high-risk situations in the future.

7. Thank the person for his or her assistance.

View the video illustration.

Introduce the video. Be sure that the videotape is wound to the beginning of the scene before starting the session. Briefly describe the video scene, emphasizing the steps involved in reporting a slip.

"Let's look at a video scene demonstrating how to report a slip. You'll see Raymond, who is overcoming a 15-year addiction to crack cocaine, report a slip to his support person, Dave. Raymond had been abstinent for 30 days before he ran into a friend who offered him a beer. Notice how Raymond describes the incident. Let's see if he uses all of the techniques that you've decided are important when it comes to reporting a slip."

Critique the model's performance. "Well, what do you think? How did Raymond do? *(Encourage discussion of the model's performance.)* Did he follow all of the steps? *(Focus comments on specific behaviors enumerated in the steps related to reporting a slip.)* Did he leave anything out?"

Elicit suggestions for improvement. "Can you think of anything that he might do to make his way of handling this situation more effective? What could he do differently?" *(Guide participants' remarks to contrast behaviors exhibited by the model with the requisite steps for reporting a slip. Politely interrupt digressions from the criterion behaviors.)*

Choose a person to role-play.

Select a group member who you believe will be successful in the role-play. Encourage cooperation by modeling the role-play scenario with the co-trainer. If a co-trainer is not available, select a person who will effectively demonstrate the skills.

Describe the role-play and demonstrate the steps (flip chart 57).

"Okay, I want *(co-trainer or group member)* to play the role of a person to whom a slip will be reported. *(Name group member)*, you'll use the techniques listed on the board to report a slip. Practicing these techniques will help you to stay clean and maintain a strong alliance with the people who support you.

"Let's review the techniques so that you don't leave any of them out." *(Point to items listed on flip chart 57. Provide a rationale for each item.)*

1. Greet the person politely. Maintain eye contact. Use a pleasant voice tone. A pleasant approach will get the person's attention. It makes it easier for him or her to listen to you and lets him or her know that you have something important to discuss.

2. Be direct. Don't beat around the bush. Tell the person that you have slipped. Indicate how you feel. However, don't let your feelings get in the way of staying on track.

3. Tell the person that you would like to discuss the circumstances surrounding your slip. This will let him or her know that you intend to stay focused on your program and it helps keep the conversation on track.

4. Describe the high-risk situation and how you escaped from it. Emphasize the fact that you did not go on a drug binge. Knowing that you escaped will help the person to see that you mean business.

5. Remark about the things that you have been doing recently to keep your sobriety program intact (attending groups, carrying your emergency card, meeting with your support person). This will help to alleviate the person's concerns and enlist his or her cooperation.

6. Ask the person to help you figure out how to prevent entering into similar high-risk situations in the future. This shows that you're not overconfident. It also lets the other person know that you need his or her help to stay clean. People are more likely to back you up if they feel needed.

7. Thank the person for his or her assistance. Pleasantness helps strengthen your relationship.

Conduct the role-play.

The following is a sample role-play. The group member's responses are in italic. This role-play portrays a group member reporting a slip to his support person. However, similar dialogue could be used to report a slip to a doctor or any member of the clinical team, a family member, or a friend. Use this as a guideline to conduct a role-play with each group member. Instruct group members to read the steps listed on the board as they engage in the role-play if they have difficulty remembering what to say.

Set up the role-play. "Imagine a situation in which it becomes necessary to report a slip. Try to think of a situation that could actually happen in the future or one that has happened in the past. Who would be the best person for you to speak to about a slip? *(Elicit the person's name—support person, member of the clinical team, friend, family member.)* Okay, now tell me, where would such an encounter most likely take place in your case? *(Elicit a specific site.)* What emotions might you be feeling as you ask for assistance? *(Pause for response.)* Is there anything else I should know about the situation to make it as realistic as possible?"

"What is *(trainer/co-trainer's)* role in this situation?"

A person to whom I will report a slip.

"What is your role in this situation?"

To be myself.

"What is your task in this situation?"

To report a slip and get help preventing future occurrences.

"Okay, let's give it a try. *(Name group member)*, you begin by saying, 'Hi *(name)*, I'm glad you could meet with me today."

Sample Role-Play Dialogue

Hi_____. I'm glad you could meet with me today.

"What's up? You sounded serious when you asked if we could meet."

Well, I have some bad news. I slipped yesterday. I didn't have a full-blown relapse, but I came close. I escaped before I went on a binge.

"I'm glad you're letting me know."

I'd like to tell you about it. Maybe you can help me figure out how to avoid similar situations in the future.

"Good idea. What happened?"

Well, I was walking to the store when a car pulled up and an old buddy of mine jumped out. He said, 'Hey, I haven't seen you for ages. What do you say we get something to eat and catch up on old times?' It sounded good at the time, so I hopped into his car. As we were driving to the restaurant, he decided to go by his house. When we got there, he walked into the bedroom and came out with a bag of weed. It caught me off guard. He lit a joint, took a drag, and passed it to me.

"What did you do?"

I knew I shouldn't take it, but the situation just got the best of me. I took a hit. With each drag I felt more and more guilty. I felt so bad that I put the joint down on the table and said I had to go. He couldn't believe it. But I just kept going. Then I called you.

"It really must have been hard to stop."

It really was. He really wanted me to stay. I kind of wanted to talk to him too, but I knew that if I stayed I'd end up using crack.

"What did you do to get away?"

I just told him that I don't use anymore. He wanted me to stay, but I just kept repeating that I had to go and walked out the door.

"You did a good job stopping early."

Yeah, it was terrible though. It's a miracle that I didn't use after I left his house. I guess I've learned a lot in the groups I've been going to, but I don't want this to happen again. Do you have any suggestions?

"One thing you might do is to refuse to associate with old buddies that you used to use with."

You're right, and I have been, but this guy caught me by surprise.

"Now that you have had an experience slipping in this type of high-risk situation, maybe it will be easier for you to deal with your old buddies next time. At least it gave you a chance to practice one of your coping techniques."

Yeah, you're right. But I should have let him know that I don't use anymore as soon as I saw him.

"Yes. You know, maybe that's something you could practice in your SAMM group."

Good idea. I'll bring it up at the next session.

"You should let the people on your clinical team know about this too."

Yes, I'll do it right away.

"You're really working at your program. Keep it up."

Thanks for your help. I feel like I'm back on track.

Review the role-play: Elicit positive feedback from group members. Provide positive feedback with respect to specific behaviors that were effective. Elicit positive comments from group members by asking them to comment on specific verbal and nonverbal behaviors that increased the effectiveness of the performance. Politely interrupt or reframe negative comments. Follow these steps when reviewing the role-play:

1. First, ask the role-player what he or she thought was most effective about the performance. Embellish the group member's responses, emphasizing the criterion behaviors listed on the board.
2. Elicit positive feedback from group members. Guide the process by eliciting remarks about specific verbal and nonverbal behaviors that enhanced the performance.
3. Ask the other player to give specific feedback to the role-player.
4. Summarize effective behaviors and reinforce the role-player with group applause.

Provide corrective feedback and repeat the role-play. Make constructive suggestions that will enhance the role-player's performance. Model skills (specific behaviors), annotating each suggestion as it is demonstrated. Repeat the role-play, giving constructive feedback as described above. Practice the role-play as many times as necessary to achieve an effective response. Practice with each group member until all have mastered the techniques for reporting a slip.

Challenge participants.

When participants have demonstrated an acceptable level of mastery, challenge them further by throwing them a curve. That is, repeat the role-play scenario with each participant, but this time introduce an obstacle that requires extending the responses described above. Having participants respond to a range of situations that require reporting a slip will increase self-confidence and help promote generalization of the skills learned.

Challenge can be made more realistic by asking participants for suggestions about circumstances that are likely to overwhelm the skills required for reporting a slip. Remember, learning is optimized by creating realistic, meaningful scenarios and finding ways to personalize them for each group member. Suggest challenge scenarios if participants are unable to pinpoint useful examples. For instance, try repeating the role-play above, only this time have the person playing the role of the individual to whom the participant is reporting the slip express frustration or annoyance that the participant has allowed this to happen. Alternatively, ask the person playing the role of a member of the clinical team to suggest doubt about the participant's sincerity or ability to remain abstinent.

Elicit challenge scenarios. "I can see that all of you are learning how to report a slip. Now I want to challenge you by making things a little more difficult. What do you think would make it hard for you to stick to the techniques that you've learned for reporting a slip to a member of your clinical team or to your support person?"

1. List suggestions on the board.
2. Ask what it is about each situation mentioned that makes it difficult for participants.
3. Identify a situation that the majority agree is likely to occur.
4. Determine whether the skill steps outlined above apply as they are or whether some modification is required.
5. Choose a person to role-play. Select a group member who you believe will be successful.
6. Conduct the role-play.
7. Review the role-play and elicit feedback from group members.
8. Provide corrective feedback.

Skill 3

REFUSING DRUGS
OFFERED BY A DEALER

OVERVIEW

Working on this skill and the next (refusing drugs offered by a friend or relative) will help patients escape high-risk situations. Be sure to point out that it would be better to avoid high-risk situations altogether, but in case they wind up in one, it's a good idea to know how to refuse drugs.

Drug dealers are terrific salesmen. They've practiced selling drugs countless times and will exploit any weakness in your patients. They don't take no for an answer. Even if a patient has firmly refused drugs, the dealer may put free drugs right into your patient's hands. The dealer knows that once your patient has used the free drugs he will crave more. Some patients refer to this intense craving for more drugs as being "sprung."

Because dealers are so skillful, you must do more than teach patients to "*just* say no." You must teach them to say no firmly and convincingly and to block any attempt by the dealer to change their mind. Two symptoms of schizophrenia can make it difficult for your patients to refuse drugs firmly and effectively. First, many people with schizophrenia tend to say things in a bland way, without much emotion showing on their face, in their tone of voice, or in their gestures. Psychiatrists refer to this lack of emotional expression as a flat or blunted affect. Dealers might take your patient's bland refusal as a sign that they might be able to make a sale anyway. Instead of a bland refusal, you will teach patients to use their facial expression, tone of voice, and gesture to convey an unequivocal refusal. Another reason that people with schizophrenia may have trouble refusing drugs is that ambivalence is a common feature of schizophrenia. Many patients find it particularly difficult to make a decision and then stick to it. Dealers may exploit their lack of resolve. To counter this, you

SESSION SUMMARY*

1. Introduce the goal (flip chart 58).

2. Make sure patients can repeat the goals.

3. Review the term "high-risk situation" (flip chart 59).

4. Develop the skill steps (flip charts 60, 61).

5. View the video illustration.

6. Choose a person to role-play.

7. Describe the role-play and demonstrate the steps (flip chart 62).

8. Conduct the role-play (set up, conduct, review, positive feedback, corrective feedback, repeat).

9. Challenge participants.

*Usually requires 2–4 sessions (see p. 73).

will teach patients to avoid a variety of behaviors that give dealers a chance to talk them into buying drugs. For example, many patients feel compelled to explain their drug refusal. They may say, "Sorry, I'm broke," to which some dealers will respond with a discount, credit, or even free drugs.

Some patients will tell you that by the time they are talking with a dealer, they have already decided to buy and use drugs. Therefore, they see no sense in practicing drug refusal. This is a very realistic concern and it can be difficult to convince some patients that there is any point to learning this skill. The key is to make sure they practice it, even if they think it's useless. But first listen to their concerns. Let them know you understand why it may seem pointless. Explain that drug dealers may approach them when they have made no plans to use and the skill will be useful in such situations. Many patients will admit that even as they are making plans to buy drugs, they are thinking, "I can't believe I'm doing this again. I promised myself I'd quit." Tell such patients that this thought will become stronger as they progress through this training and you want them to have the skill to say no to a dealer, even if they had initially planned to buy drugs. Some patients will remain skeptical. Ask them to bear with you and do the exercise anyway.

SAMPLE THERAPIST SCRIPT

Introduce the goal (flip chart 58).

"It's good to see you all here today! Welcome to skills training. In the next few classes, you'll learn the do's and don'ts of drug refusal and practice how to refuse drugs offered by a drug dealer. This can be a tough one. Let's get started!"

Make sure patients can repeat the goal.

"What is the goal of today's class?"

To learn the do's and don'ts of drug refusal and practice how to refuse drugs from a drug dealer.

"What is the main goal of the module?"

To say no to drugs and yes to healthy pleasures.

Review the term "high-risk situation" (flip chart 59).

"We talked a lot about high-risk situations during basic training. What is a **high-risk situation?** *(Pause for responses.)* That's right, a high-risk situation is any situation that makes it really hard not to use drugs *(flip chart 59).* Who can give me an example? *(Pause for responses.)* Those are good examples. An example of an extremely high-risk situation is when you're approached by a pushy dealer. This is a particularly difficult situation because drug dealers don't like to take no for an answer. Isn't that right? *(Pause for responses.)*

"Have any of you ever been approached by a pushy drug dealer? You know, somebody who just won't take no for an answer. *(Pause for responses.)* These situations are among the hardest to get out of. Some dealers really come on strong. They're so pushy that you feel like you can't get away from them. Do you know anybody like that? *(Pause for responses.)* When you run into one of these guys, you're definitely in a high-risk situation because it's really hard not to use. There are a lot of these folks out there and it's likely that you're going to run into a few. So, you need to be sure that you have the skills it takes to get out of these situations when they come up."

Develop the skill steps (flip charts 60, 61).

"Now tell me, what's the main thing you should do if you encounter a pushy dealer? *(Pause for responses.)* You bet! Get away as fast as you can. But, getting away from one of these guys might not be as easy as it sounds. Getting away quickly requires good **drug-refusal skills**. What do you suppose I mean by drug-refusal skills? *(Pause for responses.)* Exactly! Drug-refusal skills are the techniques you can use to get out of a high-risk situation before it's too late. Let's think about what some of those techniques might be. There are some do's and don'ts. *(Ask co-trainer to list do's and don'ts on the board as you elicit them from group members.)* Let's think about what it would take to get away as fast as you can. What are the Do's? *(Shape responses into the following lists [flip charts 60, 61].)*

Do's

1. Look away.
2. Walk fast.

3. Look serious.

4. Stand tall.

5. Wave him off.

6. Say, "No, I don't want any" over and over.

"Terrific! That's an excellent list. You can see how these techniques could help. Now, what are the don'ts?"

Don'ts

1. Look at him.

2. Slow down or stop walking.

3. Smile.

4. Use a soft voice.

5. Start making excuses.

6. Get into a conversation.

7. Let him put anything in your hand.

"Okay, let's see if these ideas can work. Imagine a situation in which you might encounter a pushy drug dealer. Where might such an encounter take place? *(Pause for responses.)* Right! Now let's see how this might actually go."

View the video illustration.

Introduce the video. Be sure that the videotape is wound to the beginning of the scene before starting the session. Briefly describe the video scene, emphasizing the steps involved in refusing drugs from a dealer.

"You really have to be at your best whenever you're approached by a drug dealer. Drug dealers can be persistent and pushy. They don't like to take no for an answer. Let's watch a video scene demonstrating how to refuse drugs from a dealer. You'll see George as he walks through the park on his way to visit a friend. Let's see what he does when he encounters a drug dealer along the way. See if he uses all of the steps for refusing drugs. Is there anything that he could do to be more effective?"

Critique the model's performance. "Well, what do you think? How did George do? *(Encourage discussion of the model's performance.)* Did he follow all of the steps? *(Focus comments on specific behaviors enumerated in the steps related to refusing drugs from a dealer.)* Did he leave anything out?"

Elicit suggestions for improvement. "Can you think of anything that he might do to make his way of handling this situation more effective? What could he do differently?" *(Guide participants' remarks to contrast behaviors exhibited by the model with the requisite steps for refusing drugs from a dealer. Politely interrupt digressions from the criterion behaviors.)*

Choose a person to role-play.

Select a group member who you believe will be successful in the role-play. Encourage cooperation by modeling the role-play scenario with the co-trainer. If a co-trainer is not available, select a person who will effectively demonstrate the skills.

Describe the role-play and demonstrate the steps (flip chart 62).

"Okay, I want *(co-trainer or group member)* to play the role of a pushy drug dealer or someone who wants you to buy drugs. You'll use the techniques listed on the flip chart to get out of the situation as quickly as you can. Practicing these techniques will help you to stay in control and get away quickly.

"Let's review the techniques so that you don't leave any of them out." *(Point to items listed on flip chart 62. Provide a rationale for each item.)*

1. Avert your gaze, don't make eye contract with the dealer. Looking him in the eye makes it too easy for him to get your attention.

2. Turn your head away from the dealer and wave him off with a hand gesture. Turning away will help you to avoid eye contact. Gesture by waving as if you are pushing him away. A firm hand gesture shows him that you mean what you say.

3. Stand tall and lean forward. This will help you to look strong and determined. If your stance is meek, you'll look vulnerable.

4. Walk past the dealer at a brisk pace. Moving quickly away from the dealer makes it harder for him to follow you. It shows him that you're not interested.

5. Keep your hands close to you so that the dealer can't put anything in your hand. If he succeeds in putting the drugs in your hand, he's got you. Don't even give him a chance.

6. Use a firm voice tone and keep repeating "I don't want any" over and over again. Don't let him get a word in edgewise. Use a loud voice. This way he can't give you an argument.

Conduct the role-play.

The following is a sample role-play. The group member's responses are in italic. Use it as a guideline to conduct a role-play with each group member. Instruct group members to read the steps listed on the board as they engage in the role-play if they have difficulty remembering what to say.

Set up the role-play. "Imagine a situation in which a pushy drug dealer approaches you. It's best to think of a situation that is quite likely to happen in the future or one that has happened in the past. Okay, now tell me, where would such an encounter most likely take place in your case? *(Elicit a specific site.)* Who would be involved? Are you likely to be with somebody or alone? *(Permit the group member to use a general designation such as 'a friend'—group members are often reluctant to mention specific names for fear of causing problems for others.)* What emotions might you be feeling as you notice the dealer approaching you? *(Pause for response.)* Is there anything else I should know about the situation to make it as realistic as possible?"

"What is *(co-trainer's)* role in this situation?"

A pushy drug dealer who wants to sell me drugs.

"What is your role in this situation?"

To be myself.

"What is your task in this situation?"

To refuse buying any drugs and get away as quickly as I can.

"Okay, let's give it a try."

Sample Role-Play Dialogue

"Hey, I've got something for you today."

(Averts gaze, stands erect, leans forward, and starts walking quickly away.)

"Come on, man, try some of this."

(Using a hand gesture to wave off the dealer) No, I don't want any.

"Come on, this is good stuff."

(Pulls hands in close and continues walking away.)

"Okay, maybe you're down on your luck right now. Here, you can pay me later (looks for opportunity to place drugs in role-player's hand)."

No, I don't want any.

(Follows role-player for a short distance, attempting to hand put drugs in his hand.)

(Walking quickly away) I don't want any. I don't want any.

Review the Role-play: Elicit positive feedback from group members. Provide positive feedback with respect to specific behaviors that were effective. Elicit positive comments from group members by asking them to comment on specific verbal and non-verbal behaviors that increased the effectiveness of the performance. Politely interrupt or reframe negative comments. Follow these steps when reviewing the role-play:

1. First, ask the role-player what he or she thought was most effective about the performance. Embellish the group member's responses, emphasizing the criterion behaviors listed on the board.

2. Elicit positive feedback from group members. Guide the process by eliciting remarks about specific verbal and nonverbal behaviors that enhanced the performance.

3. Ask the other player to give specific feedback to the role-player.

4. Summarize effective behaviors and reinforce the role-player with group applause.

Provide corrective feedback and repeat the role-play. Make constructive suggestions that will enhance the role-player's performance. Model skills (specific behaviors), annotating each suggestion as it is demonstrated. Repeat the role-play, giving constructive feedback as described above. Practice the role-play as many times as necessary to achieve an effective response. Practice with each group member until all have mastered this drug-refusal technique.

Challenge participants.

When participants have demonstrated an acceptable level of mastery, challenge them further by throwing them a curve. That is, repeat the role-play scenario with each participant, but this time introduce an obstacle that requires extending the responses described above. Having participants respond to a range of situations revolving around encounters with drug dealers will help promote generalization of the skills learned and increase self-efficacy.

Challenge can be made more realistic by asking participants for suggestions about circumstances that are likely to overwhelm drug-refusal skills. Remember, learning is optimized by creating realistic, meaningful scenarios and finding ways to personalize them for each group member.

Suggest challenge scenarios if participants are unable to pinpoint useful examples. For instance, you might repeat the role-play above, only this time have a succession of two or three drug dealers approach the role-player as he walks down the street. Alternatively, ask the person playing the role of a drug dealer to indicate that he can arrange a meeting with a prostitute if the role-player will agree to purchase the drug.

Elicit challenge scenarios. "I can see that all of you are catching on to how to handle a pushy dealer. Now I want to challenge you by making things a little more difficult. What do you think would make it hard for you to stick to the techniques that you've learned for refusing drugs from a pushy dealer?"

1. List suggestions on the board.
2. Ask what it is about each situation mentioned that makes it difficult for participants.
3. Identify a situation that the majority agree is likely to occur.
4. Determine whether the skill steps outlined above apply as they are or whether some modification is required.
5. Choose a person to role-play. Select a group member who you believe will be successful.
6. Conduct the role-play.
7. Review the role-play and elicit feedback from group members.
8. Provide corrective feedback.

Skill 4

REFUSING DRUGS OFFERED BY A FRIEND OR RELATIVE

OVERVIEW

In many ways, saying no to a friend or relative is very different from saying no to a dealer. One difference is that the patient may need to maintain the relationship even though there is some risk that the friend or relative will offer drugs again. This is especially true of people with schizophrenia who may be unable to work and must depend on others for basic needs. That's why the steps in this skill are designed to accomplish three things: (1) successfully refuse drugs, (2) maintain any healthy aspects of the relationship, and (3) get the friend or relative not to offer drugs in the future. However, if the friend or relative responds in a way that suggests he'll continue to offer drugs, then the skill allows the patient to leave the situation without using drugs.

SAMPLE THERAPIST SCRIPT

Introduce the goal (flip chart 63).

"It's good to see you all here today! Welcome to skills training. In the next few classes, you'll learn and practice how to refuse drugs offered by a friend or relative. The steps for refusing drugs from someone you know well are different steps than those for refusing drugs from a dealer. Let's take a look!"

SESSION SUMMARY*

1. Introduce the goal (flip chart 63).
2. Make sure patients can repeat the goal.
3. Review the term "high-risk situation."
4. Develop the skill steps.
5. View the video illustration.
6. Choose a person to role-play.
7. Describe the role-play and demonstrate the steps (flip chart 64).
8. Conduct the role-play (set up, conduct, review, positive feedback, corrective feedback, repeat).
9. Challenge participants.

*Usually requires 2–4 sessions (see p. 73).

Make sure patients can repeat the goal.

"What is the goal of today's class?"

To learn and practice how to refuse drugs from a friend or relative.

"What is the main goal of the module?"

To say no to drugs and yes to healthy pleasures.

Review the term "high-risk situation."

"We've been learning how to handle high-risk situations. What is a **high-risk situation?** *(Pause for responses.)* That's right, a high-risk situation is any situation that makes it really hard not to use drugs. You've learned how to escape from a pushy dealer. Now, let's consider some other types of high-risk situations. Can you give me a couple of examples? *(Pause for responses.)* Those are good examples. Another example of a high-risk situation is when you're approached by a relative or a friend who offers you drugs. This is a particularly difficult situation because you may be concerned that he or she will be offended if you decline the offer. Has anyone ever been in a situation like this? *(Pause for responses; encourage group members to briefly describe the circumstances and the emotions they were feeling at the time.)* You can see from these examples that these are difficult situations to get out of. But, would you agree with me that a true friend or a relative, one who really cares about you, will understand when you say that you don't want to use drugs anymore? *(Pause for responses.)* People who really care about you don't try to force you to do things against your will. Drug-refusal skills will help you escape if you find yourself in this type of high-risk situation. So, today, we're going to learn some more drug-refusal techniques. You have already learned how to get away from a pushy drug dealer. Now, we'll concentrate on how to decline drugs when they are offered by a friend or family member."

Develop the skill steps.

"Let's think about techniques we can use to escape from a high-risk situation in which a friend or relative offers you drugs. *(Ask co-trainer to write suggestions on the board as you elicit them from group members.)* Let's think about what it would take to refuse a drug offer without offending a person who cares about you. What are some things to do?" *(Shape responses into the following list.)*

Techniques for Refusing a Drug Offer from a Friend or Relative

1. Be direct. Make eye contact and use a firm, sincere voice tone. Tell the person that you're not interested.
2. Use the broken record technique. Repeat yourself if necessary.
3. Level with the person. Tell him or her that drugs were causing you problems and it's better for you to leave drugs alone.
4. Suggest an alternative. Request to do something other than use drugs.
5. Express your feelings directly. Tell the other person how you feel about being pressured.
6. Leave the situation. Tell the person that you are serious about sobriety.

View the video illustration.

Introduce the video. Be sure that the videotape is wound to the beginning of the scene before starting the session. Briefly describe the video scene, emphasizing the steps involved in refusing drugs from friends or family members.

"The techniques for refusing drugs from a friend or family member are different from the techniques used to refuse drugs from a dealer. In the video scene that I'm about to show you, you'll see Raymond decline an offer to share a joint with his friend Donnie. Raymond and Donnie have been good friends since high school. They also served together in the Army. They enjoy getting together when they have some free time. Raymond is fighting an addiction to marijuana and crack. Donnie uses marijuana from time to time but does not consider himself to have a drug problem. He invites Raymond out on the patio to smoke a cigarette but when he opens the pack, he pulls out a joint and proceeds to light it. Watch how Raymond handles the situation. See if he does all of the things that you suggested for refusing drugs from a friend."

Critique the model's performance. "Well, what do you think? How did Raymond do? *(Encourage discussion of the model's performance.)* Did he follow all of the steps? *(Focus comments on specific behaviors enumerated in the steps related to refusing drugs from a friend or family member.)* Did he leave anything out?"

Elicit suggestions for improvement. "Can you think of anything that he might do to make his way of handling this situation more effective? What could he do differently?" *(Guide participants' remarks to contrast behaviors exhibited by the model with the requisite steps for refusing drugs from a friend or family member. Politely interrupt digressions from the criterion behaviors.)*

Choose a person to role-play. Select a group member who you believe will be successful in the role-play. Encourage cooperation by modeling the role-play scenario with the co-trainer. If a co-trainer is not available, select a person who will effectively demonstrate the skills.

Describe the role-play and demonstrate the steps (flip chart 64).
"In this role-play, you will play yourself and *(co-trainer or group member)* will play the role of a friend or relative who offers you drugs. Use the steps on the board to get out of this high-risk situation. Practicing these techniques will help you to stay in control without offending your friend or relative.

"Let's review the techniques so that you don't leave any of them out." *(Point to items listed on flip chart 64. Provide the rationale for each item.)*

1. Use direct refusal. Remember to look the person right in the eye. Politely but firmly say, "No thank you. I don't care to use drugs anymore." This shows that you mean business.

2. Use the broken record technique. Repeat yourself more firmly by saying in a louder, firmer voice. "No thank you! I really don't want any." This makes it harder for the person to insist that you take some. Most people probably won't go beyond this point with you.

3. Level with the person. Tell him that using drugs caused serious problems in your life. Let them know that staying sober is a struggle for you and that your struggle is made harder when people you care about offer you drugs.

4. Suggest an alternative. Ask the person to do something else with you instead of using drugs. This shows that you want to be with the other person, but you don't want to do drugs. It also shifts the topic away from drugs.

5. Express your feelings directly. Tell the person how you feel—angry, frustrated, pressured—about being pushed to do something you don't care to do. This is the

most difficult step, but it almost always gets results. Expressing your feelings directly makes it hard for the other person to continue pushing drugs on you.

6. Leave the high-risk situation immediately. If you are still being pressured after attempting to use the previous steps, leave by saying politely, "I can see that you won't take no for an answer, so I'd better be on my way." This shows that you're determined to stay clean.

Conduct the role-play.

The following is a sample role-play. The group member's responses are in italic. Use it as a guideline to conduct a role-play with each group member. Instruct group members to read the steps listed on the board as they engage in the role-play if they have difficulty remembering what to say.

Set up the role-play. "Imagine a situation in which a friend or relative offers you drugs. It's best to think of a situation that is quite likely to happen in the future or one that has happened in the past. Now, who would be involved? Are you likely to be with others or alone with your friend? *(Remember, group members are often reluctant to mention specific names for fear of causing problems for others. Suggest that the group member make up a name to use in place of the person's actual name if need be.)* Where might such an encounter take place in your case? *(Elicit a specific site.)* What emotions might you be feeling as your friend or relative offers you drugs? *(Pause for response.)* Is there anything else I should know about the situation to make it as realistic as possible?"

"What is *(co-trainer's)* role in this situation?"

To play the role of a friend or relative who wants me to use drugs.

"What is your role in this situation?"

To be myself.

"What is your task in this situation?"

To use the steps on the board to refuse drugs.

"Okay, let's see how it might go."

Sample Role-Play Dialogue

"Hi _____. It's good to see you today. Look what I have.

Yeah, what is it?

"I ran into Joe and he sold me some great crack. Let's try it."

Oh, that's risky for me. No thanks.

"Ah, come on. I've never known you to refuse crack."

No, thanks. I don't use anymore.

"Come on, man. I've got plenty."

Look, I said that I don't use anymore. Drugs were causing serious problems in my life. It's really hard for me to stay sober. Please don't make it impossible for me.

"What are you talking about? Come on, let's get high. You can't tell me that you don't want any of this."

I mean what I said. I don't use anymore. I want to stay clean. I'd rather do something else. How about if we go to a movie or go to shoot some pool?

"You want to go out when we can stay here and have a great time? Come on, let's get high!"

That's right, I would. Please stop pressuring me. I'm starting to get angry because you're trying to get me to do something that I don't want to do.

"Hey, I don't mean to pressure you. If you don't want to use that just means more for me. We can play some pool after I smoke this crack."

Nope. Like I said, I don't use anymore. I've got something else I would rather do. I don't have any intentions of using with you ever again. I'm leaving.

Review the role-play: Elicit positive feedback from group members. Provide positive feedback with respect to specific behaviors that were effective. Elicit positive comments from group members by asking them to comment on specific verbal and non-verbal behaviors that increased the effectiveness of the performance. Politely interrupt or reframe negative comments. Follow these steps when reviewing the role-play:

1. First, ask the role-player what he or she thought was most effective about the performance. Embellish the group member's responses, emphasizing the criterion behaviors listed on the board.

2. Elicit positive feedback from group members. Guide the process by eliciting remarks about specific verbal and nonverbal behaviors that enhanced the performance.

3. Ask the other player to give specific feedback to the role-player.

4. Summarize effective behaviors and reinforce the role-player with group applause.

Provide corrective feedback and repeat the role-play. Make constructive suggestions that will enhance the role-player's performance. Model skills (specific behaviors), annotating each suggestion as it is demonstrated. Repeat the role-play, giving constructive feedback as described above. Practice the role-play as many times as necessary to achieve an effective response. Practice with each group member until all have mastered this drug-refusal technique.

Challenge participants.

When participants have demonstrated an acceptable level of mastery, challenge them further by throwing them a curve. That is, repeat the role-play scenario with each participant, but this time introduce an obstacle that requires extending the responses described above. Having participants respond to a range of situations revolving around encounters with friends or family members who offer them drugs will help promote generalization of the skills learned and increase self-efficacy.

Challenges can be made more realistic by asking participants for suggestions about circumstances that are likely to overwhelm drug-refusal skills. Remember, learning is optimized by creating realistic, meaningful scenarios and finding ways to personalize them for each group member.

Suggest challenge scenarios if participants are unable to pinpoint useful examples. Try repeating the role-play above with a slight modification. For example, have the person playing the role of the friend or family member suggest that the group member use alcohol as an alternative to cocaine. Alternatively, set up a situation that would be particularly difficult to leave. For example, the transaction could take place in an automobile. Or, have the friend or family member ask if it is all right to use with the understanding that the participant doesn't want any.

Elicit challenge scenarios. "You all seem to be getting comfortable handling friends and family members who offer drugs. Now I want to challenge you by making things a little more difficult. What do you think would make it hard for you to stick to the techniques that you've learned for refusing drugs from a friend or family member?"

1. List suggestions on the board.
2. Ask what it is about each situation mentioned that makes it difficult for participants.
3. Identify a situation that the majority agree is likely to occur.
4. Determine whether the skill steps outlined above apply as they are or whether some modification is required.

5. Choose a person to role-play. Select a group member who you believe will be successful.

6. Conduct the role-play.

7. Review the role-play and elicit feedback from group members.

8. Provide corrective feedback.

Skill 5

GETTING AN APPOINTMENT WITH A BUSY PERSON

OVERVIEW

Your patients need help from a variety of busy people, including nurses, physicians, psychologists, social workers, representative payees, and many others. Getting an appointment with such individuals can be difficult for anyone, but is especially difficult for people with schizophrenia and addictions. There are several reasons for this. First, they have a variety of symptoms that make interpersonal communications difficult, such as trouble expressing emotion (blunted affect) and trouble sticking to the point (tangential speech). In addition, we have noticed that many treatment providers are uncomfortable working with people with such a difficult combination of problems and tend to avoid committing to appointments. To overcome these obstacles, you will teach patients how to get a busy person to pay attention to them, to understand the importance and urgency of their needs, and to either discuss the problem immediately or set a time discuss the problem latter.

SAMPLE THERAPIST SCRIPT

Introduce the goal (flip chart 65).

"It's good to see you all here today! Welcome to skills training. In the next few classes, you'll learn and practice how to get an appointment with a busy person. Let's get started!"

SESSION SUMMARY*

1. Introduce the goal (flip chart 65).

2. Make sure patients can repeat the goal.

3. Introduce the skill.

4. Develop the skill steps.

5. View the video illustration.

6. Choose a person to role-play.

7. Describe the role-play and demonstrate the steps (flip chart 66).

8. Conduct the role-play (set up, conduct, review, positive feedback, corrective feedback, repeat).

9. Challenge participants.

Usually requires 2–4 sessions (see p. 73).

Make sure patients can repeat the goal.

"What is the goal of today's class?"

To learn and practice how to get an appointment with a busy person.

"What is the main goal of the module?"

To say no to drugs and yes to healthy pleasures.

Introduce the skill.

"Have you ever tried to get an appointment with a busy person? *(Pause for responses.)* It isn't always easy. When people are busy, they don't always want to take time for another person, even when it's important. Have you ever been in a situation like that? *(Pause for responses.)* Knowing how to get a person's attention when you need their assistance is an important skill to have in preventing a drug relapse. For example, suppose you want to talk with your payee or your support person and she doesn't seem to have time for you? What can you do? Let's see if we can list some techniques for getting the help you need when you need it."

Develop the skill steps.

"How do you go about getting a person to stop what he or she is doing and give you the help you want? Let's think about what some of those techniques might be. *(Ask co-trainer to write each suggestion on the board as you elicit them from group members.)* Let's think about what it would take to get the help you need. What are some techniques?"

(Shape responses into the following list.)

> *Techniques for Getting an Appointment with a Busy Person*
> 1. Greet the person politely.
> 2. Maintain eye contact and use a pleasant but firm voice tone.
> 3. Tell the person that you need his or her help.
> 4. Tell the person that it is important.
> 5. Indicate that it will take only a few minutes of her time.
> 6. If the person refuses to meet now, ask for an appointment.
> 7. Ask the person to be specific as to the time and place to meet.
> 8. Restate the time and place of the meeting and thank the person.

"Terrific! That's an excellent list. Now, let's see if these ideas can work."

View the video illustration.

Introduce the video. Be sure that the videotape is wound to the beginning of the scene before starting the session. Briefly describe the video scene, emphasizing the steps involved in getting an appointment with a busy person.

"In this scene, you'll see Michael attempt to make an appointment with Karen, who is serving as his payee. Michael encounters Karen just as she is leaving her office to rush to a meeting. She's very busy and always in a hurry. Michael needs to see Karen right away but she insists that she doesn't have time for him. Watch how Michael gets an appointment before Karen gets away. See if he uses all of the steps that you suggested for getting an appointment with a busy person."

Critique the model's performance. "Well, what do you think? How did Michael do? *(Encourage discussion of the model's performance.)* Did he follow all of the steps? *(Focus comments on specific behaviors enumerated in the steps related to getting an appointment with a busy person.)* Did he leave anything out?"

Elicit suggestions for improvement. "Can you think of anything that he might do to make his way of handling this situation more effective? What could he do differently?" *(Guide participants' remarks to contrast behaviors exhibited by the model with the requisite steps for getting an appointment with a busy person. Politely interrupt digressions from the criterion behaviors.)*

Choose a person to role-play. Select a group member who you believe will be successful in the role-play. Encourage cooperation by modeling the role-play scenario with the co-trainer. If a co-trainer is not available, select a person who will effectively demonstrate the skills.

Describe the role-play and demonstrate the steps (flip chart 66). "Okay, I want (co-trainer or group member) to play the role of a busy person. (Name group member), you'll use the techniques listed on the board to get an appointment. Practicing these techniques will make it easier for you to get help when you need it.

"Let's review the techniques so that you don't leave any of them out." (Point to items listed on flip chart 66. Provide a rationale for each item.)

1. Greet the person politely. A pleasant approach will get the person's attention. He or she will be much more likely to listen to what you have to say.
2. Maintain eye contact and use a pleasant but firm voice tone. This will help you to keep the person's attention while you tell her what you want.
3. Tell the person that you need his or her help. Telling the person that you need her will make it harder for her to decline your request.
4. Tell the person that it's important. Emphasizing the urgency of your request will accentuate the need to discuss your concerns now. It may stop her from putting you off.
5. Indicate that it will take only a few minutes of her time. This way, she is more likely to take time for you.
6. If the person refuses to meet now, ask for an appointment. This way, you can be sure that you will have the time you need, even if it isn't possible to meet at the moment.
7. Ask the person to be specific as to the time and place to meet. This seals the deal. If you set a specific time and place, the meeting is much more likely to take place.
8. Restate the time and place of the meeting. This will ensure that there is no mistake. It also shows that you're determined.

Conduct the role-play. The following is a sample role-play. The group member's responses are in italic. Use it as a guideline to conduct a role-play with each group member. Instruct group members to read the steps listed on the board as they engage in the role-play if they have difficulty remembering what to say.

Set up the role-play. "Imagine a situation in which you approach a busy person to ask for help. It's best to think of a situation that is quite likely to happen in the future or one that has happened in the past. Who might be the person that you need to see? (Elic-

it name of the person.) Okay, now tell me, where would such an encounter most likely take place? *(Elicit a specific site.)* What emotions might you be feeling as you approach this person? *(Pause for responses.)* Is there anything else I should know about the situation to make it as realistic as possible?"

"What *is (co-trainer's)* role in this situation?"

A busy person (payee/support person).

"What is your role in this situation?"

To be myself.

"What is your task in this situation?"

To get the person to give me the help that I need.

"Okay, let's give it a try. *(Name group member),* start by saying, 'Excuse me, I need to talk with you.'"

Sample Role-Play Dialogue

Excuse me, _____. I need to talk with you.

"I'm sorry, but I'm really busy now."

I see that you are, but I really need to talk with you.

"I told you, I don't have time."

I know you're in a hurry, but this is important.

"I'm sure it is, but I can't discuss it right now."

It will only take a few minutes. I promise not to take long.

"I'm sorry. I just can't take the time now."

Okay, I won't bother you anymore now. Is there another time that would be convenient for you to meet with me?

"Catch me sometime after lunch today."

All right, when and where would you like to meet?

"Be at my office today at one o'clock."

You bet. I'll be at your office today at one o'clock. Thanks.

"See you then."

Review the role-play: Elicit positive feedback from group members. Provide positive feedback with respect to specific behaviors that were effective. Elicit positive comments from group members by asking them to comment on specific verbal and non-verbal behaviors that increased the effectiveness of the performance. Politely interrupt or reframe negative comments. Follow these steps when reviewing the role-play:

1. First, ask the role-player what he or she thought was most effective about the performance. Embellish the group member's responses, emphasizing the criterion behaviors listed on the board.

2. Elicit positive feedback from group members. Guide the process by eliciting remarks about specific verbal and nonverbal behaviors that enhanced the performance.

3. Ask the co-trainer to give specific feedback to the role-player.

4. Summarize effective behaviors and reinforce the role-player with group applause.

Provide corrective feedback and repeat the role-play. Make constructive suggestions that will enhance the role-player's performance. Model skills (specific behaviors), annotating each suggestion as it is demonstrated. Repeat the role-play, giving constructive feedback as described above. Practice the role-play as many times as necessary to achieve an effective response. Practice with each group member until all have mastered the techniques for getting an appointment with a busy person.

Challenge participants.

As soon as participants have demonstrated an acceptable level of mastery, challenge them further by repeating the role-play scenario, but, this time introduce an obstacle that requires extending the responses described above. Having participants respond to a range of situations representing varying degrees of difficulty in getting an appointment with a busy person will promote generalization of the skills learned and increase self-efficacy.

Challenges can be made more realistic by asking participants for suggestions about circumstances that are likely to overwhelm the skills required to get an appointment with a busy person. Remember, learning is optimized by creating realistic, meaningful scenarios and finding ways to personalize them for each group member. Suggest challenge scenarios if participants are unable to pinpoint useful examples. For instance, you might alter the role-play above by having the role-player approach the busy person in a hallway while on the way to an important meeting. Alternatively, ask the person playing the role of a busy person to express annoyance at the role-player's persistence when it has been made clear that he or she is late for an appointment.

Elicit challenge scenarios. "It seems that everyone has mastered the skills required to get an appointment with a busy person. Now I want to challenge you by making things a little more difficult. What do you think would make it hard for you to stick to the techniques that you've learned for getting the cooperation of a busy person?"

1. List suggestions on the board.
2. Ask what it is about each situation mentioned that makes it difficult for participants.
3. Identify a situation that the majority agree is likely to occur.
4. Determine whether the skill steps outlined above apply as they are or whether some modification is required.
5. Choose a person to role-play. Select a group member who you believe will be successful.
6. Conduct the role-play.
7. Review the role-play and elicit feedback from group members.
8. Provide corrective feedback.

Skill 6
GETTING A SUPPORT PERSON

OVERVIEW

Most people need a support person, a reliable and concerned person, to help them through tough times as they try to reduce and finally quit using drugs and alcohol. A support person can help a patient identify warning signs, develop U-turns, and establish healthy habits. However, it can be especially hard for people with schizophrenia to enlist a support person for two reasons. First, their social networks are often very small. They may not speak regularly with anyone other than drug dealers. Second, even when they know someone who would make a good support person, they may lack the social and verbal skills needed to persuade the person to serve as a support person.

Your job is to help each patient find and enlist the help of a support person. First, you will teach them to recognize a good support person. Next, you will teach them how to ask someone to serve as their support person.

SAMPLE THERAPIST SCRIPT

Introduce the goal (flip chart 67).
  "It's good to see you all here today! Welcome to skills training. In the next few classes, you'll learn what makes a good support person and practice how to ask someone to be your support person. We have a lot of material to cover, so let's start."

Make sure patients can repeat the goal.
  "What is the goal of today's class?"

SESSION SUMMARY*

1. Introduce the goal (flip chart 67).
2. Make sure patients can repeat the goal.
3. Review the term "support person" (flip chart 68).
4. Review the qualities of a good support person (flip chart 69).
5. Develop the skill steps.
6. View the video illustration.
7. Choose a person to role-play.
8. Describe the role-play and demonstrate the steps (flip chart 70).
9. Conduct the role-play (set up, conduct, review, positive feedback, corrective feed back, repeat).
10. Challenge participants.

*Usually requires 2–4 sessions (see p. 73).

To learn what makes a good support person and practice asking someone to be my support person.

"What is the main goal of the module?"

To say no to drugs and yes to healthy pleasures.

Review the term "support person" (flip chart 68).

"I think that we can all agree that quitting drugs is one of the hardest things a person can ever do. But, as I've said before, as hard as it is, it isn't impossible. Because if it was impossible, nobody would ever succeed. And the truth is, a lot of people succeed in quitting drugs. Right? *(Pause for responses.)* You know, quitting drugs is so hard that nobody can do it completely alone. You need all the support you can get. That's why it's so important to have a **support person** on your side. What is a support person anyway? *(Pause for responses.)* That's right! A support person is someone you can count on in a time of need (flip chart 68). A support person can help you through tough situations. What are some things that a support person can do to help? Who can give me some examples? *(Pause for responses.)* You bet! Support persons can help you deal with cravings. They can help you remember why you decided to quit. And, they can help you develop healthy habits and healthy pleasures."

Review the qualities of a good support person (flip chart 69).

"Let's think about the qualities or traits of a good support person. What kind of traits would you like to see in a person that you would choose to be your personal support person?" *(Ask the co-trainer to list suggestions on the board as you elicit them from group members. Shape responses into the following list [flip chart 69].)*

A Good Support Person is Someone:
- I know well.
- I trust.
- I talk to frequently.
- who does not abuse drugs or alcohol.
- who is available when needed.
- who will give me time when I ask.
- who wants to help me.

Develop the skill steps.

"Once you have decided who might make a good support person for you, the next step is to get his or her cooperation. What do you suppose would be the steps involved in getting someone to agree to be your support person? What would you have to do?" *(Ask co-trainer to write each suggestion on the board as you elicit them from group members. Shape responses into the following list.)*

1. Tell the person that you need his or her help.
2. Explain why you need a support person.
3. Be direct in asking the person to serve as your support person.
4. Answer any questions the person asks about his or her responsibilities.
5. If the person agrees, show your emergency card and ask if you can write his or her telephone number on it.
6. Thank the person for agreeing to help you.

"Well, let's see if these techniques will work. Let's imagine a situation in which you might have this discussion with a prospective support person. Where might such an encounter take place? *(Pause for responses.)* Okay, let's see how this might actually go."

View the video illustration.

Introduce the video. Be sure that the videotape is wound to the beginning of the scene before starting the session. Briefly describe the video scene, emphasizing the steps involved in enlisting a support person.

"Quitting drugs is never easy. Having a support person is essential. In the video scene that I'm about to show you, you'll see Raymond enlist his friend Dave as a support person. Raymond has been attending a substance abuse treatment program. Staff members in the program have emphasized the value and the importance of having a support person to call on when feeling troubled or when tempted to use drugs. Raymond has known Dave for a long time and he knows that Dave never uses drugs. Raymond drops by Dave's house to ask him to be his support person. Let's see if Raymond uses all of the steps that you recommended."

Critique the model's performance. "Well, what do you think? How did Raymond do? *(Encourage discussion of the model's performance.)* Did he follow all of the steps? *(Focus comments on specific behaviors enumerated in the steps related to enlisting a support person.)* Did he leave anything out?"

Elicit suggestions for improvement. "Can you think of anything that he might do to make his way of handling this situation more effective? What could he do differently?" *(Guide participants' remarks to contrast behaviors exhibited by the model with the requisite steps for enlisting a support person. Politely interrupt digressions from the criterion behaviors.)*

Choose a person to role-play.

Select a group member who you believe will be successful in the role-play. Encourage cooperation by modeling the role-play scenario with the co-trainer. If a co-trainer is not available, select a person who will effectively demonstrate the skills.

Describe the role-play and demonstrate the steps (flip chart 70).

"In this role-play, you will play yourself and *(co-trainer or group member)* will play the role of a prospective support person. You will use the steps listed on the board to get the other person's cooperation. Practicing these techniques will help you to feel more comfortable asking for help.

"Let's review the techniques so that you don't leave any of them out." *(Point to items listed on flip chart 70. Provide the rationale for each item.)*

1. Tell the person that you need his or her help. This will get his attention and encourage him to assist you.

2. Explain why you need a support person. Knowing exactly what is expected will go a long way toward getting the person to accept your request.

3. Be direct in asking the person to serve as your support person. Don't beat around the bush. The direct approach will keep the conversation from getting bogged down.

4. Answer any questions the person asks about his or her responsibilities. Clarifying your responsibilities and those of the other person will show that it is a serious commitment.

5. If the person agrees, show your emergency card and ask if you can write his or her telephone number on it. Showing your emergency card lets the person know that you mean business. Asking for his telephone number tells him that you plan to call if you get tempted to use.

6. Thank the person for agreeing to help you. Be cordial. Kindness makes it easier for the person to cooperate.

Conduct the role-play.

The following is a sample role-play. The group member's responses are in italic. Use it as a guideline to conduct a role-play with each group member. Instruct group members to read the steps listed on the board as they engage in the role-play if they have difficulty remembering what to say.

Set up the role-play. "Imagine a situation in which you might ask someone to be your support person. It's best to think of a situation that is quite likely to happen in the future. Who would you ask? *(Pause for response.)* Where might such an encounter take place in your case? *(Elicit a specific site.)* What emotions might you be feeling as you ask the person to be your support person? *(Pause for response.)* Is there anything else I should know about the situation to make it as realistic as possible?"

"What is *(co-trainer's)* role in this situation?"

To play the role of someone who can be my support person.

"What is your role in this situation?"

To be myself.

"What is your task in this situation?"

To get the person's cooperation.

"Okay, let's give it a try."

Sample Role-Play Dialogue

"Hi_____, it's good to see you."

Thanks, it's good to see you too. I wanted to talk with you because I need your help with something.

"Oh, how can I help you?"

Recently, I got into a program to help me stop using drugs.

"Great! That's good news."

Thanks. The program is a big help to me, but I need all the help I can get. Quitting drugs is one of the hardest things a person can do.

"Yes, I know. But how can I help you?"

Well, in my program they talk about the importance of having a support person.

"What's a support person?"

A support person is someone who I know and trust. It should be someone who I see frequently and who will be accessible to me when I need help. Most importantly, it has to be someone who doesn't use drugs. That's why I picked you.

"Well, what does a support person do?"

A support person could help me get out of high-risk situations, like when I have cravings or I'm tempted to use drugs. He would help me think about alternatives to using.

"How's that?"

For example, there might be times when I find myself thinking about using or maybe I will have a slip. It would be helpful to be able to talk to you about it. Discussing it with you might help get me back on track.

"Oh, I see, a support person helps you get through tough times."

Yes, exactly. I find it easy to talk with you. I want you to be my support person. Will you do it?

"Yes, I want to see you do well. If I can be of help, I'll be glad to be your support person."

Great! Do you have any other questions?

"Yes, I have one question. Do I have to be available 24 hours a day?"

No you don't. Let me show you something. This is my emergency card. You can see that

I've listed emergency telephone numbers as well as some coping techniques that I can use when I'm in a high-risk situation. It's helpful, but it also would be good to know that I have somebody on my side. I'll call you if these techniques aren't enough.

"I see."

I'd like to put your telephone number on my emergency card so that it's handy. Would that be all right?

"Yes, of course."

What is your number?

"My telephone number is 555-1234."

(Writes telephone number on the emergency card) Great! Thanks again for agreeing to be my support person.

"You're welcome."

Review the role-play: Elicit positive feedback from group members. Provide positive feedback with respect to specific behaviors that were effective. Elicit positive comments from group members by asking them to comment on specific verbal and non-verbal behaviors that increased the effectiveness of the performance. Politely interrupt or reframe negative comments. Follow these steps when reviewing the role-play:

1. First, ask the role-player what he or she thought was most effective about the performance. Embellish the group members' responses, emphasizing the criterion behaviors listed on the board.
2. Elicit positive feedback from group members. Guide the process by eliciting remarks about specific verbal and nonverbal behaviors that enhanced the performance.
3. Ask the other player to give specific feedback to the role-player.
4. Summarize effective behaviors and reinforce the role-player with group applause.

Provide corrective feedback and repeat the role-play. Make constructive suggestions that will enhance the role-player's performance. Model skills (specific behaviors), annotating each suggestion as it is demonstrated. Repeat the role-play, giving constructive feedback as described above. Practice the role-play as many times as necessary to achieve an effective response. Practice with each group member until all have mastered how to enlist the cooperation of a support person.

Challenge participants.

When participants have demonstrated an acceptable level of mastery, challenge them further by throwing them a curve. That is, repeat the role-play scenario with each participant, but this time introduce an obstacle that requires extending the responses described above. Having participants respond to a range of situations will help promote generalization of the skills learned and increase self-efficacy.

Challenges can be made more realistic by asking participants for suggestions about circumstances that are likely to require more skill. Remember, learning is optimized by creating realistic, meaningful scenarios and finding ways to personalize them for each group member. Suggest challenge scenarios if participants are unable to pinpoint useful examples. For instance, you might repeat the role-play above, only this time have the person playing the role of the support person indicate that he or she does not have the time to serve as a support person, or that he or she feels unqualified to take on the responsibility.

Elicit challenge scenarios. "I can see that all of you are catching on to the techniques of getting a support person. Now I want to challenge you by making things a little more difficult. What do you think would make it hard for you to stick to the techniques that you've learned for encouraging a support person to help?"

1. List suggestions on the board.
2. Ask what it is about each situation mentioned that makes it difficult for participants.
3. Identify a situation that the majority agree is likely to occur.
4. Determine whether the skill steps outlined above apply as they are or whether some modification is required.
5. Choose a person to role-play. Select a group member who you believe will be successful.
6. Conduct the role-play.
7. Review the role-play and elicit feedback from group members.
8. Provide corrective feedback.

Skill 7

REPORTING SYMPTOMS AND SIDE EFFECTS TO A DOCTOR

OVERVIEW

Many patients believe that they use drugs and alcohol to relieve symptoms or medication side effects. For example, some patients report that alcohol seems to reduce auditory hallucinations or that cocaine relieves the sedative effects of antipsychotic medication. Using addictive drugs in this way is often called "self-medication." The extent to which self-medication plays a role in addiction remains unclear. However, in patients who are self-medicating, symptoms and medication side effects may be viewed as warning signs of impending drug and alcohol use. You will teach patients to respond to these warning signs, not by self-medicating but by making a U-turn and seeking the advice of their psychiatrist. This might lead to changes in medications that relieve the very symptoms or side effects that were leading the patient to self-medicate with drugs and alcohol.

SAMPLE THERAPIST SCRIPT

Introduce the goal (flip chart 71).

"It's good to see you all here today! Welcome to skills training. In the next few classes, you'll learn and practice how to tell your doctor about symptoms and side effects that make it harder to avoid drugs. This is a very important skill. Let's begin!"

SESSION SUMMARY*

1. Introduce the goal (flip chart 71).
2. Make sure patients can repeat the goal.
3. Review the terms "healthy pleasure," "healthy habit," and "U-turn" (flip charts 72, 73, 74).
4. List common side effects and symptoms of schizophrenia (flip charts 75, 76).
5. Develop the skill steps.
6. View the video installation.
7. Chose a person to role-play.
8. Describe the role-play and demonstrate the steps (flip chart 77).
9. Conduct the role-play (set up, conduct, review, positive feedback, corrective fee back, repeat).
10. Challenge participants.

Usually requires 2–4 sessions (see p. 73).

Make sure patients can repeat the goal.
"What is the goal of today's class?"

To learn how to tell my doctor about symptoms and side effects that make it harder for me to avoid drugs.

"What is the main goal of the module?"

To say no to drugs and yes to healthy pleasures.

Review the terms "healthy pleasure," "healthy habit," and "U-turn" (flip charts 72, 73, 74).
"We've been talking about the importance of healthy habits and healthy pleasures. Tell me again, what is a healthy pleasure? *(Pause for responses.)* That's right! It's something that feels good and is good for you (flip chart 72). And, what's a healthy habit? *(Pause for responses.)* Yes, exactly! Healthy habits are the steps you take to get to healthy pleasures (flip chart 73). Getting on the road to healthy pleasures requires knowing how to make U-turns. Who can tell me what a U-turn is? *(Pause for responses.)* Exactly! A U-turn is any step that takes you away from the road to relapse. U-turns move you in the direction of healthy pleasures (flip chart 74). The need to make a U-turn comes up in a lot of situations. For example, the temptation to use drugs increases when you are bothered by medical or psychiatric symptoms. Annoying medication side effects can also be a

risk. Have any of you ever used drugs to try to relieve symptoms or side effects? (*Pause for responses.*) Today we are going to practice one particular type of U-turn: reporting symptoms and side effects to your doctor. Your doctor may then be able to help relieve those symptoms or side effects so that you are less tempted to use drugs or alcohol."

List common side effects and symptoms of schizophrenia (flip charts 75, 76).

"First, let's list on the board some of the typical symptoms of schizophrenia and some of the more common side effects that people have. (*Ask co-trainer to list symptoms and side effects on the board as you elicit them from the group.*) Let's start with medication side effects. What are some of the side effects associated with the medications you take? (*Examples include drowsiness, blurry vision, dry mouth, constipation, diarrhea, restlessness, muscle stiffness, shakes, tremors, and other abnormal involuntary movements.*) Great! Those are terrific examples. Now let's list some of the common symptoms of schizophrenia. (*Examples include hearing voices, seeing visions, paranoia, lack of interest, fear, low energy, anxiety, depression, sleep disturbance, poor concentration, and social withdrawal.*) Wow, you guys really know your stuff."

Develop the skill steps.

"Now let's think about some of the techniques you should use to report symptoms and side effects to your doctor. (*Ask co-trainer to write suggestions on the board as you elicit them from the group.*) What are the things to keep in mind?" (*Shape responses into the following list.*)

Techniques for Reporting Symptoms and Side Effects to a Doctor

1. Greet your doctor politely. Make eye contact and use a pleasant tone of voice.
2. Describe the symptom or side effect in detail.
3. Say how long you've had the symptom or side effect.
4. Describe the severity of your problem by explaining how it interferes with your daily activities.
5. Ask directly for your doctor's help.
6. Repeat the doctor's instructions.
7. Ask how long it will take to get relief.
8. Thank the doctor for his or her assistance.

"Okay, let's see if these ideas have a chance to work. Let's imagine a situation in which you might need to report symptoms or side effects to your doctor. Where might such an encounter take place? (*Pause for responses.*) Right! Now let's see how this might actually go."

View the video illustration.

Introduce the video. Be sure that the videotape is wound to the beginning of the scene before starting the session. Briefly describe the video scene, emphasizing the steps involved in reporting symptoms and side effects to a doctor.

"Psychiatric symptoms and medication side effects can certainly set the stage for a relapse, so knowing how to report these problems to your doctor is vitally important when it comes to quitting drugs. I'm going to show you a video scene in which Joe, a young man who's been attending a drug treatment program, reports a medication side effect to his doctor. Joe has been bothered by muscle tightness in his neck. It worries him because he knows that in the past he has used drugs to relieve his distress. Let's see if Joe uses all of the techniques that you suggested for reporting symptoms and side effects to a doctor."

Critique the model's performance. "Well, what do you think? How did Joe do?" *(Encourage discussion of the model's performance.)* Did he follow all of the steps? *(Focus comments on specific behaviors enumerated in the steps for reporting symptoms and side effects to a doctor.)* Did he leave anything out?"

Elicit suggestions for improvement. "Can you think of anything that he might do to make his way of handling this situation more effective? What could he do differently?" *(Guide participants' remarks to contrast behaviors exhibited by the model with the requisite steps for reporting symptoms and side effects to a doctor. Politely interrupt digressions from the criterion behaviors.)*

Choose a person to role-play.

Select a group member who you believe will be successful in the role-play. Encourage cooperation by modeling the role-play scenario with the co-trainer. If a co-trainer is not available, select a person who will effectively demonstrate the skills.

Describe the role-play and demonstrate the steps (flip chart 77).

"Okay, I want *(co-trainer or group member)* to play the role of your doctor. Use the techniques listed on the board to get your doctor's assistance. Practicing these techniques will help you to stay in control and learn how to make a U-turn when you're experiencing symptoms or medication side effects.

"Let's review the techniques so that you don't leave any of them out." *(Point to items listed on flip chart 77. Provide a rationale for each item.)*

1. Greet your doctor politely. Make eye contact and use a pleasant tone of voice. A pleasant approach will get your doctor's attention and increase interest in your concerns.

2. Describe the symptom or side effect in detail. Tell your the doctor precisely what bothers you. A clear understanding of your problem will help the doctor decide exactly what to do to help you.

3. Say how long you've had the symptom or side effect. A clear description emphasizes the duration of discomfort in addition to providing useful diagnostic information.

4. Describe the severity of your problem by explaining how it interferes with your daily activities. Knowing that your symptom or side effect prevents you from doing things that you need to do will increase your doctor's responsiveness.

5. Ask directly for your doctor's help. This makes it clear that you are not simply reporting a problem. It emphasizes the fact that you want treatment.

6. When your doctor offers advice, repeat his or her instructions. This reduces the possibility of a mistake. Repeating your doctor's instructions ensures that you understand exactly what to do.

7. Ask how long it will take to get relief. This will let you know what to expect. It also lets your doctor know that you mean business.

8. Thank your doctor for his or her assistance. A friendly approach will go a long way toward ensuring that your doctor will help the next time you ask for assistance.

Conduct the role-play.

The following is a sample role-play. The group member's responses are in italic. Use it as a guideline to conduct a role-play with each group member. Instruct group members to read the steps listed on the board as they engage in the role-play if they have difficulty remembering what to say.

Set up the role-play. "Imagine a situation in which you have been experiencing a symptom or side effect for three days. Choose one from the list on the board. Pick one that you have actually experienced and think of the things you needed to do that were made difficult by the symptom or side effect. For example, hand tremors can make it difficult to drive a car and sign your name. Tremors may also attract the attention of others even when you don't want their attention. It's best to think of a situation that has happened in the past or one that is likely to happen in the future. Okay, which symptom or side effect do you want to use? *(Pause for response.)* All right, that's a good one. Now, tell me, where would you most likely discuss this with your doctor? *(Elicit a specific site.)* Who would be involved? Are you likely to visit the doctor alone or with somebody? *(Pause for responses.)* What emotions might you be feeling as you have this discussion with your doctor? *(Pause for response.)* Is there anything else I should know about the situation to make it as realistic as possible?"

"What is (co-trainer's) role in this situation?"

To take the role of my doctor.

"What is your role in this situation?"

To be myself.

"What is your task in this situation?"

To make a U-turn by reporting a symptom or side effect to my doctor.

"Okay, let's give it a try. Begin with a pleasant greeting and be sure to tell the doctor your name."

Sample Role-play Dialogue

Hello Dr._____. My name is _____. Thank you for meeting with me today.

"Hello _____ . How can I help you?"

I've been extremely restless.

"Hmmm. Sounds awful. Why don't you have a seat in that chair and tell me more about it."

Okay (sits in chair, moves restlessly, frequently shifting position). It's like I'm real nervous.

"Is it more like nervousness or more like restlessness?"

It's more like restlessness. It's like I have anxiety, only I'm not apprehensive. I just have trouble sitting still. People in my family tell me to sit down and relax but I feel like I need to pace.

"I see."

It started several days ago but has gotten steadily worse over the past three days.

"It sounds like it's really bothering you."

Yes, it is. It's so bad that I can't sit through a television program without walking all around the room. And then the people in my family complain. I'm even having trouble sleeping because of it. I couldn't sit still on the bus coming here today. I stood up in the aisle and the driver told me that I would have to either sit down or get off the bus.

"No wonder you're upset."

Doctor, can you please help me with this?

"I'm sure going to try. I think that the restlessness you're having is a side effect of your antipsychotic medication. It's nothing to worry about. Restlessness is a common side effect and it's usually quite treatable."

What can you do?

"I'm going to give you a prescription for a side-effect medication. This should help reduce the restlessness."

Thanks a lot.

"Take one tablet in the morning and one at bedtime."

Okay, I'll take two tablets every day: one in the morning and one at bedtime.

"That's correct."

How long will it take before I get some relief?

"You should notice a difference within a couple of hours. Make an appointment to see me again next week. The problem should be cleared up by then."

I sure will. Thank you for your help.

Review the role-play: Elicit positive feedback from group members. Provide positive feedback with respect to specific behaviors that were effective. Elicit positive comments from group members by asking them to comment on specific verbal and nonverbal behaviors that increased the effectiveness of the performance. Politely interrupt or reframe negative comments. Follow these steps when reviewing the role-play:

1. First, ask the role-player what he or she thought was most effective about the performance. Embellish the group member's responses, emphasizing the criterion behaviors listed on the board.
2. Elicit positive feedback from group members. Guide the process by eliciting remarks about specific verbal and nonverbal behaviors that enhanced the performance.
3. Ask the other player to give specific feedback to the role-player.
4. Summarize effective behaviors and reinforce the role-player with group applause.

Provide corrective feedback and repeat the role-play. Make constructive suggestions that will enhance the role-player's performance. Model skills (specific behaviors), annotating each suggestion as it is demonstrated. Repeat the role-play, giving constructive feedback as described above. Practice the role-play as many times as necessary to achieve an effective response. Practice with each group member until all have mastered techniques for reporting symptoms and side effects to the doctor.

Challenge participants.

After participants have demonstrated an acceptable level of mastery, challenge them further by throwing them a curve. Repeat the role-play scenario with each participant, but this time introduce an obstacle that requires extending the responses described above. Having participants respond to a range of situations in which it would be advisable to report symptoms or side effects to the doctor will promote generalization of the skills learned and increase self-confidence.

Challenges can be made more realistic by asking participants for suggestions about circumstances that are likely to overwhelm the skills needed to report symptoms and side effects to the doctor. Remember, learning is optimized by creating realistic, meaningful scenarios and finding ways to personalize them for each group member. Suggest challenge scenarios if participants are unable to pinpoint useful examples. For example, repeat the role-play above, but this time instruct the person playing the role of the doctor to be in a hurry or in a bad mood or to dismiss the participant's complaint as unimportant. For example, after the participant complains about a particular symptom or side effect, the doctor could reply nonchalantly, "Oh, don't worry about that. Symptoms (or side effects) like that are quite common with your diagnosis."

Elicit challenge scenarios. "I can see that all of you are catching on to how to report symptoms and side effects to your doctor. Now I want to challenge you by making things a little more difficult. What do you think would make it hard for you to stick to the techniques that you've learned for reporting symptoms and side effects?"

1. List suggestions on the board.
2. Ask what it is about each situation mentioned that makes it difficult for participants.
3. Identify a situation that the majority agree is likely to occur.
4. Determine whether the skill steps outlined above apply as they are or whether some modification is required.
5. Choose a person to role-play. Select a group member who you believe will be successful.
6. Conduct the role-play.
7. Review the role-play and elicit feedback from group members.
8. Provide corrective feedback.

Skill 8

ASKING SOMEONE TO JOIN YOU IN A HEALTHY PLEASURE

OVERVIEW

The theme of the Substance Abuse Management Module is "how to say no to drugs and yes to healthy pleasures." The idea is to encourage behaviors that don't involve drugs and that promote physical health and emotional well-being. The trouble is that drugs are powerful reinforcers that have shaped behavior into a drug-using habit. Replacing this drug habit with healthy habits requires strong reinforcers—strong enough to compete with the power of drugs to shape behavior.

When we asked patients what they wanted most out of life, they put close, caring relationships at the top of their list. Many asked us to help them re-establish such relationships with family members or establish new ones with friends or potential romantic partners. Such relationships (with non-addicted individuals) can reinforce a whole host of healthy habits, from personal hygiene to regular exercise to productive work. Building these relationships is a complex and highly varied process, but the first step often involves asking someone to join you in a fun activity. While this comes naturally to many people, it is hard for others and especially difficult for people with schizophrenia. In the next session you will teach patients how to take this early step in building healthy relationships.

SAMPLE THERAPIST SCRIPT

Introduce the goal (flip chart 78).

SESSION SUMMARY*

1. Introduce the goal (flip chart 78).
2. Make sure patients can repeat the goal.
3. Review the term "healthy pleasure" (flip chart 79).
4. Develop the skill steps.
5. View the video illustration.
6. Choose a person to role-play.
7. Describe the role-play and demonstrate the steps (flip chart 80).
8. Conduct the role-play (set up, conduct, review, positive feedback, corrective feedback, repeat).
9. Challenge participants.

Usually requires 2–4 sessions (see p. 73).

"It's good to see you all here today! Welcome to skills training. In the next few classes, you'll learn and practice how to ask someone to join you in doing something fun and healthy. This way, you can be sure to avoid using drugs. Let's get started!"

Make sure patients can repeat the goal.

"What is the goal of today's class?"

To learn how to ask someone to join me in doing something fun and healthy.

"What is the main goal of the module?"

To say no to drugs and yes to healthy pleasures.

Review the term "healthy pleasure" (flip chart 79).

"Who can tell me the difference between a healthy pleasure and an unhealthy pleasure? *(Pause for responses.)* That's it exactly! An unhealthy pleasure is something that feels good but is bad for you; a healthy pleasure is something that feels good and is good for you. Why is it important for people to have healthy pleasures in their lives? *(Pause for responses.)* You bet! Healthy pleasures help make it easier to avoid using drugs. If you have lots of healthy pleasures to occupy your time, you are less likely to have cravings and you don't think about using drugs as often. You can do some types of healthy pleasures all alone. Other healthy pleasures are more fun if you do them with another person. Would you agree that it's good to have both kinds of healthy pleasures in your schedule? *(Pause for responses.)* Great!

"Let's create a list of some healthy pleasures that you can do alone and others that you can do with someone whose company you enjoy. *(Ask co-trainer to list suggestions on the board as you elicit them from group members.)* Let's start with healthy pleasures that you can do alone. *(Pause for responses.)* Excellent! These are all good ideas. Now, let's list some healthy pleasures that are more fun to do with someone you like. *(Pause for responses.)* Terrific! That's an excellent list. Let's compare your list to the flip chart and see if we missed anything (flip chart 79). Now, you have lots of ideas about healthy pleasures that you can do."

Develop the skill steps.

"You know, when it comes to trying to quit drugs, it's usually better to do healthy pleasures with another person. Can you tell me why? *(Pause for responses.)* Exactly, it makes it easier not to use. So, it might be helpful to think about how to go about asking someone to join you in a healthy pleasure. It's not all that hard, of course, but there are some techniques that make it easier for the other person to say yes. Let's think about what they might be. *(Ask co-trainer to write each suggestion on the board as you elicit them from the group.)* What's the best way to approach a person who you want to join you in an activity?" *(Shape responses into the following list).*

Techniques for Asking Someone to Join You in a Healthy Pleasure

1. Use a pleasant greeting. Make eye contact and speak in a happy voice tone.
2. Tell the person how much you enjoy his or her company.
3. Pick at least two activities that you are certain the person will enjoy.
4. Describe the activities and when they take place.
5. Ask the person to join you. Be direct. Don't beat around the bush. Get to the point quickly.
6. If the person says that he or she has another engagement at that time, suggest an alternate activity or ask when he would have time.
7. If it becomes clear that the person doesn't want to join you in an activity, tell him or her that you understand and thank him for considering your offer.
8. If the person accepts your offer, set a time and place to meet, and thank him.

"Okay, let's see if these ideas can work. Let's imagine a situation in which you might ask someone to join you in a healthy pleasure. Where might such an encounter take place? *(Pause for responses.)* Right! Now let's see how this might actually go."

View the video illustration.

Introduce the video. Be sure that the videotape is wound to the beginning of the scene before starting the session. Briefly describe the video scene, emphasizing the steps involved.

"You've come up with some good ideas about how to ask someone to join you in a healthy pleasure. Let's watch a video scene to get an idea how it might go if you decide to give it a try. In this scene, you'll see Curtis ask Diane to go to a movie and the beach with him. Curtis and Diane have been working together in a factory for the past several months. Curtis enjoys Diane's company but, until now, he has never asked her out. Let's see how he does it. See if you can think of anything that he could do to make his approach even more effective."

Critique the model's performance. "Well, what do you think? How did Curtis do? *(Encourage discussion of the model's performance.)* Did he follow all of the steps? *(Focus comments on specific behaviors enumerated in the steps you've listed on the board).* Did he leave anything out?"

Elicit suggestions for improvement. "Can you think of anything that he might do to make his way of handling this situation more effective? What could he do differently?" *(Guide participant's remarks to contrast behaviors exhibited by the model with the requisite steps for asking someone to join in a healthy pleasure. Politely interrupt digressions from the criterion behaviors specified.)*

Choose a person to role-play.

Select a group member who you believe will be successful in the role-play. Encourage cooperation by modeling the role-play scenario with the co-trainer. If a co-trainer is not available, select a person who will effectively demonstrate the skills.

Describe the role-play and demonstrate the steps (flip chart 80).

"Okay, I want *(co-trainer or group member)* to play the role of someone whose company you enjoy. Using the techniques listed on the board, ask him to join you in an activity. Practicing these techniques will make it easier for him or her to accept your offer."

"Let's review the techniques so that you don't leave any of them out." *(Point to items listed on flip chart 80. Provide a rationale for each item.)*

1. Use a pleasant greeting. Make eye contact and speak in a happy voice tone. A pleasant approach will get the person's attention and help put him or her in a good mood.
2. Tell the person how much you enjoy his or her company. This will cue him that you are about to ask him out.
3. Pick at least two activities that you are certain the person will enjoy. Suggesting

two activities increases the chances that he or she will accept one of them.

4. Describe the activities and when they take place. This lets the person know when to be available. It also relieves him of the burden of having to ask questions.

5. Ask the person to join you. Be direct. Don't beat around the bush. Get to the point quickly. The direct approach keeps the conversation on track and will help you not to get bogged down.

6. If the person says that he or she has another engagement at that time, suggest an alternate activity or ask when he would have time. Giving the person another option increases the likelihood that he will accept your offer. It also gives him a cue to level with you if he doesn't care to join you in any activity.

7. If it becomes clear that the person doesn't want to join you in an activity, tell him or her that you understand and thank him for considering your offer. Remain cordial and consider another person that you might ask.

8. If the person accepts your offer, set a time and place to meet. Don't leave it open-ended. Making a plan on the spot increases the chances that you will get together.

Conduct the role-play.

The following is a sample role-play. The group member's responses are in italic. Use it as a guideline to conduct a role-play with each group member. Instruct group members to read the steps listed on the board as they engage in the role-play if they have difficulty remembering what to say.

Set up the role-play. "Imagine a situation in which you might ask someone to join you in a healthy pleasure. It's best to think of a situation that could actually happen in the future. Okay, now tell me, who would you like to ask to join you in a healthy pleasure? *(Pause for responses.)* Where are you likely to be when you ask? *(Elicit a specific site.)* What emotions might you be feeling as you ask the person to join you? *(Pause for response.)* Is there anything else I should know about the situation to make it as realistic as possible?"

"What is *(co-trainer's)* role in this situation?"

A *person whose company I enjoy (names person to be approached).*

"What is your role in this situation?"

To be myself.

"What is your task in this situation?"

To ask _____ to join me in a healthy pleasure.

"Okay, let's give it a try. Start by greeting your friend pleasantly. Tell _____ that you're glad to see him (or her)."

Sample Role-Play Dialogue

Hi _____. I'm really glad to see you.

"Hi _____. How are you doing?"

Things are great, but I'd like to get out more. You know I really enjoy your company. It would be fun to do something together.

"Oh, what did you have in mind?"

Well, I like shopping and movies. How about you, what do you like to do?

"Well, I like shopping too."

How about if we meet at the food court in the mall this Saturday at 10:00?

"I can't. I have an appointment Saturday morning that I have to keep."

How about another time? Is there a time that would be good for you?

"I could meet you Saturday afternoon at 4:00."

Great, I'll meet you at 4:00 this Saturday at the food court in the mall on Main Street.

"I'll see you there Saturday. Maybe we could see a movie after shopping. There's a theater near the food court."

Sounds great! See you Saturday.

Review the role-play: Elicit positive feedback from group members. Provide positive feedback with respect to specific behaviors that were effective. Elicit positive comments from group members by asking them to comment on specific verbal and non-verbal behaviors that increased the effectiveness of the performance. Politely interrupt or reframe negative comments. Follow these steps when reviewing the role-play:

1. First, ask the role-player what he or she thought was most effective about the performance. Embellish the group member's responses, emphasizing the criterion behaviors listed on the board.
2. Elicit positive feedback from group members. Guide the process by eliciting remarks about specific verbal and nonverbal behaviors that enhanced the performance.

3. Ask the other player to give specific feedback to the role-player.

4. Summarize effective behaviors and reinforce the role-player with group applause.

Provide corrective feedback and repeat the role-play. Make constructive suggestions that will enhance the role-player's performance. Model skills (specific behaviors), annotating each suggestion as it is demonstrated. Repeat the role-play, giving constructive feedback as described above. Practice the role-play as many times as necessary to achieve an effective response. Practice with each group member until all have mastered asking an acquaintance to join them in a healthy pleasure.

Challenge participants.

As soon as participants have demonstrated an acceptable level of mastery, challenge them further by throwing them a curve. That is, repeat the role-play scenario with each participant, but this time introduce an obstacle that requires extending the responses described above. Having participants respond to a range of situations in which they ask someone to join them in a healthy pleasure will promote generalization of the skills learned and increase self-confidence.

Challenges can be made more realistic by asking participants for suggestions about circumstances that are likely to overwhelm the skills required to ask someone to join them in a healthy pleasure. Remember, learning is optimized by creating realistic, meaningful scenarios and finding ways to personalize them for each group member. Suggest challenge scenarios if participants are unable to pinpoint useful examples. For instance, you might repeat the role-play above, but this time when the participant requests the company of the other, have the other person consistently decline. This way, the participant gains practice in gracefully accepting refusal.

Elicit challenge scenarios. "It looks like all of you are learning how to ask someone to join you in a healthy pleasure. Now, let's try it again—only this time I want to challenge you by making things a little more difficult. What do you think would make it hard for you to stick to the techniques that you've learned for asking someone to join you in a healthy pleasure?"

1. List suggestions on the board.

2. Ask what it is about each situation mentioned that makes it difficult for participants.

3. Identify a situation that the majority agree is likely to occur.

4. Determine whether the skill steps outlined above apply as they are or whether some modification is required.

5. Choose a person to role-play. Select a group member who you believe will be successful.

6. Conduct the role-play.

7. Review the role-play and elicit feedback from group members.

8. Provide corrective feedback.

Skill 9

NEGOTIATING WITH A REPRESENTATIVE PAYEE

OVERVIEW

Many of your patients will have representative payees who manage their disability income so that it provides for food, clothing, and shelter, rather than drugs and alcohol. Typically, the representative payee sends checks directly to those who provide the patient with shelter and food and tries to minimize the amount of cash available to the patient. However, your patients may need more money so that they can engage in healthy habits and experience healthy pleasures. For example, a patient may want to buy a new pair of running shoes so that she can continue to jog every morning with a new friend. An experienced representative payee will worry that the patient may end up spending the money on drugs and alcohol. In the next few sessions you will teach patients how to negotiate with their representative payees for the funds they need to develop new healthy habits and healthy pleasures.

SAMPLE THERAPIST SCRIPT

Introduce the goal (flip chart 78).

"It's good to see you all here today! Welcome to skills training. In the next few classes, you'll learn and practice how to ask your payee for money for healthy habits and healthy pleasures. Let's get started!"

SESSION SUMMARY*

1. Introduce the goal (flip chart 81).

2. Make sure patients can repeat the goal.

3. Introduce the skill.

4. Develop the skill steps.

5. View the video illustration.

6. Choose a person to role-play.

7. Describe the role-play and demonstrate the steps (flip charts 82, 83).

8. Conduct the role-play (set up, conduct, review, positive feedback, corrective feedback, repeat).

9. Challenge participants.

Usually requires 2–4 sessions (see p. 73).

Make sure patients can repeat the goal.

"What is the goal of today's class?"

To learn how to ask my payee for money for healthy habits and healthy pleasures.

"What is the main goal of the module?"

To say no to drugs and yes to healthy pleasures.

Introduce the skill.

"You know, we usually think that having money is a good thing. But, when it comes to quitting drugs, money can actually be bad for some people. In fact, money can be one of the biggest problems that people face when they are trying to quit drugs. What do you think? *(Pause for responses.)* Having a few dollars in your pocket is a high-risk situation for most people, especially in the early stages of recovery from drug abuse.

"Many people reduce the risk of relapse by getting a payee to help them manage their money during the early stages of recovery. Then, as they become more and more skilled at handling high-risk situations, the payee gradually turns money management back over to the person. Would you agree with me that this is a good arrangement for a lot of people? *(Pause for responses.)* Yes, having a payee is one of the most important steps a person can take when they really get serious about quitting drugs.

"I don't know whether you've ever thought about this, but it's not always easy to be a payee. It involves a lot of responsibility. Payees have to keep track of your money and make sure bills are getting paid on time and that all of your basic needs are being met. On top of that, payees have to worry about whether giving you spending money is going to lead to a relapse. I'm telling you, it's not easy!

"Working with a payee usually goes smoothly. But, if the payee worries that giving you cash will cause temptation, he or she may be a little stubborn about handing money over to you. Have any of you ever been in a situation like this? *(Pause for responses.)* At those times, it helps to have some negotiation skills. What do you suppose I mean by negotiation skills? *(Pause for responses.)* Exactly! You have good negotiation skills if you know how to strike a bargain with someone."

Develop the skill steps.

"Knowing how to strike a bargain can help if your payee gets stubborn about giving you cash when you need it for a legitimate expense. For example, let's say that you've decided to start a new healthy pleasure because you're looking for ways to make it easier not to use drugs. But you need some start-up money. What's the best way to approach your payee to get the cash you need? We need some techniques that will help you get cooperation from a payee who is worried that you might spend the money on drugs. Let's think about what some of those techniques might be. *(Ask co-trainer to write the suggestions on the board as you elicit them from the group.)* What are the steps you can take?" *(Shape responses into the following list.)*

Techniques for Negotiating with a Representative Payee

1. Greet your payee politely. Make eye contact. Use a pleasant voice tone.

2. Be direct. Tell your payee that you are looking for ways to structure your time more productively.

3. Indicate that pursuing healthy pleasures is an excellent way to make it easier for you not to use drugs.

4. Tell your payee the specific healthy pleasure that you want to pursue.

5. Let your payee know how often you plan to engage in the activity and exactly how much money you will need to pursue your healthy pleasure.

6. Remind your payee of the progress that you have made in your treatment program. Mention such areas as medication compliance, symptom reduction, drug abstinence, regular group attendance, keeping appointments with your doctor, structuring your time every day, and using coping techniques to avoid and escape high-risk situations.

7. Give your payee permission to contact a member of your clinical team to verify your progress.

8. Indicate that you will provide receipts for the money you spend on the healthy pleasure.

9. Schedule a follow-up appointment with your payee to report your progress and deliver receipts, and thank him or her.

"Okay, let's see if these ideas can work."

View the video illustration.

Introduce the video. Be sure that the videotape is wound to the beginning of the scene before starting the session. Briefly describe the video scene, emphasizing the steps involved in negotiating with a representative payee.

"Everyone knows how important it is to increase healthy pleasures when you're trying to quit drugs. Some of the best healthy pleasures are free, but when there's a cost involved, you might need to get some extra money from your payee. That's the situation that Michael runs into in the video scene that I'm about to show you. Michael has decided to start bowling so he meets with Karen, his payee, to ask for an increase in his allowance. Karen knows that in the past Michael has been tempted to use drugs whenever he has a little extra cash on hand. Naturally, she's a little apprehensive about giving Michael the money he's requesting. Let's see how Michael negotiates with Karen. See if he uses all of the steps you suggested for negotiating with a payee."

Critique the model's performance. "Well, what do you think? How did Michael do? *(Encourage discussion of the model's performance.)* Did he follow all of the steps? *(Focus comments on specific behaviors enumerated in the steps related to negotiating with a representative payee.)* Did he leave anything out?"

Elicit suggestions for improvement. "Can you think of anything that he might do to make his way of handling this situation more effective? What could he do differently?" *(Guide participants' remarks to contrast behaviors exhibited by the model with the requisite steps for negotiating with a representative payee. Politely interrupt digressions from the criterion behaviors specified.)*

Choose a person to role-play.

Select a group member who you believe will be successful in the role-play. Encourage cooperation by modeling the role-play scenario with the co-trainer. If a co-trainer is not available, select a person who will effectively demonstrate the skills.

Describe the role-play and demonstrate the steps (flip charts 82, 83).

"Okay, I want *(co-trainer or group member)* to play the role of a payee. Using the techniques listed on the board, negotiate for the money you need to start a new healthy pleasure. Practicing these techniques will help you to maintain a trusting relationship with your payee.

"Let's review the techniques so that you don't leave any of them out." *(Point to items listed on flip charts 82, 83. Provide a rationale for each item.)*

1. Greet your payee politely. Make eye contact. Use a pleasant voice tone. A pleasant greeting will get your payee's attention and let him or her know that you are sincere.

2. Be direct. Tell your payee that you are looking for ways to structure your time more productively. Knowing that you are dedicated to remaining abstinent will encourage your payee to cooperate with your request.

3. Indicate that pursuing healthy pleasures is an excellent way to make it easier for you not to use drugs. This shows your payee that you really mean business.

4. Tell your payee the specific healthy pleasure that you want to pursue. Being specific will help your payee to understand that you are sincere.

5. Let your payee know how often you plan to engage in the activity and exactly how much money you will need to pursue your healthy pleasure. Your payee will need this information to determine whether you have enough money available to pursue your goal.

6. Remind your payee of the progress that you have made in your treatment program. Mention such areas as medication compliance, symptom reduction, drug abstinence, attending groups regularly, keeping appointments with your doctor, structuring your time every day, and using coping techniques to avoid and escape high-risk situations. Reminding your payee of the many things that you do to stay sober will help convince him or her that you intend to stay away from drugs.

7. Give your payee permission to contact a member of your clinical team to verify your progress. Offering your payee a chance to discuss your progress with members of the clinical team shows that you are trustworthy.

8. Indicate that you will provide receipts for the money you spend on the healthy pleasure. Receipts offer proof that you did not use the money for drugs. It will increase your payee's trust in you.

9. Schedule a follow-up appointment with your payee to report your progress and deliver receipts. Staying in touch with your payee is the best way to encourage his or her cooperation in the future. Giving him the receipts will prove that you meant what you said.

Conduct the role-play.

The following is a sample role-play. The group member's responses are in italic. Use it as a guideline to conduct a role-play with each group member. Instruct group members to read the steps listed on the board as they engage in the role-play if they have difficulty remembering what to say.

Set up the role-play. "Imagine a situation in which you approach your payee to negotiate for some money to start a new healthy pleasure. It's best to think of a situation that is quite likely to happen in the future. Think about a healthy pleasure that you might actually need some money for. Pick the one that you might like to do first. What would that be? *(Elicit a specific and plausible healthy pleasure.)* Picture yourself with your payee. Okay, now tell me, where would such an encounter most likely take place? *(Elicit a specific site.)* What emotions might you be feeling as you encounter your payee? *(Pause for response.)* Is there anything else I should know about the situation to make it as realistic as possible?"

"What is *(co-trainer's)* role in this situation?"

To be my payee.

"What is your role in this situation?"

To be myself.

"What is your task in this situation?"

To negotiate with my payee for some money to start a healthy pleasure.

"Okay, let's give it a try."

Sample Role-Play Dialogue

"Hi _____. How can I help you?"

Hi _____. It's good to see you. I wanted to meet with you to let you know about the progress I'm making in my program.

"I know that you've been doing well. I'm really glad to see it."

Having my time occupied with constructive activities really helps a lot.

"I'm sure it does. I've noticed that you have been a lot more active lately."

Yes, I have. But there's more that I want to do.

"Really? What did you have in mind?"

I want to start a new healthy pleasure.

"Oh? What do you mean by healthy pleasure?"

A healthy pleasure is an activity that feels good and is good for me. The more healthy pleasures I schedule, the less chance I have of using drugs.

"I see what you mean."

I've been thinking about starting a new healthy pleasure.

"Yeah? What is it?"

Well, I've always been interested in bowling. I'd like to start going a couple of times a week. It's great exercise and it might give me a chance to make some new friends.

"It sounds good, but I have one concern. In the past, having extra money in your pocket was risky. It always seemed to lead straight to drugs."

Yes, that's true. But things are different now.

"How's that?"

Well, I am attending my SAMM groups, keeping all my appointments with my doctor, taking my medication regularly, and using the skills I learn in my group to avoid high-risk situations.

"You are doing a good job, but I'm concerned about your ability to handle having extra money in your pocket."

I certainly understand your concern. I know that you don't want to see me get started on drugs again.

"I sure don't."

I'll tell you what. Why don't you give the folks at the clinic a call? I'd like for you to talk to someone on my clinical team. I think they can assure you that I'm on solid ground. I want to do everything I can to earn your trust.

"Okay, I'll give them a call. You do seem to be sincere. If the people on your team feel that you can handle the cash, I'll give you the money you need to get started."

Great! I want to go twice a week. I'll need money for shoes and enough to bowl three games each time. It works out to about $22.50 a week. I could bring the receipts from the bowling alley to show you exactly where the money goes.

"That's an excellent idea."

I'd also like to schedule a follow-up appointment with you so I can let you know how I'm doing and to give you the receipts.

"Terrific!"

What do you say we meet next Monday at 2:00?

"Monday at 2:00 is fine."

Great! I'll see you then. Thanks a lot.

"You're welcome. I'm glad to do it."

Review the role-play: Elicit positive feedback from group members. Provide positive feedback with respect to specific behaviors that were effective. Elicit positive comments from group members by asking them to comment on specific verbal and non-verbal behaviors that increased the effectiveness of the performance. Politely interrupt or reframe negative comments. Follow these steps when reviewing the role-play:

1. First, ask the role-player what he or she thought was most effective about the performance. Embellish the group member's responses, emphasizing the criterion behaviors listed on the board.

2. Elicit positive feedback from group members. Guide the process by eliciting remarks about specific verbal and nonverbal behaviors that enhanced the performance.

3. Ask the other player to give specific feedback to the role-player.

4. Summarize effective behaviors and reinforce the role-player with group applause.

Provide corrective feedback and repeat the role-play. Make constructive suggestions that will enhance the role-player's performance. Model skills (specific behaviors), annotating each suggestion as it is demonstrated. Repeat the role-play, giving constructive feedback as described above. Practice the role-play as many times as necessary to achieve an effective response. Practice with each group member until all have mastered negotiating with their payee for money to start a new healthy pleasure.

Challenge participants.

When participants have demonstrated an acceptable level of mastery, challenge them further by throwing them a curve. That is, repeat the role-play scenario with each participant, but this time introduce an obstacle that requires extending the responses described above. Having participants respond to a range of situations revolving around encounters with representative payees will help promote generalization of the skills learned and increase self-efficacy.

Challenges can be made more realistic by asking participants for suggestions about circumstances that are likely to overwhelm negotiation skills. Remember, learning is optimized by creating realistic, meaningful scenarios and finding ways to personalize them for each group member. Suggest challenge scenarios if participants are unable to pinpoint useful examples. For instance, you might repeat the role-play above, but this time have the person playing the role of the representative payee indicate a degree of mistrust (for example, by suggesting that the participant has been abstinent for only a short time). Alternatively, ask the person playing the role of the representative payee to indicate unwillingness to contact members of the clinical team to verify that the participant has been consistent with all aspects of the treatment program. Another option is to indicate that the participant's payee is on vacation and the substitute handling the payee's case load is reluctant to negotiate because of a lack of knowledge pertaining to the participant's reliability.

Elicit challenge scenarios. "It's clear that all of you have become quite skilled at negotiating with your payee. Now I want to challenge you by making things a little more difficult. What do you think would make it hard for you to stick to the techniques that you've learned for negotiating with a payee?"

1. List suggestions on the board.
2. Ask what it is about each situation mentioned that makes it difficult for participants.
3. Identify a situation that the majority agree is likely to occur.
4. Determine whether the skill steps outlined above apply as they are or whether some modification is required.
5. Choose a person to role-play. Select a group member who you believe will be successful.
6. Conduct the role-play.
7. Review the role-play and elicit feedback from group members.
8. Provide corrective feedback.

PRACTICE SESSIONS

WHAT ARE PRACTICE SESSIONS?

SAMM seeks to teach participants how to say no to drugs and yes to healthy pleasures. Ideally, the therapists who teach this module would supervise participants as they practiced newly learned skills in realistic settings. However, this is usually not practical and is sometimes unsafe for trainers (for example, places where drugs are sold). Participants learn skills (for example, how to refuse drugs offered by a friend) in skills training sessions, but they may not need to use the skills right away. So, when they do need the skill, they may not have practiced it for awhile. The aim of the practice sessions is to encourage patients to use the skills in real-life situations.

We added practice sessions to give patients the opportunity to practice skills just before they need them. Here's how it works. Patients at all stages of treatment attend a 45-minute practice session twice a week. The trainer asks questions about upcoming events in which patients will need SAMM skills. For example, a patient may be anticipating a visit within a few days from a relative who always offers to share drugs. He's worried he'll relapse and not make it back to the next session. The trainer involves the entire group in reviewing relevant concepts and in setting up a role-play that will give the patient a chance to practice drug-refusal skills. Because it is a real-life example, the role-play will be highly relevant. Because the risky situation is about to happen, the role-play will be more dramatic. This will grab the attention of participants and increase the chance they will learn the skills and actually perform them outside the classroom.

HOW TO CONDUCT PRACTICE SESSIONS

Practice sessions provide opportunities to rehearse the substance abuse management skills

SESSION SUMMARY

1. Welcome group members and reinforce attendance.
2. Introduce new group members.
3. Ensure that participants can state the goals of the module and practice sessions.
4. Review homework assigned in the previous practice session.
5. Ask four questions (flip chart 4)
   - Has anyone encountered a high-risk situation since our last meeting?
   - Does anyone anticipate encountering a high-risk situation in the coming week?
   - Has anyone added a new healthy habit or healthy pleasure since our last class?
   - Is anyone planning to start a new healthy habit or pleasure before our next session?
6. Identify an emerging theme as you explore participants' responses to these questions.
7. Create a role-play scenario based on any of the nine skills that comes closest to the theme.
8. Rehearse the role-play with as many participants as time permits.
9. Give homework assignments when appropriate.
10. Remind group members of the time and place of the next practice session and end the meeting.

learned during skills training sessions. The main goal in each practice session is to quickly and efficiently identify a current "theme" related to any of the nine skills taught in skills training. Do this by following the outline shown in the gray box.

In addition to providing opportunities to consolidate skills training, practice sessions create a forum for problem solving and homework assignments. The sample session presented below demonstrates how to integrate problem-solving techniques into the group process. When homework assignments are made in relation to the concerns raised by participants, the assignment can be tailored to specific skill deficits and thus will be more relevant to the lives of the patients in question.

Because much of the group process is spontaneous, practice sessions place heavy demands on the therapist. In these sessions, the therapist often acts more like a stage director and a coach than a therapist. The therapist conducting the practice session must know the nine skills taught in skills training, and must be very directive and take charge of the session. Knowing what to do when one encounters a pushy dealer or how to negotiate with a representative payee for much needed funds often involves high drama. Consequently, practice sessions are generally fun and entertaining.

SAMPLE PRACTICE SESSION

Sample Therapist Script

Welcome group members and reinforce attendance.

"It's good to see you all here today! Welcome to the practice group. The goal of this group is to apply all the concepts and skills you have learned in basic training and skills training to what is going on in your everyday lives. Would you agree with me that practice makes perfect? The more you practice a skill, the easier it will be to use it in situations that call for that skill."

Introduce new members.

"Before we begin, I would like to introduce James to the group. James is joining us for the first time. Let's give him a hand. Welcome, James. Let's go around the group and introduce ourselves. Say your name and which part of the SAM module you're currently participating in."

Note: This is an excellent way to review the names of group members for all participants.

Ensure that participants can state the goals of the module and practice sessions.

"Let's review. Who can tell me the overall goals of the module?"

Saying no to drugs and yes to healthy pleasures.

"What is the goal of the practice group?"

To practice the skills we need to avoid drugs and start new healthy pleasures.

Review homework assigned in the previous session.

It's helpful to keep a record of assignments you've given and bring it to each group meeting as a reminder.

THERAPIST: Last time, I gave homework assignments to a few people. Let's review. Joe, last week you expressed concern about attending a family birthday party because you knew that alcohol would be served. Does everyone remember helping Joe think of ways to deal with cravings and practicing how to refuse alcohol offered by friends or relatives?
PARTICIPANTS: Yes.
THERAPIST: Joe, how did it turn out?
JOE: The birthday party was fine until my brother offered me a beer. I told him over and

over that I don't drink anymore. I even told him all about the program too.

THERAPIST: How did he respond?

JOE: At first, he said, "Okay, I'll just grab a beer for myself." But I didn't think I could hang out with him if he was drinking. My cravings were already really bad. So I suggested that we watch the game without any alcohol around.

THERAPIST: How did he react?

JOE: Great! He even decided to drink one of the sodas I brought to the party. I think we may even go to a game together next weekend.

THERAPIST: That's great Joe! You did a good job using the skills we practiced for refusing drugs or alcohol from a friend or relative. What does the class think? *(Gather positive feedback from participants about Joe's behavior, then continue until all homework assignments have been briefly reviewed.)*

THERAPIST: Gina, your assignment last week was to talk to your doctor about your medication side effects. Did you meet with your doctor?

GINA: Yeah, but I forgot to tell him that I was having side effects when I met with him.

THERAPIST: Well, what would make it easier for you to remember?

GINA: I could write it down.

THERAPIST: Okay. See me right after group and we'll get it down on paper.

GINA: Yeah, that's a good idea.

THERAPIST: I'm proud of you all. You're working hard on your homework assignments.

Ask four questions (flip chart 4).

THERAPIST: Okay, who can tell me what a high-risk situation is?

DAVID: A high-risk situation is any situation that would be very difficult not to use.

THERAPIST: Exactly! Good job, David. Now, has anyone encountered a high-risk situation since our last meeting?

JOHN: I had a close call.

THERAPIST: Okay, John. I'll put your name on the board and we'll come back to discuss the details right after I check to see if anyone else had a close call. Did anyone else encounter a high-risk situation or have a slip?

JERRY: Yeah, I slipped up this weekend. I was hanging out with some of my old friends and . . .

THERAPIST: *(Interrupting politely)* Thanks, Jerry, for reporting your slip. It's important to report slips so that you can learn how to prevent them from happening again. Let me put your name on the board and we will come back to you in a minute. Anyone else?

ELLEN: I did a healthy pleasure this weekend.

THERAPIST: That's great! We are going to cover healthy pleasures later but first let's finish our review of high-risk situations. Jerry, you mentioned that you slipped over the weekend. Let's review your drug-habit chain. First of all, when did you slip up? *(Therapist writes drug-habit chain on blackboard as Jerry describes the circumstances surrounding his slip.)*

JERRY: Sunday afternoon. I stayed sober all weekend all the way up to Sunday. Then I got terrible cravings, so I decided to go and visit some of my friends to watch the game.

THERAPIST: Have you used with these friends in the past?

JERRY: Yeah, all the time. But, I didn't go over with the intention of using. When I got there we started watching the game, but then Jeff stopped by. He had some marijuana with him and before I knew it, I took a hit.

THERAPIST: What did you do when you realized you slipped up?

JERRY: Well, I got up and left right away. But, I've been feeling pretty lousy knowing I messed up my sobriety.

THERAPIST: *(To class)* Well, let's look at the board. What did Jerry do that was effective?

FRANK: He stayed sober Friday and Saturday.

THERAPIST: Good. What else?

JOE: He left the situation as soon as he realized that he slipped. He practiced damage control.

FRANK: Yeah, and he's reporting it to the group.

THERAPIST: Excellent! Jerry, you realized you slipped up and you practiced damage control. This situation could have easily led to a full-blown relapse. It's great that you stopped early and bounced right back into treatment. *(Initiates a round of applause.)* Let's see what we can learn from this situation. Jerry, if this were to happen again, what could you do differently to prevent a slip?

JERRY: Make a U-turn earlier. Maybe not even go to see my friends when I'm craving.

THERAPIST: I agree. I'm particularly proud of you for getting up and leaving right away when you realized you were in a high-risk situation. But it seems to me that hanging out with these "old drug-using buddies" is a high-risk situation in itself. It would probably be better to avoid these situations in the first place. Let's see if others have any suggestions.

FRANK: I think it is a warning sign if he has thoughts to hang out with these guys. Whenever I get thoughts of hanging out with old buddies I do a healthy pleasure to take my mind off of it. Next time he might try going for a walk or hanging out with someone that he knows is sober.

LINDA: He could pull out his emergency card and review the disadvantages to using drugs.

THERAPIST: Good advice. Jerry, do you have a support person?

JERRY: Yes.

THERAPIST: That gives me an idea. I think a homework assignment can help here. How about reporting this slip to your support person and discussing ways to prevent this from happening in the future? Could you do that this week and tell us about it in our next session?

JERRY: Yeah, sure.

Note: Time may not permit a thorough review of all high-risk situations mentioned. Choose those that you feel will be most valuable to the majority of the participants present.

THERAPIST: Now, John, briefly tell us about your close call.

JOHN: I was walking to the bus stop when this man offered me some weed. I just waved him off and told him, "No, I don't want any and kept walking."

THERAPIST: Wow! You were able to refuse drugs from a pushy dealer. It sounds like you did it just the way we learned to do it in skills training. I think that deserves a round of applause (*initiates applause*). Okay, let's think about the week ahead. Is anyone anticipating a high-risk situation this coming week? Maybe you expect to receive money or perhaps you'll run into an old friend.

ELLEN: It's a high-risk situation for me every day. There are drugs everywhere.

Therapist: I agree. And that does make it hard. But, for now, let's focus on ways we can avoid high-risk situations.

PHIL: I have one. I need to pick up my check downtown from my sister's so I can get some new clothes this weekend. I am a little worried about running into some old friends in my sister's neighborhood.

THERAPIST: Okay, that's a good one. Let's put it on the board and come back to it in just a second. Anyone else? (*Pauses for responses*) No? Okay, if anyone thinks of anything as we go along just let me know. Any suggestions for Phil's situation?

MICHELLE: Can he wait to get his check or have his sister send it to him?

THERAPIST: That's a good suggestion. That way Phil can guarantee that his money will be used for healthy pleasures and not for drugs or alcohol. Any other ideas for Phil?

DANA: Phil, what about talking to your case manager about picking up your check and taking you shopping?

PHIL: Yeah, I guess I could talk to my case manager.

THERAPIST: That's an excellent idea! Dana, good job talking directly to Phil and using good eye contact! Phil, could you talk to your case manager this week and let us know about your plan in our next class?

PHIL: I'll talk to her this afternoon.

THERAPIST: Great! Anyone else anticipating a high-risk situation this week?

MICHAEL: I don't have any plans this week. I'm just worried because last time at this point in my sobriety I slipped up and used cocaine.

THERAPIST: Wow! You're thinking smart by recognizing your warning signs. What could you do this time to keep your mind off of drugs? What could you do to get yourself moving toward healthy pleasures?

MICHAEL: Well, I was thinking about spending more time with my support person this week and planning to do more healthy pleasures—maybe even playing miniature golf with some of the guys on Saturday.

THERAPIST: Michael, it sounds like you have already scheduled activities to help keep yourself busy. If you notice yourself getting off track at any point, let your support person know right away. Okay?

MICHAEL: Definitely!

THERAPIST: Well, speaking of healthy pleasures, has anyone started a new healthy pleasure or healthy habit since our last class? Ellen, you mentioned something earlier.

ELLEN: I went to a movie last weekend with my kids.

THERAPIST: That's a good one!

Note: If time permits, a good way to increase participation is to pose a specific question to participants. For example, you might say, "Let's go around the group and have everyone tell me one healthy pleasure you did since our last meeting. I'll make a list."

CURTIS: I started working out three times a week at the local gym.

THERAPIST: That could be a healthy habit or a healthy pleasure. That's excellent!

SARA: I would like to start working out after group. How could I go about joining a gym?

THERAPIST: Sara, that leads us into the last question: Is anyone anticipating adding a healthy pleasure this week? Let's help Sara do some planning. Curtis, how did you go about joining a gym?

CURTIS: I just talked to my case manager and she had a list of some local gyms and their prices. You could also check into the Wellness Clinic. Your doctor should be able to tell you more information about that.

THERAPIST: Thanks Curtis! That is a lot of helpful information. Sara, what about finding out more information about gyms this week?

SARA: Okay. I'll try to talk to my doctor Thursday when I meet him to review my medications.

THERAPIST: Okay, I'm going to write this down for a homework assignment. Can you follow-up with us in the next class?

SARA: Sure. I can do that.

JOE: I've been thinking about asking a friend in my sober-living home to do a healthy pleasure, but I get so nervous every time I approach her.

Identify an emerging theme as you explore participants' responses to these questions.

As the session continues, a "hot" topic or theme usually emerges. Several participants may have encountered high-risk situations that were particularly difficult to handle. Or, several members may be expecting the arrival of a disability check at the first of the month. In any case, the therapist should try to apply one of the nine skills to the emerging theme and proceed to a role-play exercise. For example, if the hot topic revolves around the advisability of initiating healthy pleasures, structure a role-play around "Asking Someone to Join You in a Healthy Pleasure."

THERAPIST: You know what, Joe? I'm really glad you brought that up. Asking someone to join you in a healthy pleasure isn't always an easy thing to do. A lot of people have trouble with that. It might be helpful for all of us to get some practice asking someone to do a healthy pleasure. Joe, what's your friend's name?

Create a role-play scenario based on any of the nine skills that comes closest to the theme.

Review the steps for "Asking Someone to Join You in a Healthy Pleasure" and set up the role-play for Joe. See "How to Conduct Skills Training Sessions" for a detailed description of how to make role-plays realistic and effective.

Depending upon the time available, it may not be possible to practice one of the nine skills in each session. If this turns out to be the case, indicate that you will start the next session with the role-play scenario that emerged in the present session. Remember that the emphasis in practice sessions is on polishing skills. Avoid distractions and stay focused on the main goal—practicing skills.

The remaining steps, rehearse the role-play, give homework assignments, and remind group members of the time and place of the next meeting, are described for each skill in the skills training section.

BIBLIOGRAPHY

We borrowed extensively from other sources to create this module. Much of the content was originally written in Marlatt and Gordon's seminal book, *Relapse Prevention: Maintenance Strategies in the Treatment of Addictive Behaviors* (New York: Guilford, 1985), including the concepts of high-risk situations, lapse versus relapse, abstinence violation effect, urge surfing (riding the wave), warning signs of drug relapse, and healthy habits and pleasures. Our approach to skills training is based on the Social and Independent Living Skills Modules developed by Liberman and his colleagues at the UCLA Intervention Research Center for Psychoses.

In addition we borrowed the idea that managing the risk of drug relapse is like the work of a forest ranger in preventing fires and putting them out quickly from Brownell's *LEARN Program for Weight Control* (Philadelphia: Brownell & Hager, 1990). The Mt. Recovery metaphor is from Sobell and Sobell's book, *Problem Drinkers: Guided Self-change Treatment* (New York: Guilford, 1993). Finally, our concept of damage control was inspired by Marlatt and Tapert's description of harm reduction in *Addictive Behaviors Across the Lifespan*, edited by Baer, Marlatt, and McMahon (Newbury Park, CA: Sage, 1993, pp. 243–273).

SUGGESTED READING

Dual Diagnosis

Bellack, A. S., & Geron, J. S. (1998). Substance abuse treatment for people with schizophrenia. *Addictive Behaviors, 23*, 749-766.

Carey, K. B. (1996). Substance use reduction in the context of outpatient psychiatric treatment: A collaborative, motivational, harm reduction approach. *Community Mental Health Journal, 32*, 291-306.

Cohen, J., & Levy, S. J. (1992). *The mentally ill chemical abuser: Whose client?* New York: Lexington.

Daley, D. C., & Campbell, F. (1993). *Coping with dual disorders: Addiction and emotional or psychiatric illness.* Center City, MN: Hazelden.

Daley, D. C., Moss, H. B., & Campbell, F. (1993). *Dual disorders: Counseling clients with chemical dependency and mental illness.* Center City, MN: Hazleden.

Drake, R. E., Antosca, L. M., Noordsy, D. L., Bartels, S. J., & Osher, F. C. (1991). New Hampshire's specialized services for the dually diagnosed. *New Directions for Mental Health Services, 50,* 57-67.

Drake, R. E., Mercer-McFadden, C., Mueser, K. T., McHugo, G. J., & Bond, G. R. (1998). A review of integrated mental health and substance abuse treatment for patients with dual disorders. *Schizophrenia Bulletin, 24,* 589-608.

Drake, R. E., Osher, F. C., & Wallach, M. A. (1991). Homelessness and dual diagnosis. *American Psychologist, 46,* 1149-1158.

Drake, R. E., Yovetich, M. A., Bebout, R. R., Harris, M., & McHugo, G. J. (1997). Integrated treatment for dually diagnosed homeless adults. *Journal of Nervous and Mental Disease, 185,* 298-305.

Evans, K., & Sullivan, J. M. (1990). *Dual diagnosis: Counseling the mentally ill substance abuser.* New York: Guilford.

Margolis, R. D., & Zweben, J. E. (1998). *Treating patients with alcohol and other drug problems: An integrated approach.* Washington, DC: American Psychological Association.

Marlatt, G. A., & Roberts, L. J. (1998). Treatment of comorbid addictive behaviors: Harm reduction as an alternative to abstinence. *In Session: Psychotherapy In Practice, 4,* 1-8.

Miller, N. S. (1994). *Treating coexisting psychiatric and addictive disorders: A practical guide.* Center City, MN: Hazelden.

Minkoff, K. (1989). An integrated treatment model for dual diagnosis of psychosis and addiction. *Hospital and Community Psychiatry, 40,* 1031-1036.

Mueser, K. T., Bellack, A. S., & Blanchard, J. J. (1992). Comorbidity of schizophrenia and substance abuse: Implications for treatment. *Journal of Consulting and Clinical Psychology, 60,* 845-856.

Mueser, K. T., Drake, R. E., & Wallach, M. A. (1998). Dual diagnosis: A review of etiological theories. *Addictive Behaviors, 23,* 717–734.

Regier, D. A., Farmer, M. E., Rae, D. S., Locke, B. Z., Keith, S. J., Judd, L. L., & Goodwin, F. K. (1990). Comorbidity of mental disorders with alcohol and other drug abuse: Results from the Epidemiological Catchment Area (ECA) study. *Journal of the American Medical Association, 264,* 2511-2518.

Riley, D. (1994). *The harm reduction model: Pragmatic approaches to drug use from the area between intolerance and neglect.* Ottawa, Canada: Canadian Centre on Substance Abuse.

Roberts, L. J., Shaner, A., Eckman, T. A., Tucker, D. E., & Vaccaro, J. V. (1992). Effectively treating stimulant-abusing schizophrenics: Mission impossible? *New Directions for Mental Health Services, 53,* 55-65.

Shaner, A., Eckman, T. A., Roberts, L. J., Wilkins, J. N., Tucker, D. E., Tsuang, J. W., & Mintz, J. (1995). Disability income, cocaine use, and repeated hospitalization among schizophrenic cocaine abusers: A government-sponsored revolving door? *New England Journal of Medicine, 333,* 777-783.

Shaner A., Roberts L. J., Eckman T. A., Racenstein J. M., Tucker, D. E., Tsuang J., & Mintz J. (1998). Sources of diagnostic uncertainty among chronically psychotic cocaine abusers. *Psychiatric Services, 49,* 684-690.

Shaner A., Roberts L. J., Eckman T. A.,Tucker D. E., Tsuang J., Wilkins J. N., & Mintz J. (1997). Monetary reinforcement of abstinence from cocaine among mentally ill patients with cocaine dependence. *Psychiatric Services, 48,* 807-810.

Shaner, A., Roberts, L. J., Eckman, T. A., & Wilkins, J. N. (1997). Skills training for substance abusing schizophrenic patients. *National Institute on Drug Abuse Research Monograph Series, 178,* 256.

Shaner A., Tucker D. E., Roberts L. J., & Eckman T. A. (in press). Disability income, cocaine use and contingency management among cocaine dependent schizophrenic patients. In S. T. Higgins & K. Silverman (Eds.), *Motivating behavior change among illicit-drug abusers: Contemporary research on contingency management interventions*. Washington, DC: American Psychological Association.

Solomon, J., Zimberg, S., & Shollar, E. (1993). *Dual diagnosis: Evaluation, treatment, training and program development*. New York: Plenum.

Tsuang, J. W., Ho, A. P., Eckman, T. A., & Shaner, A. (1997). Dual diagnosis treatment for patients with schizophrenia who are substance dependent. *Psychiatric Services, 48*, 887-889.

Harm Reduction

MacCoun, R. J. (1998). Toward a psychology of harm reduction. *American Psychologist, 53*, 1199-1208.

Marlatt, G. A. (Ed.). (1998). *Harm reduction: Pragmatic strategies for managing high-risk behaviors*. New York: Guilford.

Marlatt, G. A., Larimer, M. E., Baer, J. S., & Quigley, L. A. (1993). Harm reduction for alcohol problems: Moving beyond the controlled drinking controversy. *Behavior Therapy, 24*, 461-504.

Marlatt, G. A., & Roberts, L. J. (1998). Treatment of comorbid addictive behaviors: Harm reduction as an alternative to abstinence. *In Session: Psychotherapy in Practice, 4*, 1-8.

Marlatt, G. A., Somers, J. M., & Tapert, S. F. (1993). Harm reduction: Applications to alcohol abuse problems. In L. S. Onken, J. D. Blaine, & J. J. Boren (Eds.), *Behavioral treatments for drug abuse and dependence* (pp. 147-166). Rockville, MD: National Institute on Drug Abuse (NIDA) Research Monograph #137.

Marlatt, G. A., & Tapert, S. F. (1993). Harm reduction: Reducing the risks of addictive behaviors. In J. S. Baer, G. A. Marlatt, & R. McMahon (Eds.), *Addictive behaviors across the lifespan* (pp. 243-273). Newbury Park, CA: Sage.

Marlatt, G. A., Tucker, J. A., Donovan, D. M., & Vuchinich, R. E. (1997). Help-seeking by substance abusers: The role of harm reduction and behavioral economic approaches to facilitate treatment entry and retention. In L. S. Onken, J. D. Blaine, & J. J. Boren (Eds.), *Beyond the therapeutic alliance: Keeping the drug dependent individual in treatment* (pp. 44-84). Rockville, MD: NIDA Research Monograph #165.

O'Hare, P. A., Newcombe, R., Matthews, A., Buning, E. C., & Drucker, E. (Eds.). (1992). *The reduction of drug-related harm*. London: Routledge.

Roberts, L. J., & Marlatt, G. A. Harm reduction. In R. Tarter (Ed.), *Sourcebook of substance abuse*. Manuscript in preparation.

Relapse Prevention

Brownell, K. D., Marlatt, G. A., Lichtenstein, E., & Wilson, G. T. (1986). Understanding and preventing relapse. *American Psychologist, 41*, 765-782.

Marlatt, G. A. (1996). Models of relapse and relapse prevention: A commentary. *Experimental and Clinical Psychopharmacology, 4*, 55-60.

Marlatt, G. A., & Gordon, J. R. (1985). *Relapse prevention: Maintenance strategies in the treatment of addictive behaviors*. New York: Guilford.

Monti, P. M., Abrams, D. B., Kadden, R. M., & Cooney, N. L. (1989). *Treating alcohol dependence: A coping skills training guide*. New York: Guilford.

Roberts, L. J., & Marlatt, G. A. (1998). Guidelines for relapse prevention. In G. P. Koocher, J. C. Norcross, & S. S. Hill (Eds.), *Psychologist's desk reference* (pp. 243-247). New York: Oxford University Press.

Wilson, P. H. (1992). *Principles and practices of relapse prevention*. New York: Guilford.

Skills Training

Eckman, T. A. (1993). Teaching social and independent living skills to schizophrenic patients. *Relapse, 3,* (1), 10-11.

Eckman, T. A., & Liberman, R. P. (1990). A large-scale field test of a medication management skills training program for schizophrenics. *Psychosocial Rehabilitation Journal,13,* 31-35.

Eckman, T. A., Liberman, R. P., Phipps, C. C., & Blair, K. E. (1990). Teaching medication management skills to schizophrenic patients. *Journal of Clinical Psychopharmacology, 10,* 33-38.

Eckman, T. A., Wirshing, W. C., Marder, S. R., Liberman, R. P., Johnston-Cronk, K., Zimmermann, K., & Mintz, J. (1992). Technique for training schizophrenics in illness self-management: A controlled trial. *American Journal of Psychiatry, 149*(11), 1549-1555.

Liberman, R. P. (1988). *Psychiatric rehabilitation of chronic mental patients*. Washington, DC: American Psychiatric Press.

Liberman, R. P., DeRisi, W. J., & Mueser, K. T. (1989). *Social skills training for psychiatric patients*. Boston, MA: Allyn & Bacon.

Liberman, R. P., & Eckman, T. A. (1989). Dissemination of skills training modules to pychiatric facilities: Overcoming obstacles to the utilization of a rehabilitation innovation. *British Journal of Psychiatry, 155* (suppl. 5), 117-122.

Liberman, R. P., Eckman, T. A., Kuehnel, T. G., Rosenstein, J., & Kuehnel, J. M. (1982). Dissemination of new behavior therapy programs to community mental health centers. *American Journal of Psychiatry, 139,* 224-226.

Liberman, R. P., Mueser, K., Wallace, C. J., Jacobs, H. E., Eckman, T. A., & Massel, K. (1986). Training skills in the psychiatrically disabled: Learning coping and competence. *Schizophrenia Bulletin, 12*(4), 631-647.

Liberman, R. P., Wallace, C. J., Blackwell, G., Eckman, T. A., Vaccaro, J. V., & Kuehnel, T. G. (1993). Innovations in skills training for the seriously mentally ill: The UCLA social and independent living skills modules. *Innovations & Research, 2,* 43-60.

Other Social and Independent Living Skills Modules:

Psychiatric Rehabilitation Consultants
P.O. Box 2867
Camarillo, CA 93011-2867
Phone: (805) 484-5663
Fax: (805) 484-0735

GLOSSARY

This glossary is designed to help therapists explain key concepts to patients. For that reason, it is written as if spoken to patients.

Damage Control

What is it? Anything you do to keep a slip from becoming a full-blown relapse.

What are some examples? Stopping a slip before you run out of money; getting right back into treatment.

Why is it important? If you are able to quit using drugs and alcohol right away and never use again, that's great. However, if you do slip and use, you should stop the slip early before it does even more damage to your relationships, health, and finances. Remember, abstinence is the ideal goal, but if you do slip, it is important to quit using right away and get back into treatment. That will help keep the damage to a minimum and that's why we call it damage control.

Healthy Habits

What are they? Things you do over and over that are good for you. They aren't necessarily all that pleasurable all by themselves, but you need to do them in order to get something that would be fun. You can think of healthy habits as the steps you need to take in order to get healthy pleasures.

What are some examples? Eating balanced meals, good grooming and hygiene, fulfilling family responsibilities, exercising regularly, following medical advice.

Why are they important? The module is designed to help you replace the unhealthy habit of using drugs or alcohol with healthy habits. The idea is to learn to think and act in ways that lead you away from drugs and toward healthy pleasures that will make you want to continue healthy habits.

For example, suppose there's someone you want to know better and ask out on a date. You'll need to look presentable at least several times. You'll have to shower, shave, brush your teeth, and put on clean clothes every day. These are called healthy habits. You need to do them if you want to enjoy the healthy pleasure of dating.

Healthy Pleasures

What are they? Things you really enjoy and that are good for your health and well-being.

What are some examples? Reading, listening to music, doing a job well, taking a walk on the beach, dating, and getting a compliment from someone you respect.

Why are they important? Drugs and alcohol are unhealthy pleasures. They are pleasures because they can be very enjoyable, especially at first. But in the long run, they make you sick, lonely, and poor. That's why we call them unhealthy pleasures. When you are addicted to alcohol or drugs you spend a great deal of your time and money trying to get drugs, using them, and then recovering from their effects. Healthy pleasures are just the opposite. They tend to improve physical and emotional health. They build relationships. If you spend your time and money on healthy pleasures, two things will happen: First, you'll have less time and money to spend on drugs and, second, you'll be having too much fun to want to use drugs.

High-Risk Situation

What is it? Any situation in which it would be very hard to avoid using. By *situation* we mean a scene involving a place (e.g., public park), particular people (e.g., drug-using buddies), things (e.g., a supply of cash), what you are thinking (e.g., "I'll just use a little"), and what you are feeling (e.g., "I deserve it"). By *high-risk* we mean that if you get into such a situation, you are taking a big risk because it will be very hard to avoid using.

What are some examples? It varies from person to person. For one person, it might be going to a party at a friend's house where the guests are likely to bring drugs. Another person may have trouble refusing drugs from particular dealers in a particular part of town.

Why is it important? It will be very hard to say no if you get into a high-risk situation, so you must learn how to avoid getting into such situations in the first place. Do this by learning to recognize the warning signs that you are headed toward drug use.

Representative Payee

What is it? Someone who receives your disability income and has the responsibility of spending it for your benefit.

What are some examples? A good friend, family member, an accountant, attorney, or employee of an institution such as a hospital or a community mental health center. There are two ways to get a rep. payee: You can ask the Social Security Administration or the Veterans Benefits Administration to send the disability income to someone who has agreed to serve as your rep. payee or your doctor can ask that your disability income be sent to a rep. payee.

Why is it important? Many patients find that receiving a disability check leads to an irresistible urge to spend it on drugs or alcohol. Afterward they are broke, homeless, and hungry. To prevent this, you can have the disability check sent to a representative payee. You meet regularly with your payee and discuss how best to spend your disability income. You and your payee may decide that it would be best if he or she writes checks to your landlord and utility companies so that you don't have to handle large amounts of cash. You may decide on ways to limit the amount of spending money you have at any one time.

Support Person

What is it? Someone you can count on in a time of need; someone you know and trust, who you see frequently, who doesn't use drugs, and who has agreed to serve as your support person.

What are some examples? A good friend, family member, or one of the people you see at clinics or social service agencies.

Why are they important? Most people need a reliable and concerned person to help them through tough times as they try to reduce and finally quit using drugs and alcohol. While quitting is your responsibility, it helps to have someone who will support you in this effort. A support person can help you to clarify your reasons for quitting and, in an emergency, if your emergency card isn't working, he or she can help you remember the disadvantages of using and advantages of quitting. A support person can help you identify warning signs, develop U-turns, and establish healthy habits. If you slip and use drugs or alcohol again, a support person can also help you understand how you slipped and how to prevent another slip.

U-turns

What are they? Things you do that take you away from using drugs. We call them U-turns because when you see a warning sign that you are headed toward drug use, you should make a U-turn and head away from using drugs.

What are some examples? Getting off the bus that is headed toward the neighborhood where you usually buy drugs; calling a non-drug-using friend and doing something that doesn't involves drugs, such as seeing a movie.

Why are they so important? If you can make U-turns, you can avoid getting into high-risk situation.

Warning Signs

What are they? Anything that tells you that you might be headed toward a high-risk situation.

What are some examples? Feeling depressed or overwhelmed by voices, thinking that alcohol or drugs would make you feel better, calling drug-using or drinking buddies, cashing a big check, getting on a bus headed for a neighborhood where you usually buy drugs.

Why are they important? If you know the warning signs that you are headed toward drugs, you can do things that take you away from drugs. This is how you can avoid getting into a high-risk situation.

Appendix A

FORMS AND OTHER MATERIALS FOR SAMM

This section contains copies of forms you will need to teach SAMM.

Basic Training Attendance

Complete this form for each patient following each basic training class. This will allow you to keep track of which classes the patient attended so you will know when the patient has completed all eight sessions. The patient will be more likely to succeed in skills training if he or she has completed all eight of the basic training classes.

Skills Training Attendance

Complete this form following each skills training class to keep a record of which classes the patient attended and how well the patient performed the skill. This form will help you determine which patients need more practice. When everyone in the class has practiced and demonstrated the skill, then the class is ready to move on to a new skill.

Class Reminder Form

Complete this form following each skills training or practice class to serve as your reminder of what activities took place and what homework assignments were given. You can help patients learn skills by beginning every class with a brief review of the previous group and by asking for a report on homework assignments. Making a brief record of the group's progress and homework assignments will make it easier to remember how to start the next session of that group. This is especially important when you are conducting several different groups each week.

Clinical Urgency Form

Use this form to tell a patient's psychiatrist about worsening symptoms. Psychiatric symptoms can interfere with concentration, making it difficult for the patient to participate in the group and learn skills.

Certificate of Training

Present this to each patient when he or she completes SAMM. The certificate reinforces the patient's hard work and effort in successfully completing the module. Also, remember that every certificate you complete represents your own hard work and dedication.

Activity Schedule

The patient completes this form, listing all appointments, class times, healthy pleasures, and healthy habits. It helps patients notice how much of their time is unstructured and how much this puts them at risk for using drugs or alcohol. It also helps them set aside time for healthy habits and healthy pleasures.

Skill Prompt Cards

Skill prompt cards list the steps for each skill. Print the steps for each skill on 4 × 6 cards and give them to patients to help them remember the skills outside of the classroom. This will reduce anxiety and increase the chances the patient will perform the skill steps in the real situation.

Emergency Card Template

Patients start filling out this card during basic training. The card reminds them of key phone numbers, medical information, healthy habits, healthy pleasures, high-risk situations, warning signs, and coping skills. Make a double-sided copy of the card for patients, who will fold it twice and keep it in their wallets.

List of Healthy Pleasures

You can give patients this list of healthy pleasures to assist them in creating their own personalized list. It may help patients brainstorm healthy pleasures they may want to begin carrying out as a regular activity or just as something new and exciting to try. You may wish to create a local list of healthy pleasures.

Skills Illustration Videotape

In addition, the *Substance Abuse Management Module (SAMM) Skills Illustration Videotape* is available from W. W. Norton. This tape demonstrates the nine skills taught in the skills training sessions. Patients watch each vignette prior to practicing the skill in each session. The nine skills include quitting after a slip, reporting a slip, refusing drugs offered by a dealer, refusing drugs offered by a friend or relative, getting an appointment with a busy person, getting a support person, reporting symptoms and side effects to a doctor, asking someone to join you in a healthy pleasure, and negotiating with a representative payee. Call (800) 233-4830 to order the video.

BASIC TRAINING ATTENDANCE

Name _____   ID _____

Start Date _____   End Date _____

1	2	3	4	5	6	7	8

Total for Each Type of Session

PRACTICE ATTENDANCE

BASIC TRAINING SUMMARY

Did patient attend all 8 sessions?

Yes _____   No _____

Total Sessions Available _____

Total Sessions Attended _____

PRACTICE SUMMARY

Did patient attend at least 2 sessions per week?

Yes _____   No _____

Total Practice Sessions Available _____

Total Practice Sessions Attended _____

Date = present   A = absent

This form from *Overcoming Addictions* (W. W. Norton & Company, 800-233-4830) may be reproduced.

BASIC TRAINING ATTENDANCE

Name __Steve M.__   ID __0456__

Start Date __4/19__   End Date __5/20__

1	2	3	4	5	6	7	8
4/19	(A)	4/22	(A)	4/26	4/29	(A)	(A)
(A)	5/6	5/9	5/11	5/13	5/15	5/17	5/26

Total for Each Type of Session

1	1	2	1	2	2	1	1

PRACTICE ATTENDANCE

4/19	4/22	4/26	4/29	(A) 5/3	5/6
5/9	5/13	5/17	5/20		

BASIC TRAINING SUMMARY

Did patient attend all 8 sessions?

Yes __✓__   No_____

Total Sessions Available __16__

Total Sessions Attended __11__

PRACTICE SUMMARY

Did patient attend at least 2 sessions per week?

Yes_____   No __✓__

Total Practice Sessions Available __10__

Total Practice Sessions Attended __9__

Date = present   A = absent

SKILLS TRAINING ATTENDANCE

Name _____   ID _____

Start Date _____   End Date _____

#						Available / Attended
1					0 1 2 3	Available _____ Attended _____
2					0 1 2 3	Available _____ Attended _____
3					0 1 2 3	Available _____ Attended _____
4					0 1 2 3	Available _____ Attended _____
5					0 1 2 3	Available _____ Attended _____
6					0 1 2 3	Available _____ Attended _____
7					0 1 2 3	Available _____ Attended _____
8					0 1 2 3	Available _____ Attended _____
9					0 1 2 3	Available _____ Attended _____

PRACTICE ATTENDANCE

SKILLS TRAINING SUMMARY

Did patient attend all 8 sessions?

Yes _____   No _____

Total Sessions Available _____

Total Sessions Attended _____

PRACTICE SUMMARY

Did patient attend at least 2 sessions per week?

Yes _____   No _____

Total Practice Sessions Available _____

Total Practice Sessions Attended _____

SKILLS TRAINING ATTENDANCE

Name **Steve M.**   ID **0456**

Start Date **5/22**   End Date **7/24**

						Available / Attended
1	5/22	5/24			0 1 2 ③	Available **2** Attended **2**
2	5/29	5/31			0 1 ② 3	Available **2** Attended **2**
3	6/3	6/5			0 1 ② 3	Available **2** Attended **2**
4	6/7	6/10	6/12		0 1 ② 3	Available **3** Attended **3**
5	6/17	6/19	6/21	6/24	0 1 2 ③	Available **4** Attended **4**
6	6/26	6/28	Ⓐ 7/1	7/3	0 1 ② 3	Available **4** Attended **3**
7	7/5	7/8	7/10		0 1 ② 3	Available **3** Attended **3**
8	Ⓐ 7/12	7/15	7/17		0 1 ② 3	Available **3** Attended **2**
9	Ⓐ 7/19	7/22	7/24		0 1 2 ③	Available **3** Attended **2**

PRACTICE ATTENDANCE

5/24	5/31	6/3	6/7	6/10	6/14
6/17	6/21	6/24	6/28	7/1	7/5
7/8	Ⓐ 7/12	Ⓐ 7/15	Ⓐ 7/19	7/22	

SKILLS TRAINING SUMMARY

Did patient attend all 8 sessions?

Yes _____   No ✓

Total Sessions Available **26**

Total Sessions Attended **23**

PRACTICE SUMMARY

Did patient attend at least 2 sessions per week?

Yes _____   No ✓

Total Practice Sessions Available **17**

Total Practice Sessions Attended **14**

CLASS REMINDER FORM

Homework Assignments

NOTES ABOUT CLASS

Date _____

Class _____

CLASS REMINDER FORM

Homework Assignments **(from Friday 10/26)**

1. <u>DAVID</u> - to ask Felix to be his support person.

2. <u>JAMES</u> - to ask Carl to be his support person.

3. <u>WILLIE</u> - to think about asking Jackie to join him in a healthy
pleasure.

4. <u>KAREN</u> - to list 5 inexpensive healthy pleasures.

NOTES ABOUT CLASS

Date <u>**Monday 10/29**</u>

Class <u>**Practice Group**</u>

—Reviewed homework assignments

  - David stated Felix could serve as his support person.

  - Willie needs ideas of healthy pleasures.

—Reviewed healthy pleasures for the weekend.

—Practiced role-play of asking someone to join you in a healthy
pleasure (for Willie).

—Also practiced how to ask someone to be a support person
(for James).

CLINICAL URGENCY FORM

Date: _____

To: _____

From: _____

Patient Name: _____

Group Observed (including date and time): _____

Concerns/Observations:

CLINICAL URGENCY FORM

Date: **10/29/96**

To: **Dr. Barnett**

From: **Stacy**

Patient Name: **John M.**

Group Observed (including date and time): **10/29 - Friday 10am practice**

Concerns/Observations:

John has been very argumentative and agitated in group for the past two days. He seems extremely suspicious and is unable to stay for the full class period. I'm wondering if he's been medication compliant. Perhaps next time you speak with him you could address this issue and the issue of his participation in the day hospital.

Thank you -

Stacy

CERTIFICATE OF TRAINING

This certificate is given to

for satisfactory completion of the course in

Substance Abuse Management Module

Given at

This   day of

Saying No to Drugs and Yes to Healthy Pleasures

CERTIFICATE OF TRAINING

This certificate is given to

Joe Smith

for satisfactory completion of the course in

Substance Abuse Management Module

Given at **Dual Diagnosis Program**

This **1st** *day of* **May, 1999**

Saying No to Drugs and Yes to Healthy Pleasures

ACTIVITY SCHEDULE

	MONDAY	TUESDAY	WEDNESDAY
5:00 AM			
6:00 AM			
7:00 AM			
8:00 AM			
9:00 AM			
10:00 AM			
11:00 AM			
12:00 PM			
1:00 PM			
2:00 PM			
3:00 PM			
4:00 PM			
5:00 PM			
6:00 PM			
7:00 PM			
8:00 PM			
9:00 PM			
10:00 PM			
11:00 PM			

ACTIVITY SCHEDULE

	THURSDAY	FRIDAY	SATURDAY	SUNDAY
5:00 AM				
6:00 AM				
7:00 AM				
8:00 AM				
9:00 AM				
10:00 AM				
11:00 AM				
12:00 PM				
1:00 PM				
2:00 PM				
3:00 PM				
4:00 PM				
5:00 PM				
6:00 PM				
7:00 PM				
8:00 PM				
9:00 PM				
10:00 PM				
11:00 PM				

ACTIVITY SCHEDULE

	MONDAY	TUESDAY	WEDNESDAY
5:00 AM			
6:00 AM	GROOMING *TAKE MEDS	GROOMING *TAKE MEDS	GROOMING *TAKE MEDS
7:00 AM	BREAKFAST 7:30 - BUS	BREAKFAST 7:30 - BUS	BREAKFAST 7:30 - BUS
8:00 AM	TREATMENT GROUPS	TREATMENT GROUPS	TREATMENT GROUPS
9:00 AM			
10:00 AM		MEDICATION CLINIC	
11:00 AM			
12:00 PM	LUNCH	LUNCH	LUNCH
1:00 PM	TREATMENT GROUP	TREATMENT GROUP	TREATMENT GROUP
2:00 PM			
3:00 PM	BINGO	EXERCISE	MEET WITH SUPPORT PERSON
4:00 PM			
5:00 PM			DINNER WITH PHIL
6:00 PM	TAKE BUS DINNER	TAKE BUS DINNER	*CATCH BUS
7:00 PM	T.V.	LISTEN TO MUSIC	DOMINOES/ CARDS
8:00 PM			
9:00 PM	*TAKE MEDS GET READY	*TAKE MEDS	*TAKE MEDS BEDTIME
10:00 PM	FOR BED	BEDTIME	
11:00 PM			

ACTIVITY SCHEDULE

	THURSDAY	FRIDAY	SATURDAY	SUNDAY
5:00 AM				
6:00 AM	GROOMING *TAKE MEDS	GROOMING *TAKE MEDS		
7:00 AM	BREAKFAST 7:30 - BUS	BREAKFAST 7:30 - BUS		GROOMING *TAKE MEDS
8:00 AM	TREATMENT GROUP		*TAKE MEDS GROOMING	BREAKFAST
9:00 AM		MEET EDDIE FOR COFFEE SCHOOL	BREAKFAST W/ SUSAN	TAKE BUS HOME TO SEE FAMILY
10:00 AM				HOME
11:00 AM			WALK/ WINDOW SHOP	
12:00 PM	LUNCH	LUNCH		PICNIC
1:00 PM	TREATMENT GROUP	SCHOOL	LUNCH	&
2:00 PM			CATCH MOVIE	DAY
3:00 PM	EXERCISE	TAKE BUS HOME		IN
4:00 PM		GET READY FOR MEETING		PARK
5:00 PM		CA MEETINGS		
6:00 PM	TAKE BUS DINNER		TAKE BUS HOME	
7:00 PM		DINNER	PIZZA W/ JOE	
8:00 PM	T.V.	BINGO	SOBER DANCE	RETURN TO SOBER
9:00 PM	READ *TAKE MEDS	*TAKE MEDS		LIVING
10:00 PM	BEDTIME	BEDTIME		*TAKE MEDS BEDTIME
11:00 PM			*TAKE MEDS BEDTIME	

SKILL PROMPT CARDS
Copy for patients to use as reminders.

QUITTING AFTER A SLIP

1. Avoid eye contact with the person offering drugs.
2. Stand up and turn away from the person.
3. Start walking out of the room.
4. Say in a firm voice tone, "I gotta go."
5. Use the broken record technique by continuing to say, "I gotta go now."
6. Keep moving quickly, don't stop for anything

REPORTING A SLIP

1. Greet the person politely. Maintain eye contact. Use a pleasant voice tone.
2. Be direct. Don't beat around the bush. Tell the person that you have slipped.
3. Tell the person that you would like to discuss the circumstances surrounding your slip.
4. Describe the high-risk situation and how you escaped from it. Emphasize the fact that you escaped before you went on a full-blown relapse.
5. Remark about the things that you have been doing recently to keep your sobriety program intact (attending groups, carrying your emergency card, meeting with your support person).
6. Ask the person to help you figure out how to prevent entering into similar high-risk situations in the future.
7. Thank the person for his or her assistance.

REFUSING DRUGS OFFERED BY A DEALER

1. Avert your gaze. Don't make eye contact with the dealer.
2. Turn your head away from the dealer and wave him off with a hand gesture.
3. Stand tall and lean forward.
4. Walk past the dealer at a brisk pace.
5. Keep your hands close to you so that the dealer can't put anything in your hand.
6. Use a firm voice tone and keep repeating "I don't want any" over and over again.

REFUSING DRUGS OFFERED BY A FRIEND OR RELATIVE

1. Be Direct. Tell the person that you're not interested.
2. Use the broken record technique. Repeat yourself if necessary.
3. Level with the person. Tell him it her that drugs were causing you problems and it's better for you to leave drugs alone.
4. Suggest an alternative. Request to do something other than use drugs.
5. Express your feelings directly. Tell the other person how you feel about being pressured.
6. Leave the situation. Tell the person that you are serious about sobriety.

GETTING AN APPOINTMENT WITH A BUSY PERSON

1. Greet the person politely.
2. Maintain eye contact and use a pleasant but firm voice tone.
3. Tell the person that you need his or her help.
4. Tell the person that it is important.
5. Indicate that it will only take a few minutes of his or her time.
6. If the person refuses to meet now, ask for an appointment.
7. Ask the person to be specific as to the time and place to meet.
8. Restate the time and place of the meeting and thank the person.

GETTING A SUPPORT PERSON

1. Tell the person that you need his or her help.
2. Explain why you need a support person.
3. Be direct in asking the person to serve as your support person.
4. Answer any questions the person asks about his or her responsibilities.
5. If the person agrees, show your emergency card and ask if you can write his or her telephone number on it.
6. Thank the person for agreeing to help you.

REPORTING SYMPTOMS AND SIDE EFFECTS TO A DOCTOR

1. Greet your doctor politely. Make eye contact and use a pleasant tone of voice.
2. Describe the symptom or side effect in detail.
3. Say how long you've had the symptom or side effect.
4. Describe the severity of your problem by explaining how it interferes with your daily activities.
5. Ask directly for your doctor's help.
6. Repeat the doctor's instructions.
7. Ask how long it will take to get relief.
8. Thank the doctor for his or her help.

ASKING SOMEONE TO JOIN YOU IN A HEALTHY PLEASURE

1. Use a pleasant greeting. Make eye contact and speak in a happy voice tone.
2. Tell the person how much you enjoy his or her company.
3. Pick at least two activities that you are certain the person will enjoy.
4. Describe the activities and when they take place.
5. Ask the person to join you. Be direct. Don't beat around the bush.
6. If the person says he or she has another engagement at that time, suggest an alternative activity or ask when he would have time.
7. If it becomes clear that the person doesn't want to join in an activity, tell him or her that you understand and thank him for considering your offer.
8. If the person accepts your offer, set a time and place to meet.

NEGOTIATING WITH A REPRESENTATIVE PAYEE

1. Greet your payee politely. Make eye contact. Use a pleasant voice tone.

2. Be direct. Tell your payee that you are looking for ways to structure your time more productively.

3. Indicate that pursuing healthy pleasures is an excellent way to make it easier for you not to use drugs.

4. Tell your payee the specific healthy pleasure that you want to pursue.

5. Let your payee know how often you plan to engage in the activity and exactly how much money you will need to pursue your healthy pleasure.

6. Remind your payee of the progress that you have made in your treatment program. Mention such areas as medication compliance, symptom reduction, drug abstinence, regular group attendance, keeping appointments with your doctor, structuring your time every day, and using coping techniques to avoid and escape high-risk situations.

7. Give your payee permission to contact a member of your clinical team to verify your progress.

8. Indicate that you will provide receipts for the money you spend on the healthy pleasure.

9. Schedule a follow-up appointment with your payee to report your progress and deliver receipts, and thank him or her.

Instructions for Preparing the Emergency Card

1. Cut out this page (front and back of the emergency card) and make a double-sided copy—that is, two sides of a single sheet of paper. (Save this page for future use!)

2. On your copy, cut along the dashed line around the edges of the emergency card; fold along the solid lines.

Name:

Social security no.:

Emergency Phone no.'s:

Support Person 1: (name & phone no.)

Support Person 2: (name & phone no.)

Payee:

In case of emergency contact:

Healthy Habits

Things that I do over and over again that are good for me

- •
- •
- •
- •

Treatment program: (name & phone no.)

Hospital ER: (name & phone no.)

Crisis Line: AA #

NA #

Other #

Prescribed medications (name, dose, freq.)

Allergies:

Other important health information:

Healthy Pleasures

Something that feels good and is good for me

- •
- •
- •
- •

EMERGENCY CARD *Front Side*

High-Risk Situation

I'm heading for a drug relapse if:

- People:

- Places:

- Things:

- Thoughts:

- Emotions:

Warning Signs

I'm headed for a high-risk situation:

- People:

- Places:

- Things:

- Thoughts:

- Emotions:

I've decided to QUIT because:

U-turns and Coping Skills

Instead of using drugs I will:

- Participate in a healthy pleasure

- Call my support person

- Ride the wave

- Review why I decided to quit

-

-

EMERGENCY CARD *Back Side*

LIST OF HEALTHY PLEASURES

1. Shopping
2. Zoo
3. Observatory
4. Movies
5. Picnics
6. Theme Parks
7. Movies at home (video, cable, TV)
8. Restaurants
9. Sporting events (live/TV)
10. Libraries
11. Exercise (jogging, walking, biking, weight lifting)
12. AA, NA, CA meetings
13. Sober dances
14. Visit a friend or relative
15. Concerts
16. Church services
17. Beach
18. Museums
19. Volunteer in the community

Appendix B

KNOWLEDGE AND SKILLS TEST

This test measures the extent to which a patient learns the key concepts and skills taught in SAMM. The 120-item test contains questions about key concepts covered in the module, and structured role-plays test of each of the nine specific skills taught in the module. We used this test in an initial study of the feasibility of SAMM to determine how well patients learned what was taught. The test has proven to be a good indicator of whether the patient is learning the key concepts. You might wonder what score would be considered good enough to protect a patient against further drug use. Although we suspect that higher scores on this test mean that the patient is less likely to relapse, we have not yet demonstrated that. We include it here for several reasons. First, it highlights what we think are the most important things to teach. Second, you can use it to determine which patients most need training. Third, you can use it to determine how much your patients are learning and where they may need additional help. To do this, administer the test before starting treatment, at some point(s) during treatment, and after completing treatment. The test takes approximately 30–45 minutes to complete.

Name _____

ID Number _____

Rating Occasion _____

Date _____

Rater _____

Substance Abuse Management Module
Knowledge and Skills Test

ADMINISTRATION INSTRUCTION

First, ask which drug the patient prefers most—his or her *drug of choice*. Whenever the test refers to a drug, use the patient's *drug of choice*. For example, in the role-play for drug refusal, ask the patient what drug he or she would be most likely to buy. Whenever *drug of choice* appears in the test, substitute the name of the patient's *drug of choice*..

To Patient: "I'm interested in how much you know about drug relapse. I'm going to ask you some questions or describe situations that are related to drug relapse. Your job is to answer the questions the best you can. Each question is brief and easy to understand. However, if there are words or concepts that seem unfamiliar, just answer the question the best you can.

"The questions and situations in this test will make more sense if they involve the drugs or alcohol that you prefer. We call this your drug of choice. What is your drug of choice? Okay whenever the test refers to drugs, we will think about those questions or situations with regard to (*drug of choice*) use."

Using the "Notes" Section: The notes section appears after each question. You can use this space to record specific responses given by the patient or to record the number and wording of prompts given by the trainer.

Role-plays: For each role-play, a sample dialogue is given. This is meant to be used as a guideline. The patient does not have to use these exact wording in the responses. It is helpful to be familiar with the role-play dialogues before administering the test.

Test Scores: Test scores range from 0–120 points. You might wonder what score would be considered good, meaning that the patient knows why and how to avoid drugs. Although we suspect that higher scores on this test mean that the patient is less likely to relapse, we have not yet demonstrated that. However, in an initial test of the feasibility of this treatment, patients began treatment with a mean score of 41 (standard deviation of 11.8). At the end of four months of daily sessions, their scores improved to a mean of 102 (standard deviation of 12.6). Three months after training, patients received a mean score of 100 (standard deviation of 11.1). This means that patients can learn and retain the lessons taught in SAMM. Using the total score will give you a way to measure a patient's progress toward treatment goals. The exact score may not be as important as the change in score after the patient has completed the SAMM training. Scores on individual items and sections of the test can also be used to determine areas in which patients need additional training.

BASIC TRAINING

Emergency Card

1. In drug relapse prevention, it is helpful to carry an emergency card. Tell me, what is an emergency card?

_____It has information that helps me remember things to help quit using drugs

_____**Total Points:**   Score 0 for no correct answers

                                  Score 1 for one correct answer

        Prompts: If the patient states, "I don't know," you may prompt once by asking, "Do you have any ideas?"

*Notes:*_____

_____

If the patient is unable to answer the question, SKIP to question 6.

2. Can you tell me what information is written on the emergency card?

_____Personal drug-habit chain (or warning signs or high-risk situations)

_____Craving control measures (or coping strategies or U-turns)

_____Payee's name and phone number

_____Bad effects of using (or number one disadvantage of using drugs)

_____Support person's name and phone number

_____Telephone number of my clinic/program

_____**Total Points:**   Score 0 for no correct answers

                                  Score 1 for two correct answers

                                  Score 2 for three or more correct answers

        Prompts: You may prompt a patient a maximum of two times by asking, "Can you tell me more?"

*Notes:*_____

_____

3. **Tell me three advantages of carrying an emergency card with you.**

_____Remember how to avoid drugs

_____Remember healthy pleasures

_____Lists telephone numbers of support people or someone who can assist me if I am tempted to use.

_____Remember my personal disadvantages of using and the advantages of saying no to drugs

_____Lists telephone number of my program in case I need emergency psychiatric treatment

_____**Total Points:**   Score 0 less than three advantages

Score 1 for three advantages

Score 2 for four or more advantages

   Prompts: If the patient does not provide three answers without prompting, prompt a maximum of two times by asking, "Can you tell me more?" or "Are there any more advantages?"

_Notes:_____

_____

4. **Do you have an emergency card with you? If so, please show me the card.**

_____Shows you the emergency card

_____Does not show you the emergency card

_____**Total Points:**   Score 0 for not having the emergency card available to show you

Score 1 for showing you the emergency card

_Notes:_____

_____

5. **On the card is a section named "Instead of using I will . . ." or, in other words, a section for coping techniques. Please name three coping techniques.**

_____Ride the wave

_____Get help from a support person

_____Do a healthy pleasure

_____Do a healthy habit

_____Make a U-turn

_____**Total Points:**   Score 0 for less than three techniques

Score 1 for three techniques

Score 2 for four or more techniques

_Notes:_____

_____

High-Risk Situations

6. What is a high-risk situation?
_____A situation in which it is very difficult to avoid using drugs
_____A combination of people, places, events, and things
_____The situation is very tempting because it is easy to use
_____**Total Points:**   Score 0 for any other answer
                            Score 1 for one answer above
                            Score 2 for two or more answers above
    Prompts: If the patient does not provide one of the answers, prompt one time by asking, "Can you tell me more?"
*Notes:*_____
_____

7. Can you give me three examples of high-risk situations?
_____Having large sums of money
_____Having more than a couple of dollars in my pocket
_____Hanging out with people who use alcohol or drugs
_____Going to a neighbor's where drug dealers are available
_____When my symptoms of schizophrenia flare-up
_____If I have medication side effects that won't go away
_____Feeling depressed or lonely or angry or stressed
_____Other:_____
_____**Total Points:** When scoring this item, the answers listed above are just a few examples of the possible categories of high-risk situations, which include people, places, things, thoughts, emotions, or stating denial of the risk of using.
                Score 0 for less than two high-risk situations/categories
                Score 1 for two correct answers
                Score 2 for three or more correct answers
    Prompts: Prompt two times by asking, "Are there any more?"
*Notes:*_____
_____

If the patient is unable to answer the question, SKIP to question 9.

8. Why is it important to identify your personal high-risk situations?
_____So I can recognize when I am at a high risk to use drugs
_____If I know my high-risk situations, then I can take steps to avoid them
_____If I know my high-risk situations, then I can be prepared to refuse drugs

_____If I know my high-risk situations, then I can be better able to escape them.

_____**Total Points:**   Score 0 for no correct answer

Score 1 for two correct answers

Score 2 for three or more correct answers

Prompts: Prompt a maximum of two times by asking "Can you tell me more?"

_Notes:_____

_____

Escaping High-Risk Situations

9. **Suppose you get into a high-risk situation where you are approached by a pushy drug dealer who tells you the drugs are free and he tries to put the drugs in you hand. What would you do in that situation?**

_____I would refuse to use the drugs

_____I would leave the situation

_____**Total Points**:   Score 0 for no correct answers

Score 1 for two correct answers

Score 2 for three or more correct answers

Prompts: Prompt a maximum of two times by asking, "Is there anything else you would do?"

_Notes:_____

_____

10. **Let's suppose that you are in that situation. I am going to pretend to be a dealer and you will show me how you would refuse drugs when I offer them to you. You are standing there and I walk up to you and say:**

Sample Dialogue

"Hey, I've got something for you today."

(Averts gaze, starts walking quickly away.)

"Come on, this is good stuff."

(Pulls hand in close and continues to walk away.)

"Okay, maybe down on your luck right now. Here, you can pay me later." (Looks for an opportunity to place drugs in role-player's hand.)

No, I don't want any.

Follows role-player for a short distance while attempting to put drugs in his hand.

(Walks away quickly)

Techniques for Refusing Drugs Offered by a Dealer

Technique	Score 1 point for each technique used
States a verbal refusal anywhere in the role-play	_____
Looks away, does not make eye contact with the dealer	_____
Uses a hand gesture to wave off the dealer	_____
Keeps moving, doesn't stop to talk	_____
Keeps hands close to body so that the dealer can't put anything in his hand	_____
Total	_____

11. Suppose you got into a high-risk situation where you are approached by a friend or family member who wants you to use drugs with him. What would you do in that situation?

_____I would refuse to use the drugs

_____I would leave the situation

_____I would make a U-turn

_____**Total Points:**   Score 0 for no correct answers

Score 1 for two correct answers

Score 2 for three or more correct answers

Prompts: Prompt a maximum of two times by asking, "Is there anything else you would do?"

*Notes:*_____

_____

12. Let's suppose you are in that situation. I will be an old friend who wants you to use with me. I pull out (drug of choice) and offer it to you.

Sample Dialogue

"Hi, _____. It's good to see you today. Look what I have."

Yeah, what is it?

"I ran into Joe and he sold me some great (drug of choice). Let's try it."

Oh, that's risky for me. No thanks.

"Ah, come on. I've never known you to refuse (drug of choice)."

No, thanks. I don't use anymore.

"Come on, man. I've got plenty."

Look, I said that I don't use anymore. Drugs were causing serious problems in my life. It's really hard for me to stay sober. Please don't make it impossible for me.

"What are you talking about? Come on, let's get high. You can't tell me that you don't want any of this."

I mean what I said. I don't use anymore. I want to stay clean. I'd rather do something else. How about if we go to a movie or go to the pool hall and shoot some eight-ball?

"You want to go out when we can stay here and have a great time? Come on, let's get high."

That's right, I would. Stop pressuring me. I'm starting to get angry because you're trying to get me to do something that I don't want to do.

"Hey, I don't mean to pressure you. If you don't want to use that just means more for me. We can play some pool after I use this (drug of choice)."

Nope. Like I said, I don't use anymore. I've got something else I would rather do. I don't have any intentions of using with you ever again. I'm leaving.

Techniques for Refusing Drugs Offered by a Friend or Relative

Technique	Score 1 point for each technique used
Is direct. Says he's not interested	_____
Uses the broken record technique at least one time	_____
Levels with the person (e.g., says that drugs were causing problems and it's better to leave them alone)	_____
Suggests an alternative; requests to do something other than use drugs	_____
Expresses feelings directly; says how he feels about being pressured	_____
Leaves the situation	_____
	Total _____

Damage Control

13. When you slip and use drugs (after a period of sobriety), what kind of feelings or thoughts might you experience and what might you do because of those feelings?

_____When I slip and use drugs, I could have feelings or thoughts of failure

_____I might as well continue using drugs

_____**Total Points:**   Score 0 for any other answer

Score 1 for one answer above

Score 2 for two answers above

*Notes:*_____

_____

14. Tell me two advantages of understanding how a drug slip can affect you?

_____I can anticipate and better understand these thoughts and feelings of failure if I slip

_____I will be able to know that these thoughts and feelings are to be expected

_____I can acknowledge the feelings and then refocus my attention and get back on track

_____It will be easier to stop using early

_____I can escape the high-risk situation easier

_____I can choose to do a healthy pleasure instead

_____**Total Points:**   Score 0 for less than two advantages

Score 1 for two advantages

Score 2 for three or more advantages

Prompts: If less than two answers are provided, prompt one time by asking, "Are there any others?"

*Notes:*_____

_____

15. Suppose you are in a high-risk situation and you take a hit and realize you are on the verge of relapsing. Tell me two things you could do in that situation.

_____Remind myself that I am in a high-risk situation

_____Stop using drugs early before it does any more damage to my relationships, health, and finances

_____Refuse to use drugs any more

_____Leave

_____**Total Points**:   Score 0 for less than two answers

Score 1 for two correct answers

Score 2 for three or more correct answers

Prompts: You may prompt a maximum of two times by asking, "Is there anything else you would do?"

*Notes:*_____

_____

16. Let's say you are actually in that situation. I'm going to be the person who takes out a bag, opens it up, and puts it on the table. I offer you some (drug of choice). You take a few hits and decide you don't want to have a full-blown relapse.

Sample Dialogue

"Hey, _____. I'm really glad you came over. I've got some really good stuff. Let's get loaded. What do you say?"

(Reluctantly accepts) Uh, okay (takes one hit and passes drug to the other person).

"Here, take another hit."

(Immediately puts drug down). No, thanks. I gotta go. (Stands up, turns away, and starts to walk out).

"Hey, where are you going?"

No, I gotta go.

"What do you mean you gotta go? We're just getting started."

I gotta go (keeps walking toward the door).

"We've got enough here to last all night."

I gotta go.

"I don't believe you. Come back if you change your mind."

(Continues walking out the door)

Techniques for Damage Control

Technique	Score 1 point for each technique used
Doesn't make eye contact	_____
Stands up and turns away	_____
Starts walking out of the room	_____
Says in a firm voice tone, "I gotta go"	_____
Uses the broken record technique by continuing to say, "I gotta go now"	_____
Keeps moving, doesn't stop for anything.	_____
Total	_____

Note: If patient refuses drug but stays, score 1 for refusal technique and 0 for all remaining techniques in role play.

Support Persons

17. What is a support person?

_____Someone who I can call to get help when I am tempted to use

_____Someone with whom I can discuss drug slips and who can help me get back on track to maintain abstinence

_____Someone who can help me remember the disadvantages of using and the advantages of quitting

_____Someone who can problem-solve and help me identify alternatives to using (healthy pleasures, coping techniques, escaping, etc.)

_____**Total Points:**   Score 0 for no correct answers

Score 1 for one correct answer

Score 2 for two or more correct answers

Prompts: Prompt once by asking, "Can you tell me more?"

*Notes:*_____

_____

18. **What would you use a support person for?**

_____I can call him/her for support when I am in a high-risk situation

_____To help me problem-solve my high-risk situations

_____To help me use healthy pleasures instead of using drugs

_____To help me remember to use the skills to avoid using drugs and to do healthy pleasures

_____**Total Points:**   Score 0 for less than two correct answers

Score 1 for two correct answer

Score 2 for three or more correct answers

Prompts: Prompt a maximum of two times by asking, "Are there any others?"

*Notes:*_____

_____

19. **Tell me at least two qualities or characteristics of a good support person.**

_____Someone who I know, trust, and who cares about me

_____Someone who is accessible

_____Someone who does not use

_____**Total Points:**   Score 0 for less than two answers

Score 1 for two correct answer

Score 2 for three or more correct answers

Prompts: Prompt a maximum of two times by saying, "Are there any others?"

*Notes:*_____

_____

20. **In this situation, I will pretend to be someone who you would like to be your support person. Your task will be to ask me to be your support person.**

Sample Dialogue

"Hi, _____. It's good to see you."

Thanks. It's good to see you too. I wanted to talk with you because I need your help with something.

Oh, how can I help you?

Recently, I got into a program to help me stop using drugs.

"Great! That's good news."

Thanks. The program is a big help to me, but I need all the help I can get. Quitting drugs is one of the hardest things a person can do.

"Yes, I know. But how can I help you?"

Well, in my program they talk about the importance of having a support person.

"What's a support person?"

A support person is someone who I know and trust. It should be someone who I see frequently and who will be accessible to me when I need help. Most importantly, it has to be someone who doesn't use drugs. That's why I picked you.

"Well, what does a support person do?"

A support person could help me get out of high-risk situations, like when I have cravings or I'm tempted to use drugs. He would help think about alternatives to using.

"How's that?"

For example, there might be times when I find myself thinking about using or maybe I will have a slip. It would be helpful to be able to talk to you about it. Discussing it with you might help get me back on track.

"Oh, I see, a support person helps you get through tough times."

Yes, exactly. I find it easy to talk with you. I want you to be my support person. Will you do it?

"Yes, I want to see you do well. If I can be of help, I'll be glad to be your support person."

Great! Do you have any other questions?

"Yes, I have one question. Do I have to be available 24 hours a day?"

No you don't. Let me show you something. This is my emergency card. You can see that I've listed emergency telephone numbers as well as some coping techniques that I can use when I'm in a high-risk situation. It's helpful, but it would also be good to know that I have somebody on my side. I'll call you if these techniques aren't enough.

"I see."

I'd like to put your telephone number on my emergency card so that it's handy. Would that be all right?

"Yes, of course."

What is your number?

"My telephone number is 555-1234."

Great! Thanks again for agreeing to be my support person.

"You're welcome."

Techniques for Getting a Support Person

Technique	Score 1 point for each technique used
Tells the person he needs his/her help	_____
Explains why he needs a support person	_____
Is direct in asking the person to serve as his support person	_____
Answers any questions that the person asks about his or her responsibilities	_____
If the person agrees, shows emergency card and asks if he can write the person's telephone number on it	_____
Thanks the person for agreeing to help	_____
Total	_____

20. **It is helpful to report a drug slip to your support person. In this situation, I will play the role of your support person. You will report your drug slip to me. You visited a friend over the weekend and took a couple hits of (drug of choice) but then stopped. You come by my office to talk about it.**

Sample Dialogue

Hi, _____. I'm glad you could meet with me today.

"What's up? You sounded serious when you asked if we could meet."

Well, I have some bad news. I slipped yesterday. I didn't have a full-blown relapse, but I came close. I escaped before I went on a binge.

"I'm glad you're letting me know."

I'd like to tell you about it. Maybe you can help me figure out how to avoid similar situations in the future.

"Good idea. What happened?"

Well, I was walking to the store when a car pulled up and an old buddy of mine jumped out. He said, "Hey, I haven't seen you for ages. What do you say we get something to eat and catch up on old times? So I hopped in his car. As we were driving to the restaurant, he decided to go by his house. When we got there, he walked into the bedroom and came out with (drug of choice). It caught me off guard. He lit a joint and passed it to me and I took a hit.

"What did you do?"

I knew I shouldn't take it, but the situation just got the best of me. I took a hit. With each hit I felt more and more guilty. I felt so bad that I put it down on the table and said I had to go. He couldn't believe it. But I just kept going. Then I called you.

"It really must have been hard to stop."

It really was. He really wanted me to stay. I kind of wanted to talk to him too, but I knew that if I stayed I'd end up using more.

"What did you do to get away?"

I just told him that I don't use anymore.

"You did a good job escaping that high-risk situation."

Yeah, it was terrible though. It's a miracle that I didn't use after I left his house. I don't want this to happen again. Have you got any suggestions?

"One thing you might do is to refuse to associate with old buddies that you used to use with."

You're right, and I have been, but this guy caught me by surprise.

"Now that you have had an experience slipping in this type of high-risk situation, maybe it will be easier for you to deal with your old buddies next time. At least it gave you a chance to practice one of your coping techniques."

Yeah, you're right. But I should have let him know that I don't use anymore as soon as I saw him.

"Yes. You know, maybe that's something you could practice in your SAMM group."

Good idea. I'll bring it up at the next session.

"You should let the people on your clinical team know about this too."

Yes, I'll do it right away.

"You're really working at your program. Keep up the good work."

Thanks for your help. I feel like I'm back on track.

Techniques for Reporting a Slip

Technique	Score 1 point for each technique used
Greets the person politely	_____
Is direct, doesn't beat around the bush	_____
Says he would like to discuss the circumstances surrounding his slip	_____
Describes the high-risk situation and how he escaped from it	_____
Remarks about the things he has been doing recently to keep his sobriety program intact (attending groups, carrying emergency card, meeting with support person)	_____
Asks for help in figuring out how to prevent entering into a similar high-risk situation in the future	_____
Thanks the person for assistance	_____
Total	_____

Payees

22. When quitting drugs, some people find it helpful to have a payee. What is a payee?
_____Someone who manages or controls my use of money
_____**Total Points:**   Score 0 for any other answer
                        Score 1 for answer above
     Prompts: Prompts once by asking, "Do you have any idea what a payee is?"
*Notes:*_____

_____

If the patient is unable to answer the question, SKIP to question 26.

23. People managing drug relapse find payees to be helpful. What are two advantages of having a payee?
_____Helps me manage my money responsibly
_____Reduces the risk that I will use drugs
_____Helps me budget my money
_____Pays my rent and utilities so I won't become homeless as a result of spending all my money on drugs.
_____**Total Points:**   Score 0 for less than two answers
                        Score 1 for two correct answers
                        Score 2 for three or more answers
     Prompts: Prompt a maximum of two times by asking, "Are there any others?"
*Notes:*_____

_____

24. **How do you know if you need a payee?**

_____If one of my high-risk situations is having a large sum of money

_____If I have trouble paying my bills and rent on time and end up homeless as a result

_____If I give my money away when my symptoms flare up or go on spending sprees for items other than drugs

_____**Total Points**:   Score 0 points for no correct answers

Score 1 for one answer

Score 2 for two or more answers

Prompts: You may prompt one time by asking, "Are there any others?"

_Notes:_____

_____

25. **If you decided to get a payee, how would you go about getting one?**

_____Ask my case manager/social worker

_____Ask my group leader

_____Ask my doctor

_____I have a court-appointed conservator so that's like having a payee for me

_____Ask my support person

_____Seek advice from any available community agencies who provide this service

_____The court assigns one for me

_____**Total Points**   Score 0 for no correct answers

Score 1 for two correct answers

Score 2 for three or more correct answers

_Notes:_____

_____

26. **Let's suppose that you approach your payee to negotiate for some money to start a new healthy pleasure. The healthy pleasure that you have decided to do is to go bowling every week. I will play the role of your payee and you will be yourself. Your task is to approach me in order to negotiate for more money so that you can start going bowling every week.**

Sample Dialogue

"Hi,_____. How can I help you?"

_Hi, _____. It's good to see you. I wanted to meet with you to let you know about the progress that I'm making in the program._

"I know that you've been doing well. I'm really glad to see it."

Having my time occupied with constructive activities really helps a lot.

"I'm sure it does. I've noticed that you have been a lot more active lately."

Yes, I have. But there's more that I want to do.

"Really, what did you have in mind?"

I want to start a new healthy pleasure.

"Oh? What do you mean by "healthy pleasure?"

A healthy pleasure is an activity that feels good and is good for me. The more healthy pleasures I schedule, the less chance I have of using drugs.

"I see what you mean."

I've been thinking about starting a new healthy pleasure.

"Yeah? What is it?"

Well, I've always been interested in bowling. I'd like to start going a couple of times a week. It's great exercise and it might give me a chance to make some new friends.

"It sounds good, but I have one concern. In the past, having extra money in your pocket was risky. It always seemed to lead straight to drugs."

Yes, that's true. But things are different now.

"How's that?"

Well, I am attending the groups in my relapse prevention program, keeping all my appointments with my doctor, taking my medication regularly, and using the skills I learn in my group to avoid high-risk situations.

"You are doing a good job, but I'm concerned about your ability to handle having extra money in your pocket."

I certainly understand your concern. I know that you don't want to see me get started on drugs again.

"I sure don't."

I'll tell you what. Why don't you give the folks at the clinic a call? I'd like for you to talk to someone on my clinical team. I think that they can assure you that I'm on solid ground. I want to do everything I can to earn your trust.

"Okay, I'll give them a call. You do seem to be sincere. If the people on your team feel that you can handle the cash, I'll give you the money you need to get started."

Great! I want to go twice a week. I'll need money for shoes and enough to bowl three games *each time. It works out to about $22.50 a week. I could bring the receipts from the bowling alley to show you exactly where the money goes.*

"That's an excellent idea."

I'd also like to schedule a follow-up appointment with you so that I can let you know how I'm doing and give you the receipts.

"Terrific!"

What do you say we meet next Monday at 2:00?

"Monday at 2:00 is fine."

Great! I'll see you then! Thanks a lot.

"You're welcome. I'm glad to do it."

Techniques for Negotiating with a Payee

Technique

Score 1 point for each technique used

Greets payee politely   _____

Is direct. Says that he is looking for ways to structure his time more productively   _____

Indicates that pursuing healthy pleasures is an excellent way to make it easier not to use drugs   _____

Tells payee the specific healthy pleasure that he wants to pursue   _____

Says how often he plans to engage in the activity and exactly how much money he will need to pursue this healthy pleasure   _____

Reminds payee of the progress he has made in his treatment program (e.g., medication compliance, symptom reduction, drug abstinence, regular group attendance, keeping appointments with doctor, structuring time every day, using coping techniques to avoid and escape high-risk situations)   _____

Gives permission to contact a member of his clinical team to verify progress   _____

Indicates that he will provide receipts for the money spent on the healthy pleasure   _____

Schedules a follow-up appointment to report progress and deliver receipts   _____

Total   _____

Drug-Habit Chains

27. Tell me, what is a drug-habit chain?
_____A drug-habit chain is made up of the things that I do over and over again that lead me to drug use

_____**Total Points:**   Score 0 for no correct answers
                          Score 1 for answer above

If the patient is unable to answer the question, SKIP to question 30.

28. What is the main advantage of knowing your own drug-habit chain?
_____I can get out of the chain that leads me to drug use (like making a U-turn)
_____**Total Points**: the patient only needs to articulate the idea of getting out of the chain, and doe
  not have to use the term U-turn.
                          Score 0 for no correct answers
                          Score 1 for answer above
_Notes:_____

_____

29. Describe your #1 drug-habit chain.
_____Describes a thought that precedes drug use
_____Describes a feeling that precedes drug use
_____Describes making a plan to obtain drugs
_____Describes the action taken to obtain the drug
_____Describes using the drug in a specific situation
_____**Total Points:**   Score 0 for one category to describe his/her #1 drug-habit chain.
                          Score 1 for two categories
                          Score 2 for three or more categories
  Prompts: Prompt one time by asking, "Is there anything else?"
_Notes:_____

_____

Warning Signs

30. When it comes to drug relapse, what are warning signs?
_____A warning sign tells you that you have taken a step toward using drugs
_____Describes triggers, cravings, making a plan, getting and using the drug
_____**Total Points**:   Score 0 for no correct answers
                          Score 1 for answer above

Score 2 for two answers above

Prompts: Prompt one time by asking, "Can you tell me more?"

Notes:_____

_____

If the patient is unable to answer the question, SKIP to question 33.

31. What are the main advantages of knowing your own personal warning signs?

_____I can avoid high risk situations

_____I can do a healthy pleasure instead of using drugs

_____I can make a U-turn to escape using drugs

_____I can use coping techniques to avoid using drugs

_____**Total Points**:   Score 0 for no correct answers

Score 1 for two correct answers

Score 2 for three or more correct answers

Prompts: Prompt one time by asking, "Are there any more?"

Notes_____

_____

32. What is your highest-risk situation?

_____Having large sums of money

_____Having more than a couple dollars in my pocket

_____Hanging out with people who use

_____Going to a neighborhood where drug dealers are present

_____When my symptoms of schizophrenia flare up

_____Having side effects from my medication that won't go away

_____Feeling depressed, lonely, or angry

_____Feeling stressed

_____Other: _____

_____**Total Points**:   Score 0 for no answer

Score 1 for identifying high-risk situation

Notes:_____

_____

If the patient unable to answer the question, SKIP to question 34.

33. Think about the high-risk situation of (name the high-risk situation that the patient identi-fied in the last question). Tell me at least one warning sign for that high-risk situation.

_____Describes a thought that precedes drug use

_____Describes a feeling that precedes drug use
_____Describes a symptom that causes discomfort that precedes drug use
_____Describes making a plan to obtain the drug
_____Describes the action taken to obtain the drug
_____Describes a situation in which he/she uses drugs
_____**Total Points**:   Score 0 for no correct answer
                                    Score 1 for one warning sign
                                    Score 2 for two or three warning signs.
          Prompts: Prompt two times by asking, "Are there any more?"
_Notes:_____

_____

U-turns

34. What is the definition of a U-turn?
_____Any step that takes me further away from drugs
_____Things like healthy habits, removing triggers, riding the wave, emergency card
     (concrete examples such as taking medications, taking a shower, etc. are acceptable responses)
_____**Total Points**:   Score 0 for any other answer
                                    Score 1 for one correct answer
                                    Score 2 for two correct answers
          Prompts: Prompt one time by asking, "Can you tell me more?"
_Notes:_____

_____

If patient is unable to answer the question, SKIP to question 38.

35. Let's say that you're in the following situation. You are thinking a lot about using (drug of choice) when you get a large sum of money. What is at least one U-turn you could make in that situation?
_____Call a support person
_____Get a payee
_____Give money to support person or payee
_____Use emergency card to review disadvantages of using
_____Get someone to join me in a healthy pleasure
_____**Total Points**:   Score 0 for no correct answers
                                    Score 1 for one correct answer
                                    Score 2 for two or more correct answers
          Prompts: Prompt one time by asking, "Can you think of any others?"

*Notes:*_____
_____

36. Let's say that you are in another situation. This time you are experiencing side effects of your medication and you are thinking about using. Tell me one U-turn you could make in this situation.

_____Report troubling side effects to my doctor
_____Call my support person to talk about my discomfort
_____Use my emergency card to get telephone numbers or use coping techniques
_____Other_____
_____**Total Points**:   Score 0 for no correct answers
              Score 1 for one correct answer
              Score 2 for two or more correct answers
      Prompts: Prompt one time by asking, "Can you tell me any more?"
*Notes:*_____
_____

37. In this situation, you are at a friend's house and you are experiencing cravings. Tell me one U-turn you would make in this situation.

_____If I slip and use, stop using immediately and leave
_____Say no to drug offers
_____Report a lapse to support person or treatment team
_____Call a support person
_____Get a friend to join me in a healthy pleasure instead of using
_____Use my emergency card to review coping techniques
_____**Total Points**:   Score 0 for no correct answers
              Score 1 for one correct answer
              Score 2 for two or more correct answers
      Prompts: Prompt one time by asking, "Can you tell me any more?"
*Notes:*_____
_____

Healthy Pleasures

38. What is a healthy pleasure?
_____Healthy pleasures are things that feel good
_____Healthy pleasures are good for you
_____**Total Points**:   Score 0 for no correct answers
              Score 1 for one correct answer
              Score 2 for two or more correct answers

Prompts: Prompt one time by asking, "Can you tell me more?"

*Notes:*_____

_____

If patient is unable to answer the question, SKIP to question 40.

39. What are some of your favorite healthy pleasures?

_____1._____

_____2._____

_____3._____

_____**Total Points:**   Score 0 for no correct answers

Score 1 for one correct answer

Score 2 for two or more correct answers

Prompts: Prompt one time by asking, "Are there any more?"

*Notes:*_____

_____

40. Suppose you wanted to ask someone to go bowling with you. How would you go about asking him or her to do this? I will play the role of a friend. Your task is to try and get me to go bowling with you.

Sample Dialogue

Hi, _____. I'm really glad to see you.

"Hi, _____. How are you doing?"

Things are great, but I'd like to do more recreational activities. You know I really enjoy your company. It would be fun to do something together.

"Oh, what did you have in mind?"

Well, I enjoy bowling and playing golf. How about you? What do you like to do?

"Well, I like bowling too."

How about if we meet at the bowling alley this Saturday at 10:00?

"I can't. I have an appointment Saturday morning that I have to keep."

How about another time? Is there a time that would be good for you?

"I could meet you Saturday afternoon at 4:00."

Great, I'll meet you at 4:00 this Saturday at the bowling alley on Main Street.

"I'll see you there Saturday. Maybe we could get a bite to eat after bowling. There's a great little diner across the street."

Sounds great! See you Saturday!

Techniques for Asking Someone to Join You in a Healthy Pleasure

Technique	Score 1 point for each technique used
Uses a pleasant greeting	
Says how much he enjoys the person's company	_____
Mentions two activities	_____
Asks the person to join him; is direct, doesn't beat around the bush.	_____
When the person says he has another engagement at that time, suggests an alternate activity or asks when he would have time.	_____
If it becomes clear that the person doesn't want to join him, tells him that he understands and thanks him for considering his offer	_____
If the person accepts, sets up a time and place to meet	_____
Total	_____

Healthy Habits

41. What is a healthy habit?
_____Healthy habits are things that you do over and over that lead to healthy pleasures
_____**Total Points:**   Score 0 for incorrect answer
                              Score 1 for correct answer above

*Notes:*_____
_____

If patient is unable to answer question, SKIP to question 42.

42. What are three healthy habits that are very important to you?
_____1._____
_____2._____
_____3._____
_____**Total Points:**   Score 0 for less than three correct answers.
                              Score 1 for three correct answers
                              Score 2 for three correct answers, UNPROMPTED
     Prompts: If less than three answers are given, prompt a maximum of two times by asking, "Are there any more?"
*Notes:*_____
_____

43. Suppose you wanted to attend all the groups at the program each week. You need to get a schedule of the programs from your case manager who is very busy. You know it will be difficult to get an appointment with your case manager. I'll pretend to be your case manager and you show me how you would go about getting the schedule for groups at your program.

Sample Dialogue

Excuse me,_____. I need to talk with you.

"I'm sorry, but I'm really busy right now."

I see that you are, but I really need to talk.

"I told you, I don't have any time."

I know that you're in a hurry, but this is really important.

"I'm sure that it is, but I can't discuss it right now."

It will only take a few minutes. I promise not to take long.

"I'm sorry. I just can't take the time right now."

Okay, I won't bother you any more now. Is there another time that would be convenient for you to meet with me?

"Catch me sometime after lunch today."

Great! When and where would you like to meet?

"Be at my office today at 1:00."

You bet! I'll be at your office today at 1:00. Thanks!

"See you then."

Techniques for Getting an Appointment with a Busy Person

Technique	Score 1 point for each technique used
Greets the person politely	_____
Says he needs his help	_____
Says it is important	_____
Indicates that it will only take a few minutes	_____
When the person refuses to discuss it now, asks for an appointment	_____
Asks the person to be specific as to the time and place to meet	_____
Restates the time and place of the meeting	_____
Total	_____

44. It is helpful to report side effects of antipsychotic medication. Side effects can cause great discomfort and for some this can be a reason to use drugs. In this situation, suppose you were having a side effect of your antipsychotic medication. I will play the role of your doctor and you will be you. Your task is to report the side effect to me. You have an appointment to see me.

Sample Dialogue

Hello Dr._____. My name is_____. Thank you for meeting with me today.

"Hello, _____. How can I help you?"

I've been extremely restless.

"Hmm. Sounds awful. Why don't you have a seat in that chair and tell me more about it."

Okay (sits in chair, moves restlessly, frequently shifting position). It's like I'm real nervous.

"Is it more like nervousness or more like restlessness?"

It's more like restlessness. It's like I have anxiety, only I'm not apprehensive. I just have trouble sitting still. People in my family tell me to sit down and relax but I feel like I need to pace.

"I see."

It started several days ago but has gotten steadily worse over the past three days.

"It sounds like it's really bothering you."

Yes, it is. It's so bad that I can't sit through a television program without walking all around the room. And then the people in my family complain. I'm even having trouble sleeping because of it. I couldn't sit still on the bus coming here today. I stood up in the aisle and the driver told me that I would have to either sit down or get off the bus.

"No wonder you're upset."

Doctor, can you please help me with this?

"I'm sure going to try. I think that the restlessness you're having is a side effect of your antipsychotic medication. It's nothing to worry about. Restlessness is a common side effect and it's usually quite treatable."

What can you do?

"I'm going to give you a prescription for a side-effect medication. This should help reduce the restlessness."

Thanks a lot.

"Take one tablet in the morning and one at bedtime."

Okay, I'll take two tablets daily: one in the morning and one at bedtime.

"That's correct."

How long will it take for me to get some relief?

"You should notice a difference within a couple of hours. Make an appointment to see me again next week. The problem should be cleared up by then."

I sure will. Thank you for your help.

Techniques for Reporting Symptoms and Side Effects to a Doctor

Technique	Score 1 point for each technique used
Greets doctor politely	_____
Describes the symptom or side effect in detail	_____
Describes how long the symptom or side effect has been present	_____
Describes the severity of the problem by explaining how it interferes with daily activities	_____
Asks directly for doctor's help	_____
Repeats the doctor's instructions	_____
Asks how long it will take to get relief	_____
Thanks doctor for assistance	_____
Total	_____

Appendix C

THERAPIST COMPETENCE AND ADHERENCE SCALE

This scale assesses the therapist's ability to perform specific instructional activities demanded of SAMM trainers. We used the test in research to ensure that the therapist followed the manual closely and competently. A trained observer watched the SAMM therapist lead a group and rated the therapist on various performance and adherence subscales, with items rated on a four-point Likert-type scale. We include it here because it highlights what we think is most important for a therapist to do during treatment sessions.

Substance Abuse Management Module
Therapist Competence and Adherence Scale

INTRODUCTION TO TOPIC AND GOAL-SETTING

1. Therapist acknowledges attendance and participation (e.g., indicates pleasure at seeing participants and reinforces efforts).

Poor	Fair	Good	Excellent

2. Therapist verbally relates contents of current session to previous and future sessions.

Poor	Fair	Good	Excellent

3. Therapist states specific goals for the session.

Poor	Fair	Good	Excellent

4. Therapist states goals in behavioral terms.

Poor	Fair	Good	Excellent

5. Therapist states goals succinctly.

Poor	Fair	Good	Excellent

6. Therapist states rationale for goals.

Poor	Fair	Good	Excellent

7. Therapist elicits group members' rationale for goals.

Poor	Fair	Good	Excellent

8. Therapist elicits approval and understanding of goals.

Poor	Fair	Good	Excellent

9. Global rating of introduction to topic and goal-setting.

_____   _____   _____   _____
Poor   Fair   Good   Excellent

EDUCATING GROUP MEMBERS

10. Therapist conveys contents accurately.

_____   _____   _____   _____
Poor   Fair   Good   Excellent

11. Therapist conveys contents succinctly.

_____   _____   _____   _____
Poor   Fair   Good   Excellent

12. Therapist elicits verbal contributions from all group members.

_____   _____   _____   _____
Poor   Fair   Good   Excellent

13. Therapist asks group members appropriate questions to insure that they are paying attention and understand.

_____   _____   _____   _____
Poor   Fair   Good   Excellent

14. Therapist responds in an appropriate manner to incorrect answers (praises efforts, then redirects to correct response).

_____   _____   _____   _____
Poor   Fair   Good   Excellent

15. Therapist verifies understanding.

_____   _____   _____   _____
Poor   Fair   Good   Excellent

16. Therapist includes all members in discussion.

_____   _____   _____   _____
Poor   Fair   Good   Excellent

17. Global rating of educating group members.

_____   _____   _____   _____
Poor   Fair   Good   Excellent

DIRECTING ROLE-PLAYS

18. Therapist elicits the benefits of learning the skill from group members

    _____   _____   _____   _____
    Poor   Fair   Good   Excellent

19. Therapist involves all members in eliciting resources needed to perform the designated skill.

    _____   _____   _____   _____
    Poor   Fair   Good   Excellent

20. Therapist reviews methods for obtaining all mentioned resources.

    _____   _____   _____   _____
    Poor   Fair   Good   Excellent

21. Therapist describes scene clearly.

    _____   _____   _____   _____
    Poor   Fair   Good   Excellent

22. Therapist ensures that all members understand the goals to be achieved by the role-play.

    _____   _____   _____   _____
    Poor   Fair   Good   Excellent

23. Therapist ensures that all members understand their roles.

    _____   _____   _____   _____
    Poor   Fair   Good   Excellent

24. Therapist describes the setting that the role-play simulates.

    _____   _____   _____   _____
    Poor   Fair   Good   Excellent

25. Therapist sets the stage by arranging furniture and providing props.

    _____   _____   _____   _____
    Poor   Fair   Good   Excellent

26. Therapist coaches during the role-play by cueing and prompting.

    _____   _____   _____   _____
    Poor   Fair   Good   Excellent

27. Therapist stops the role-play when undesirable behaviors are being displayed and keeps the duration relatively brief.

    _____   _____   _____   _____
    Poor   Fair   Good   Excellent

28. Global rating of role-play direction skills.

    _____   _____   _____   _____
    Poor   Fair   Good   Excellent

GIVING FEEDBACK

29. Therapist elicits and gives feedback after role-plays.

    Poor   Fair   Good   Excellent

30. Therapist elicits and gives positive feedback first.

    Poor   Fair   Good   Excellent

31. Therapist elicits and gives feedback on specific target behaviors.

    Poor   Fair   Good   Excellent

32. Therapist provides feedback in behavioral terms.

    Poor   Fair   Good   Excellent

33. Therapist avoids overwhelming the role-player by selecting fewer than four target behaviors per role-play.

    Poor   Fair   Good   Excellent

34. Global rating of feedback skills

    Poor   Fair   Good   Excellent

VERBAL REINFORCEMENT

35. Therapist praises specific behaviors immediately following their occurrence (e.g., attending to group activities, engaging in role-play, completing homework assignment, answering questions).

    Poor   Fair   Good   Excellent

36. Therapist's intonations are consistent with statements of praise and communicates warmth and enthusiasm (e.g., tone, volume, inflection, duration of speech).

    Poor   Fair   Good   Excellent

37. Therapist's nonverbal behavior is consistent with statements of praise and communicates warmth and enthusiasm (e.g., hand gestures, facial expression, eye contact).

| _____ | _____ | _____ | _____ |
| Poor | Fair | Good | Excellent |

38. Therapist capitalizes on opportunities to reinforce.

| _____ | _____ | _____ | _____ |
| Poor | Fair | Good | Excellent |

39. Global rating of reinforcement skills.

| _____ | _____ | _____ | _____ |
| Poor | Fair | Good | Excellent |

MODELING BEHAVIORS

40. Therapist utilizes modeling when appropriate (e.g., when patient fails to follow verbal instructions).

| _____ | _____ | _____ | _____ |
| Poor | Fair | Good | Excellent |

41. Modeling is kept appropriately brief.

| _____ | _____ | _____ | _____ |
| Poor | Fair | Good | Excellent |

42. Behaviors to be modeled are clearly demonstrated and annotated.

| _____ | _____ | _____ | _____ |
| Poor | Fair | Good | Excellent |

43. Therapist elicits members' understanding of modeled behaviors.

| _____ | _____ | _____ | _____ |
| Poor | Fair | Good | Excellent |

44. Global rating of modeling skills.

| _____ | _____ | _____ | _____ |
| Poor | Fair | Good | Excellent |

GIVING INSTRUCTIONS

45. Therapist gives instructions and prompts before behaviors are practiced.

| _____ | _____ | _____ | _____ |
| Poor | Fair | Good | Excellent |

46. Instructions specify behavior to be displayed.

    Poor   Fair   Good   Excellent

47. Therapist limits instructions to avoid overwhelming the members.

    Poor   Fair   Good   Excellent

48. Therapist states instructions succinctly and coherently.

    Poor   Fair   Good   Excellent

49. Global rating of instructions.

    Poor   Fair   Good   Excellent

THERAPEUTIC ALLIANCE

50. Therapist displays warmth and enthusiasm.

    Poor   Fair   Good   Excellent

51. Therapist displays empathy or makes comments to set members at ease.

    Poor   Fair   Good   Excellent

52. Global rating of therapeutic alliance-building skills.

    Poor   Fair   Good   Excellent

Appendix D

CONSUMER SATISFACTION QUESTIONNAIRE

This questionnaire asks patients to rate the usefulness of SAMM. You can use it to get a picture of SAMM from the patients' perspectives—what they like and don't like, what they would like to see changed, and their overall impression of the impact of SAMM on their treatment.

Substance Abuse Management Module
Consumer Satisfaction Questionnaire

Please use this form to evaluate the SAMM program. Your opinion is important to us. Be sure to respond to every item. Place a check mark on the line that best expresses your opinion.

BASIC TRAINING

1. The information I learned in basic training was easy to understand.

_____	_____	_____	_____	_____
Strongly Disagree	Moderately Disagree	Unsure	Moderately Agree	Strongly Agree

2. The information I learned in basic training has increased my knowledge of drug abuse.

_____	_____	_____	_____	_____
Strongly Disagree	Moderately Disagree	Unsure	Moderately Agree	Strongly Agree

3. The information I learned in basic training has helped me to cope with drug abuse.

_____	_____	_____	_____	_____
Strongly Disagree	Moderately Disagree	Unsure	Moderately Agree	Strongly Agree

4. The information I learned in basic training has helped me to quit using drugs.

_____	_____	_____	_____	_____
Strongly Disagree	Moderately Disagree	Unsure	Moderately Agree	Strongly Agree

5. I enjoyed participating in the basic training groups.

_____	_____	_____	_____	_____
Strongly Disagree	Moderately Disagree	Unsure	Moderately Agree	Strongly Agree

6. The information I learned in basic training prepared me adequately for skills training.

_____	_____	_____	_____	_____
Strongly Disagree	Moderately Disagree	Unsure	Moderately Agree	Strongly Agree

SKILLS TRAINING

7. The techniques I learned in skills training were easy to understand.

___	___	___	___	___
Strongly Disagree	Moderately Disagree	Unsure	Moderately Agree	Strongly Agree

8. The techniques I learned in skills training have increased my knowledge of drug abuse.

___	___	___	___	___
Strongly Disagree	Moderately Disagree	Unsure	Moderately Agree	Strongly Agree

9. The techniques I learned in skills training have helped me to cope with drug abuse.

___	___	___	___	___
Strongly Disagree	Moderately Disagree	Unsure	Moderately Agree	Strongly Agree

10. The techniques I learned in skills training have helped me to quit using drugs.

___	___	___	___	___
Strongly Disagree	Moderately Disagree	Unsure	Moderately Agree	Strongly Agree

11. I enjoyed participating in the skills training groups.

___	___	___	___	___
Strongly Disagree	Moderately Disagree	Unsure	Moderately Agree	Strongly Agree

12. The techniques I learned in the SAMM program have improved the quality of my life.

___	___	___	___	___
Strongly Disagree	Moderately Disagree	Unsure	Moderately Agree	Strongly Agree

GROUP LEADERS

13. The group leaders made the module contents easy to understand.

___	___	___	___	___
Strongly Disagree	Moderately Disagree	Unsure	Moderately Agree	Strongly Agree

14. The group leaders were genuinely concerned about how well I learned.

___	___	___	___	___
Strongly Disagree	Moderately Disagree	Unsure	Moderately Agree	Strongly Agree

15. The group leaders gave me ample opportunity to ask questions during the groups.

Strongly Disagree	Moderately Disagree	Unsure	Moderately Agree	Strongly Agree

16. The group leaders gave me ample opportunity to practice skills during the groups.

Strongly Disagree	Moderately Disagree	Unsure	Moderately Agree	Strongly Agree

17. I was satisfied with the group leaders.

Strongly Disagree	Moderately Disagree	Unsure	Moderately Agree	Strongly Agree

COMPARED TO OTHER PROGRAMS

18. The information and skills that I learned in the SAMM program was easier to understand than any other program that I have attended.

Strongly Disagree	Moderately Disagree	Unsure	Moderately Agree	Strongly Agree

19. The SAMM program has given me more knowledge about drug abuse than any other treatment program that I have attended.

Strongly Disagree	Moderately Disagree	Unsure	Moderately Agree	Strongly Agree

20. I learned more coping techniques in the SAMM program than in any other treatment program that I have attended.

Strongly Disagree	Moderately Disagree	Unsure	Moderately Agree	Strongly Agree

21. The SAMM program helped curb my drug use more than any other program that I have attended.

Strongly Disagree	Moderately Disagree	Unsure	Moderately Agree	Strongly Agree

GENERAL SATISFACTION

22. I would recommend the SAMM program to other people who need help with drug addiction.

_____	_____	_____	_____	_____
Strongly Disagree	Moderately Disagree	Unsure	Moderately Agree	Strongly Agree

23. My drug use has decreased as a direct result of the information and skills I learned in the SAMM program.

_____	_____	_____	_____	_____
Strongly Disagree	Moderately Disagree	Unsure	Moderately Agree	Strongly Agree

23. Overall, I would rate the SAMM program as:

_____	_____	_____	_____
Poor	Fair	Good	Excellent

24. What did you like *best* about the SAMM program?

_____

_____

_____

25. What did you like *least* about the SAMM program?

_____

_____

_____

26. Can you think of anything that would improve the SAMM program?

_____

_____

_____

Appendix E
FLIP CHART

The chart provides quick access to content from basic training and skills training. Therapists create the chart by copying the figures in this appendix onto a blank flip chart pad attached to an easel. These are available from most office supply stores and catalogues. Attaching tabs to the pages helps the therapist find frequently used pages. The SAMM flip chart serves three purposes: (1) helps the therapist learn the material as he or she creates the flip chart, (2) increases patient understanding, and (3) keeps the therapist on track during sessions.

SUBSTANCE ABUSE MANAGEMENT MODULE (SAMM)

Flip Chart

1

GOAL OF THE MODULE

Say no to drugs and yes to healthy pleasures.

2

MODULE GROUPS

- Basic Training
  -8 sessions
  -Graduate to skills training
- Skills Training
  -27 sessions
- Practice Sessions
  -Ongoing

3

PRACTICE SESSION QUESTIONS

- Did you encounter a high-risk situation?
- Are you anticipating a high-risk situation?
- Did you add a healthy habit or healthy pleasure?
- Are you anticipating adding a healthy habit or healthy pleasure?

4

Basic Training   Session 1
DAMAGE CONTROL

- Session Goal
  To learn why it is important to stop a relapse early.
- Module Goal
  To say no to drugs and yes to healthy pleasures.

5

HIGH-RISK SITUATIONS

Situations that make it hard to avoid using drugs.

6

DAMAGE CONTROL

If I get into a high-risk situation and use drugs, I should

STOP DRUG USE EARLY

before it does any more damage to my health, relationships, and finances.

7

SLIP OR FULL-BLOWN RELAPSE

What's the difference?

- How long did it last?
- How much money did I spend?
- What were the negative consequences?
- How did I feel about myself and my behavior?

8

MT. RECOVERY

9

CONTINUUM OF HARM

EXCESSIVE USE ⟷ ABSTINENCE

- Lonely
- Sick
- Homeless
- Jailed
- Broke

- Friends
- Health
- Decent home
- Job
- Money

10

ABSTINENCE VIOLATION EFFECT (AVE)

- Now I've blown it; might as well keep using.
- This may happen when I break (violate) a goal of abstinence.
- This is how slips sometimes become full-blown relapses.

11

BOUNCING BACK INTO TREATMENT

- Call my support person.
- Talk with my doctor.
- Discuss this slip in group and figure out how to prevent it next time.

12

Basic Training Session 2
EMERGENCY CARD

- ## Session Goals
  To learn the importance of an emergency card.

  To create my own personal emergency card to remember how and why to avoid drugs.

- ## Module Goal
  To say no to drugs and yes to healthy pleasures.

13

Basic Training Session 3
HABITS AND CRAVING CONTROL

- ## Session Goals
  To see that drug abuse is learned and can be unlearned.

  To learn what causes cravings and how to deal with them.

- ## Module Goal
  To say no to drugs and yes to healthy pleasures.

14

HABITS

Things I do
over and over again.

15

HABITS:
HEALTHY OR UNHEALTHY?

- ## Healthy Habits
  Brushing my teeth, eating regular healthy meals, taking prescribed medication

- ## Unhealthy Habits
  Driving too fast, smoking cigarettes, drinking too much coffee, drinking too much alcohol, using illegal drugs

16

CRAVING

A strong urge or desire
to use drugs or alcohol.

17

I WANT TO QUIT—
WHY DO I CRAVE?

- Withdrawal
- Conditioning

18

GETTING HIGH

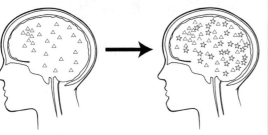

△ = Your brain's own feel-good chemicals
☆ = Addicting drugs

1 9

YOUR BRAIN ADJUSTS TO DRUGS

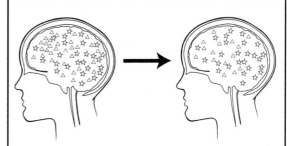

Your brain cuts down on its production of
natural feel-good chemicals.

2 0

WITHDRAWAL

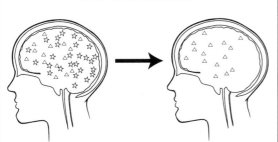

When the drug is gone, there's not enough of
your brain's own feel-good chemicals.

2 1

LEARN TO PREDICT CRAVING

- Do I crave in a particular situation?
- With certain people?
- At particular times?
- When I am in a certain mood?

2 2

CONDITIONED CRAVING

- PAVLOV'S DOGS

Meat	⟶	Drooling
Meat + Bell	⟶	Drooling
Bell	⟶	Drooling

- ADDICTION

Drug	⟶	Craving
Drugs + Trigger	⟶	Craving
Drug	⟶	Craving

2 3

Basic Training Session 4
HIGH-RISK SITUATIONS

- Session Goal
To learn my high-risk situations and why I
should avoid them.

- Module Goal
To say no to drugs and yes to healthy
pleasures.

2 4

HIGH-RISK SITUATIONS

Situations that
make it hard
to avoid using drugs.

25

THE PARTS OF A HIGH-RISK SITUATION

PEOPLE: drug dealer, drinking buddy, strawberry

PLACES: liquor store, park, or neighborhood known for drugs

THINGS: paraphernalia (pipes, screens, lighters, brillo pads, syringes), cash

THOUGHTS: "I'm going to have just one beer."

EMOTIONS: angry, sad, nervous, lonely, worthless

26

WARNING SIGNS AND U-TURNS

- Warning signs
  Things that say "Warning! High-risk situation ahead."

- U-Turns
  Things I do that lead me away from high-risk situations and drugs.

  I should make U-turns when I see warning signs.

27

HEALTHY PLEASURES

Things that feel good
and
are good for me.

28

Basic Training Session 5
WARNING SIGNS

- Session Goal
  To learn how to avoid high-risk situations by knowing my warning signs.

- Module Goal
  To say no to drugs and yes to healthy pleasures.

29

HIGH-RISK SITUATIONS

Situations that
make it hard
to avoid using drugs.

30

WARNING SIGNS

Things that warn me
that I might be headed
toward a high-risk
situation.

31

DRUG-HABIT CHAIN

Things I do
over and over
in order to use
drugs and alcohol.

32

TYPES OF WARNING SIGNS

PEOPLE: calling your drug dealer or drug-using buddies, looking for strawberries

PLACES: taking a "walk" in the park or neighborhood known for drugs

THINGS: handling or buying paraphernalia (pipes, screens, lighters, brillo pads, syringes), cashing a check

THOUGHTS: "A beer would really cut down on these voices."

EMOTIONS: angry, sad, nervous, lonely, worthless

33

HOW TO AVOID USING DRUGS

Healthy Pleasures
U-turn
Escape
Warning Sign
Quit Early
High-Risk Situation
Slip
Full-Blown Relapse

34

Basic Training   Session 6
HEALTHY PLEASURES AND HEALTHY HABITS

• Session Goals
  To learn how healthy pleasures and healthy habits will help me avoid drugs and alcohol.

• Module Goal
  To say no to drugs and yes to healthy pleasures.

35

HEALTHY PLEASURES

Things that feel good
and
are good for me.

36

HEALTHY PLEASURES

- Watching TV
- Reading
- Listening to music
- Fishing
- Taking a walk on the beach
- Eating an ice cream cone
- Teaching a child something new
- Getting a compliment from someone I respect
- Cooking
- Doing a job well
- Dating

37

HEALTHY HABITS

- Healthy = Good for me.
- Habits = I do them over and over.
- Not always fun but often lead to healthy pleasures.

38

HEALTHY HABITS

- Taking prescribed medication
- Buying food
- Buying clothing
- Waking up on time
- Going to bed on time
- Washing my clothes
- Combing my hair
- Taking a shower
- Brushing my teeth
- Shaving
- Saving money
- Attending meetings
- Exercising regularly

39

ACTIVITIES SCHEDULE

- Write-in important appointments: attending clinic, meeting support person, going to school, going to work.
- Schedule time for healthy habits.
- Schedule time for healthy pleasures.

40

Basic Training Session 7
WHY QUIT USING DRUGS?

- Session Goals
  To compare advantages and disadvantages of using drugs.
  To decide why I want to quit.

- Module Goal
  To say no to drugs and yes to healthy pleasures.

41

ADVANTAGES OF USING DRUGS

- Euphoria: It feels good.
- Strawberries and sex.
- Feel like I fit in.
- Have fun with others.
- Worries go away, feel better fast.

42

DISADVANTAGES OF USING DRUGS

- Lose trust and respect of family and friends
- Lose job
- No money for rent, food, or clothing
- Become homeless
- Beg or steal from others
- Injured in accidents
- Get robbed or assaulted
- Get arrested; go to jail
- Voices and paranoia
- Depression
- Suicidal thoughts
- Physical illnesses, including HIV

43

Using Drugs and Alcohol
ADVANTAGES VS. DISADVANTAGES

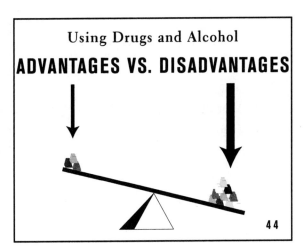

44

ADVANTAGES OF NOT USING DRUGS

- Enough money for an apartment
- Save money for healthy pleasures
- Self-respect
- Gain trust of family and friends
- Feel healthy
- Decreased voices and paranoia
- Feel stable and in control

45

SUPPORT PERSON

- Someone I can count on in time of need.

- A support person can help me
  -deal with cravings.
  -remember why I decided to quit.
  -develop healthy habits and healthy pleasures.

46

A GOOD SUPPORT PERSON IS SOMEONE

- I know well.
- I trust.
- I talk to frequently.
- Who does not abuse drugs or alcohol.
- Who is available when needed.
- Who will give me time when I ask.
- Who wants to help me.

47

Basic Training Session 8
MONEY MANAGEMENT

- Session Goal
  To make sure my money takes care of me instead of going to drugs that harm me.

- Module Goal
  To say no to drugs and yes to healthy pleasures.

48

MONEY CAN BE A

- Trigger.
- Warning sign.
- High-risk situation.

49

FLIP PAGES FOR SKILLS TRAINING

- Quitting after a slip
- Reporting a slip
- Refusing drugs offered by a dealer
- Refusing drugs offered by a friend or relative
- Getting an appointment with a busy person
- Getting a support person
- Reporting symptoms and side effects to a doctor
- Asking someone to joining you in a healthy pleasure
- Negotiating with a representative payee

50

Skills Training
QUITTING AFTER A SLIP

- **Session Goal**
  To learn how to stop using before a slip becomes a full-blown relapse.

- **Module Goal**
  To say no to drugs and yes to healthy pleasures.

51

DAMAGE CONTROL

If I get into a high-risk situation and use drugs, I should

STOP DRUG USE EARLY

before it does any more damage to my health, relationships, and finances.

52

MT. RECOVERY

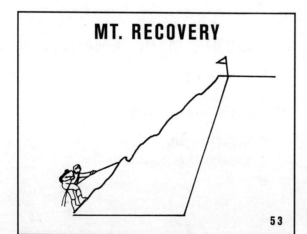

53

HOW TO AVOID USING DRUGS

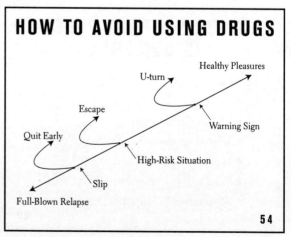

54

QUITTING AFTER A SLIP

1. Avoid eye contact.
2. Stand up and turn away.
3. Walk toward the door.
4. Say "I gotta go!" firmly.
5. Use broken record technique.
6. Keep moving quickly, don't stop for anything.

55

Skills Training
REPORTING A SLIP

- Session Goal
  To learn how to tell a support person that you slipped and used drugs or alcohol.

- Module Goal
  To say no to drugs and yes to healthy pleasures.

56

HOW TO REPORT A SLIP

1. Greet the person politely (good eye contact)
2. Be direct. Say you slipped (pleasant voice tone).
3. Ask to discuss how it happened.
4. Describe the high-risk situation (and how you quit).
5. Review treatment efforts (groups, support person).
6. Ask for help in avoiding such risky situations.
7. Thank the person.

57

Skills Training
REFUSING DRUGS OFFERED BY A DEALER

- Session Goal
  To learn the do's and don'ts of drug refusal and practice how to refuse drugs from a drug dealer.

- Module Goal
  To say no to drugs and yes to healthy pleasures.

58

HIGH-RISK SITUATIONS

Situations that
make it hard
to avoid using drugs.

59

DO'S

- *Do* look away.
- *Do* walk fast.
- *Do* look serious.
- *Do* stand tall.
- *Do* wave him off.
- *Do* say, "No, I don't want any" over and over.

60

DON'TS

- *Don't* look at him.
- *Don't* slow down or stop walking.
- *Don't* smile.
- *Don't* use a soft voice.
- *Don't* start making excuses.
- *Don't* get into a conversation.
- *Don't* let him put anything in my hand.

61

REFUSING DRUGS OFFERED BY A DEALER

1. Avert your gaze.
2. Turn your head away and wave him off.
3. Stand tall and lean forward.
4. Walk past at a brisk pace.
5. Keep your hands close.
6. Use a firm voice tone and say, "I don't want any!" over and over.

62

Skills Training
REFUSING DRUGS OFFERED BY A FRIEND OR RELATIVE

- ## Session Goal
  To learn and practice how to refuse drugs offered by a friend or relative.

- ## Module Goal
  To say no to drugs and yes to healthy pleasures.

63

REFUSING DRUGS OFFERED BY A FRIEND OR RELATIVE

1. Be direct. Tell the person you're not interested.
2. Use broken record technique.
3. Level with the person.
4. Suggest an alternative.
5. Express your feelings directly.
6. Leave the situation.

64

Skills Training
GETTING AN APPOINTMENT WITH A BUSY PERSON

- ## Session Goal
  To learn and practice how to get an appointment with a busy person.

- ## Module Goal
  To say no to drugs and yes to healthy pleasures.

65

GETTING AN APPOINTMENT WITH A BUSY PERSON

1. Greet the person politely.
2. Maintain good eye contact and pleasant, firm voice.
3. Say you need his or her help.
4. Say it's important.
5. Say it'll take just a few minutes.
6. If not now, ask for an appointment.
7. Get a specific time and place to meet.
8. Restate time and place to meet, thank the person.

66

Skills Training

GETTING A SUPPORT PERSON

- ## Session Goal
  To learn what makes a good support person and practice asking someone to be my support person.

- ## Module Goal
  To say no to drugs and yes to healthy pleasures.

67

A SUPPORT PERSON

- Is someone I can count on in a time of need.

- Can help me
  -deal with cravings.
  -remember why I decided to quit.
  -develop healthy habits and healthy pleasures.

68

A GOOD SUPPORT PERSON IS SOMEONE

- I know well.
- I trust.
- I talk to frequently.
- Who does not abuse drugs or alcohol.
- Who is available when needed.
- Who will give me time when I ask.
- Who wants to help me.

69

GETTING A SUPPORT PERSON

1. Say you need his or her help.
2. Explain why.
3. Ask him to be your support person.
4. Answer questions about responsibilities.
5. Write telephone number on emergency card.
6. Thank him for agreeing to help you.

70

Skills Training

REPORTING SYMPTOMS AND SIDE EFFECTS TO A DOCTOR

- ## Session Goal
  To learn how to tell my doctor about symptoms and side effects that make it harder to avoid drugs.

- ## Module Goal
  To say no to drugs and yes to healthy pleasures.

71

HEALTHY PLEASURES

Things that feel good
and
are good for me.

72

HEALTHY HABITS

- *Healthy* = Good for me.
- *Habits* = I do them over and over.
- Not always fun but often lead to healthy pleasures.

73

HOW TO AVOID USING DRUGS

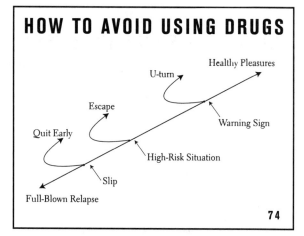

Healthy Pleasures

U-turn

Escape

Warning Sign

Quit Early

High-Risk Situation

Slip

Full-Blown Relapse

74

MEDICATION SIDE EFFECTS

- Drowsiness
- Blurry vision
- Dry mouth
- Constipation
- Diarrhea

- Restlessness
- Muscle stiffness
- Tremors
- Jerky muscle movements

75

SYMPTOMS OF SCHIZOPHRENIA

- Hearing voices
- Seeing things
- Paranoia
- Lack of interest
- Fear

- Sadness
- Trouble sleeping
- Poor concentration
- Avoiding people

76

REPORTING SYMPTOMS AND SIDE EFFECTS TO A DOCTOR

1. Greet your doctor politely (eye contact/pleasant voice tone).
2. Describe the symptoms or side effects.
3. Say how long you've had it.
4. Say how it interferes with daily activities
5. Ask for the doctor's help.
6. Repeat the doctor's instructions.
7. Ask how long it will take to get relief.
8. Thank the doctor for assistance.

77

Skills Training

ASKING SOMEONE TO JOIN YOU IN A HEALTHY PLEASURE

- Session Goal
  To learn to ask someone to join me in doing something fun and healthy.

- Module Goal
  To say no to drugs and yes to healthy pleasures.

78

HEALTHY PLEASURES TO SHARE WITH OTHERS

- Playing tennis
- Going on a picnic
- Rowing on a lake
- Playing checkers
- Going to a movie
- Going out to dinner
- Dancing
- Making love
- Going on a drive in the country
- Walking on the beach
- Camping
- Watching a sporting event
- Going to a jazz concert
- Watching a favorite TV program
- Talking on the phone

7 9

ASKING SOMEONE TO JOIN YOU IN A HEALTHY PLEASURE

1. Use a pleasant greeting (eye contact/happy voice tone).
2. Tell the person you enjoy his or her company.
3. Pick two activities.
4. Describe the activities (include when).
5. Ask the person to join you.
6. If not available, suggest other activity or ask when he or she would have time.
7. If he doesn't want to, say you understand and thank him for considering your offer.
8. If he accepts, set a time and place to meet.

8 0

Skills Training

NEGOTIATING WITH A REPRESENTATIVE PAYEE

- ## Session Goal
  To learn to ask my payee for money for healthy habits and healthy pleasures.

- ## Module Goal
  To say no to drugs and yes to healthy pleasures.

8 1

NEGOTIATING WITH A REPRESENTATIVE PAYEE

1. Greet your payee politely (eye contact/pleasant voice).
2. Tell him you want to structure your time more productively.
3. Indicate that healthy pleasures would help you not to use drugs.
4. Say which healthy pleasure you want to do.
5. Say how much money you need and how often.

continued . . .

8 2

NEGOTIATING
(continued)

6. Remind your payee of treatment progress (medication compliance, drug abstinence, regular group attendance, keeping appointments with your doctor, structuring your time every day, and avoiding high-risk situations).
7. Give payee permission to contact clinical team.
8. Say you'll provide receipts.
9. Schedule a follow-up appointment, and thank your payee.

8 3

NOTES

NOTES

NOTES

NOTES

NOTES

NOTES

NOTES

NOTES

NOTES